$5

Proceed
to Peshawar

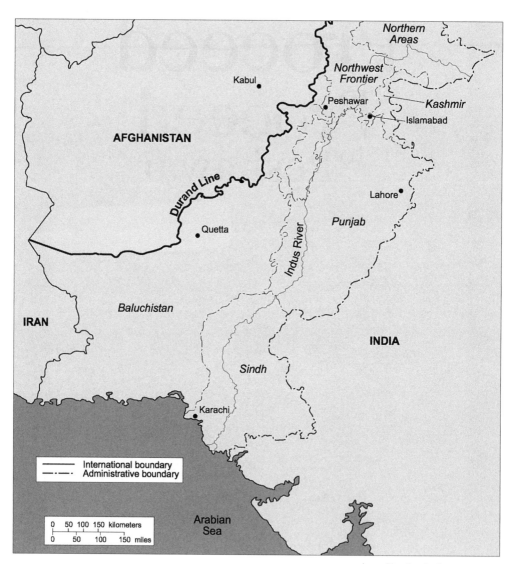

Northern
Areas

Kabul •

Northwest
Frontier

AFGHANISTAN

Peshawar •

Kashmir

Islamabad

Durand Line

Lahore •

Quetta •

Punjab

Indus River

Baluchistan

IRAN

INDIA

Sindh

International boundary
Administrative boundary

Karachi •

0 50 100 150 kilometers
0   50   100   150 miles

Arabian
Sea

Charles D. Grear

Proceed
to Peshawar

The Story of a U.S. Navy Intelligence
Mission on the Afghan Border, 1943

George J. Hill

NAVAL INSTITUTE PRESS
Annapolis, Maryland

Naval Institute Press
291 Wood Road
Annapolis, MD 21402

Library of Congress Cataloging-in-Publication Data
Hill, George J.
  Proceed to Peshawar : the story of a U.S. Navy intelligence mission on the Afghan
border, 1943 / George J. Hill, Captain, Medical Corps, USNR (Ret.).
    pages cm
  Summary: "Proceed to Peshawar is a story of adventure in the Hindu Kush
Mountains and of a previously untold military and naval intelligence mission during
World War II by two American officers along 800 miles of the Durand Line, the po-
rous border between Afghanistan and Pakistan. They passed through the tribal areas
and the princely states of the North-West Frontier Province, and into Baluchistan.
This appears to be the first time that any American officials were permitted to travel
for any distance along either side of the Durand Line. Many British political and
military officers believed that India would soon be free, and that the Great Game
between Russia and Britain in the nineteenth and early twentieth centuries would
then come to an end. Some of them thought that the United States should, and
would, assume Britain's role in Central Asia, and they wanted to introduce America
to this ancient contest. "— Provided by publisher.
  Includes bibliographical references and index.
  ISBN 978-1-61251-280-8 (pbk.)
  1. Khyber Pakhtunkhwa (Pakistan)—History, Military. 2. World War, 1939-
1945—Military intelligence—United States. 3. Enders, Gordon B. (Gordon
Bandy) 4. Zimmermann, Albert Walter. 5. Military intelligence—United States—
History—20th century. 6. Intelligence officers—United States—Biography. 7.
Khyber Pakhtunkhwa (Pakistan)—Description and travel. 8. Khyber Pakhtunkhwa
(Pakistan)—History—20th century. I. Title. II. Title: Story of a U.S. Navy intelli-
gence mission on the Afghan border, 1943.
  DS392.N67H55 2013
  940.54'8673—dc23
                                                                   2013029603

♾ Print editions meet the requirements of ANSI/NISO z39.48–1992
(Permanence of Paper).
Printed in the United States of America.

21 20 19 18 17 16 15 14 13   9 8 7 6 5 4 3 2 1
First printing

Front cover: Photograph of two American military officers in a U.S. Army jeep,
crossing the Lowari Pass into Chitral, North-West Frontier Province of India (now
Khyber Pakhtunkhwa Province of Pakistan), on 18 November 1943. Lieutenant
Albert W. Zimmermann, USNR, at right, looking at the camera; Major Gordon B.
Enders, USAR, driving, mostly hidden by an officer of the Chitrali Scouts. The Hindu
Kush Range is in the background. The photograph was taken by Major Sir Benjamin
Bromhead, OBE. This was the first motor vehicle crossing of the Lowari Pass.

To our fathers and mothers

"They also serve who only stand and wait."
(John Milton)

And to

Warren, Babs, and Tom
. . . who kept the promise of silence.

When everyone is dead the Great Game is finished.
Not before.

—Rudyard Kipling, *Kim*

Comments on the trip taken by Enders, Zimmermann, and Bromhead,
November–December 1943:

This trip—It was all about the Great Game.

—Colonel Harry Reginald Antony Streather, MBE, OBE
Aide-de-camp to governor, North-West Frontier Province
Member of first ascent party of Tirish Mir, Hindu Kush Range, 1950
Survived fall on K-2 in 1953

Yes, the trip was a part of the Great Game.

—Roderick K. Engert, Office of Strategic Services in India
Son of Cornelius Engert, minister to Afghanistan
Yale University, class of 1950

Contents

Foreword

Proceed to Peshawar is unexpectedly interesting to read. I say "unexpectedly" because this book, describing a visitor's trip through Afghanistan
in 1943, masquerades as the history of an American officer's trip through
the Afghan border territories during that year. Yes, we do read about his
military mission and the people whom he met during that trip, but the
really interesting parts of this book are the descriptions that Lieutenant
Albert Zimmermann (referred to in the book as AZ), a keen observer,
writes of the people and their surroundings. Starting with his comments
on Day 1, Friday 11 November 1943, where AZ reports comments by Major
Sir Benjamin Bromhead delivered at the Peshawar Club to the effect that
"The tribes [in the tribal area] have never really been conquered and
the present set up seems to be the best solution of a bad situation. . . .
The tribes have their own laws, with offences against property taking
precedence over [offenses against] lives." AZ then crosses into the tribal
territory at Shabkadar on Monday 15 November with Major Bromhead,
where "all villages were fortified and there were no schools, to avoid
blood feuds." AZ observed that, in his opinion, education appeared to be
the only way to bring the people under peaceful government. Later, on
9 December, AZ comments in a letter to his wife, "Most of this country
is pretty God-forsaken. You marvel that anyone can scratch a living out
of it. That's partly the trouble—some can't—so they take to plunder &
pillaging."

A considerable number of very interesting quotes are included from other visitors to Afghanistan, especially Gordon Bandy Enders, the instigator and driving force behind AZ's trip, and Lowell Thomas, who had visited the region and written about it some twenty years before. These quotes provide counterpoints to AZ's narrative and help the reader understand the current situation.

Gordon Enders is a fascinating man. Born in Essex, Iowa, in 1897, his family in 1901 went to India as missionaries; in 1906 they settled in Almora near the border of India and Tibet. Gordon lived in India from the age of four until he was fifteen, and actually lived a childhood very much like that of Kipling's Kim. Extensive quotes in this book come from two long letters, each composed over several days, that Enders typed and sent to his wife in 1941 after he had been commissioned an intelligence officer in the U.S. Army. They show great insight into local conditions and traditions, and even by themselves make this book into a must read for anyone interested in that era.

In the background of this story is the Afghan government that, during World War II, adopted a policy of strict neutrality, and confirmed it with a loya jirga (large council) in 1941. In October 1941 the British and Soviet governments delivered parallel ultimatums to the Afghan government, demanding the expulsion of the two hundred or so German and Italian citizens from the country. This caused much resentment among the Afghans, particularly in view of their policy of neutrality, but in practice they had to comply. For this reason, AZ had to travel with a British Army representative like Major Bromhead while in the country.

As things happen, I had occasion twenty-eight years later in 1971 to spend ten days in Afghanistan, where I visited some of the places AZ described. As far as I can remember, virtually nothing had changed from the conditions described by AZ. I remember traveling through the mountains near Kabul in a Jeep with an Afghan National Army officer who, when we saw in a valley in front of us some local tribesmen living in some black tents, told our driver to turn around instantly and go off in a different direction, commenting to me, "This is not a safe place to be—those are dangerous people who do not obey our laws." And yet, when I visited Baghe Babur, the burial gardens of the Emperor Babur (died 1530), the founder of the Moghul Dynasty of India, which are located near Kabul, the scene was absolutely peaceful, with gardeners watering the roses just as they did back home. In the mountains, though, I saw villagers eating their meals of lamb stew and rice with their right hands dipping into the pot just as AZ reported in a letter to his wife. And the approaches to the Khyber Pass appeared to be almost unchanged from those described by AZ during the first days of his trip. My principal memory of Afghanistan is that of a land where nothing ever really changes, particularly tribal customs and the way the local people behave.

Illustrations are an integral part of this book. AZ took more than one hundred pictures of local people and conditions while on this trip, even though he did not know until later if his borrowed camera would even work. But the camera did work, and many of the resulting photographs are reproduced in this book, providing fascinating glimpses of a world that is completely foreign to most Americans. AZ took this trip seventy years ago, but the backgrounds to these images could have been taken any time during the past seven hundred years (except for the methods of transportation).

In conclusion, reading this book produces an understanding of the immutable nature of this part of our world that is very relevant to an understanding of the problems faced by our troops in this very ancient and traditional country, and I heartily recommend it as such.

Denis B. Woodfield, D.Phil. (Oxon.)
Honorary Fellow, Lincoln College
Oxford University
April 2012

Preface

At about 9:00 in the morning on Tuesday 16 November 1943, a U.S. Army jeep pulled away from the Services Hotel in Peshawar, North-West Frontier Province, India. Three men were on board, and the jeep was fully loaded. It was getting under way on what all of the passengers knew would be a dangerous and—if successful—historic journey.

The jeep was driven by a forty-six-year-old man wearing a military aviator's sheep-lined leather jacket and the gold maple leaves of a U.S. Army major on his shirt collars. His round face, black eyebrows, and deeply tanned skin gave him an almost oriental appearance. He squinted grimly under the brim of his dark brown officer's hat. Although he was usually very talkative, the major was uncommonly quiet as the jeep pulled out. He had been expected a day earlier, but he had been delayed and he was not in a good mood. In the right front passenger seat was a large man, forty-three years old, dressed comfortably in a tweed jacket and khaki trousers that might or might not be of military origin. He wore a soft civilian cap and horn-rim glasses. With his easy smile, bald head, and moustache, he looked more like a professor than a soldier. But he, too, was a major, and when he chose to wear his badges of rank, they were British. Another man, this one in an American uniform, sat in the back seat. At forty-one, he was the youngest of the three Allied officers. Blue-eyed, tanned, trim, and rather handsome, he wore the silver bars of a U.S. Navy lieutenant on each lapel. Later in the trip the Navy man would share the back seat with a uniformed officer of the local militia. The militia officer was to assist the safe passage of the jeep and its passengers as it proceeded through tribal territory. The militia officer would be replaced at each stage of the trip by another khassadar (tribal policeman) who would vouchsafe and guide the Westerners through his own territory.

The three Allied officers knew from previous experience that they were now players in what had for nearly four decades been known as the Great Game—the struggle for dominance in Central Asia, in which India was the prize. And they knew this was the first time that American military officers had joined the game, armed and under orders, as the saying goes.

This book will tell the story of the remarkable month-long journey along the Indian–Afghan border that these three Allied officers took in the late fall of 1943. The participants and those to whom they reported, and those who received the reports of the journey, are all dead—most of them a long time ago. The reports that they wrote about the trip have long since been filed away and forgotten, or destroyed. However, we now know that the area traversed by these officers is an area of vital interest to the United States—indeed to the entire world—and it therefore may be instructive to see what they encountered, and what lessons we may learn from their experiences. At the very least, by reviewing the report of this journey we can see that a brave spirit and willingness to push on against the odds is neither new in our own time, nor has it been forgotten. Success in dangerous endeavors is not for the faint hearted.

Acknowledgments

I gratefully acknowledge my father-in-law, Lieutenant Albert W. Zimmermann, USNR, who served in India in World War II, and his wife, Barbara (Shoemaker) Zimmermann, who could "only stand and wait" until the war was over. These were dangerous times, and no one was really safe, especially overseas. They believed in what they were doing—he for the Navy and for his country, and she taking care of their home and their young family, and volunteering in a canteen for service members. Barbara Zimmermann saved the crucial documents that made it possible to construct this book, in files of letters, notes, and documents; a scrapbook and photo album; and loose photos and two reels of sixteen-millimeter movies. She put them away after the war, in about 1947, and no one examined them again for nearly sixty years.[1]

I also acknowledge the previous work of others on the history and literature of the Great Game, and especially Rudyard Kipling, whose book *Kim* popularized this expression for the contest in Central Asia between Britain and Russia. I published a brief account of this trip, accompanied by three photos, in Appalachia in 2008. I thank the Appalachian Mountain Club for the opportunity to introduce this story to the public. Correspondence from readers of that article helped me to find other sources that have enriched my understanding of the trip and the travelers.

I give special thanks to the Zimmermann children: Barbara Warren "Babs" Zimmermann Johnson and her husband Melvin Thornton Johnson; my wife, Helene "Lanie" Zimmermann Hill; Ambassador Warren

Zimmermann and his wife Corinne "Teeny" (Chubb) Zimmermann; and Dr. Albert W. Zimmermann Jr. and his wife Lenore Marie (Lisbinski) Zimmermann.

Friends of Al and Barbara Zimmermann contributed much to this story: Mrs. Amelie (Sexias) Kane, widow of Commander (selected) Jack Kane; and her daughter, Sheila Kane; Jack Thayer's daughter "Dodie" Thayer; First Lieutenant Clarence Lewis, USMC, OSS; Lieutenant Lewis' wife Mrs. Georgiana "Sam" (Wetherill) Lewis; their daughter Susan Lewis Lillien; and Anne and Crosby Lincoln, daughters of Lieutenant Colonel Joseph Freeman Lincoln, USAR, OSS, and his wife Virginia "Ginny" Lincoln.

I am grateful to the Enders family and their friends: Dr. Gertrude "Trudy" (Enders) Huntington, and Dr. Allen Coffin Enders. I thank David M. Hovde, Purdue University, and Sarah Uschak, Office of Alumni Relations, The College of Wooster, for their help in locating records of Gordon Enders; Maynard Creel, who shared his memories of Gordon Enders; the descendants of Cornelius and Sara Engert: his son, Roderick K. Engert and his granddaughter, Jane Morrison Engert; and Colonel "Tony" Streather, who served in Pakistan in 1950 and recalled his experiences there.

Thanks to the staff of the Franklin Delano Roosevelt Library; Amanda A. Hegge of the Patrick J. Hurley Collection, Oklahoma University Library; staff members of the New York Public Library; Georgetown University Special Collections; and Nate Patch and Paul Brown, Military Archive Section, National Archives and Records Administration (NARA II).

And most of all, I thank my wife, Helene "Lanie" Zimmermann Hill, Ph.D., who was so patient and helpful during the writing of this book.

Key Documents and Players

The trip began simply enough, but many details can be teased out of the letter asking for a U.S. Naval intelligence officer to go on the trip, and from his orders. These two documents are the earliest that mention the trip:

EXPRESS—SECRET & PERSONAL—NO. 9732
INTELLIGENCE BUREAU
QUETTA
26TH OCT., 1943

Dear John,

I have just heard from Major Sir Benjamin Bromhead of the N.W.F.P. Public Relations Bureau that with the blessing of the Governor N.W.F.P. he is taking Major Enders, U.S. Military Attaché, Kabul, on a personally conducted tour of the Frontier and Baluchistan from Chitral to Quetta with the idea of making it clear to the American Legation in Kabul what are our frontier problems and our ideas and policy in dealing with them and the Afghans.

I promptly asked him whether he could also take one of the American officers from the U.S. Naval Liaison Office if they would like to send one. He replied in the affirmative subject to the Governor's sanction which he said he thought would certainly be forthcoming.

Would you put the offer to Smith and ask him to telegraph me a reply so as to reach me by 1st November, just saying whether they would like to send an officer and if so whom.

Bromhead's dates are:

10.XI.43 leave Peshawar for the Kurram (Parachinar)
15.XI.43 return Peshawar.
18.XI.43 leave for Chitral.
25.XI.43 return Peshawar.
29.XI.43 leave for Waziristan.
10.XII.43 finish tour in Quetta or Peshawar.

As you can see, it means a month away from H.Qs.

I don't know if Smith would be interested in this somewhat unique opportunity of getting a first-class background for his own office and Naval H.Qs. at Washington to use in connection with any reports emanating from U.S. sources in Kabul or Delhi, or whether he could spare an officer for so long. You will readily appreciate the necessity for carefully picking the officer so that he does not get hold of the wrong end of the stick or miss important points.

How Smith would explain to Enders and Engert the presence of this officer would be Smith's headache and not ours!

If Smith's wire contains an affirmative reply I will wire Bromhead in Peshawar to get H.E.'s sanction and convey same direct to Smith, including instructions regarding date and place where the officer should report. After wiring Bromhead as above I fade out of the picture and negotiations between Smith and Bromhead are then direct.

Smith will realize that the weather will be bitterly cold with the possibility of snow in Waziristan and Chitral, so warm clothes are essential.

Bromhead's address in Peshawar is:

>Major Benjamin Bromhead, OBE, IA,
>Deputy Public Relations Officer,
>Frontier Tribes, PESHAWAR. (N.W.F.P.)

Will you please convey this message to Smith?

Yours sincerely,

/s/

J. R. Harris, Esq., I.P.
Central Intelligence Officer, Karachi.

Copy to Major Sir Benjamin Bromhead, OBE, IA, in continuation of our conversation of yesterday's date.

The designation and address of the American Naval Liaison Office in Karachi is:—
United States Naval Liaison Office
254 Ingle Road, KARACHI, and the telegraphic address is ALUSLO, Karachi. The Commanding Officer is Lt. Com-mander F. Howard Smith, U.S.N.

As will be seen, the trip was a dream of one of the travelers for a long time. How that came to fruition will become apparent in due time. We next see the document that sends AZ on the trip. The time between the message to Harris on 26 October 1943 and the issuance of the orders on 8 November was but two weeks. It is clear that AZ got the nod—he was the man who could be trusted not to get hold of the wrong end of the stick.

OFFICE OF THE UNITED STATES NAVAL LIAISON OFFICE
KARACHI, INDIA
CABLE ADDRESS—205065—8 NOVEMBER 1943
"ALUSLO"
EN3–11(KA)P16–4/00/A-1/JAH
SERIAL 558

From: The United States Naval Liaison Officer, Karachi
To: Lieutenant Albert W. Zimmermann, I-V(S), USNR.
Subject: ORDERS, Temporary Additional Duty
Reference: (a) SecNav letter to all Ships and Stations dated
             April 30, 1943.

1. Upon receipt of these orders and when directed by proper authority, on or about 11 November 1943, you will proceed via transportation furnished by the United States Army, to Peshawar, North West Frontier Province, India, and such other places as may be deemed necessary for the proper performance of the duties assigned you. Upon completion of this temporary duty you will return to this office and resume your regular duties.

2. Transportation to Peshawar, North West Frontier Province, India, is to be furnished by the United States Army and you are authorized to defray any additional travel, including transportation by military or commercial aircraft, subject to reimbursement by the government.

3. Per diem allowances while traveling in obedience to these orders is authorized in accordance with reference (a).

Francis H. Smith
FRANCIS H. SMITH
cc BuPers

FIRST ENDORSEMENT—U.S. NAVAL LIAISON OFFICER—
NOVEMBER 12 1943
EN3–11(KA)P16–4/00/A-1/JAH—KARACHI, INDIA

From: The United States Naval Liaison Officer, Karachi.
To: Lieutenant Albert W. ZIMMERMANN, I-V(S), USNR

1. You departed at *1540* this date.

Francis H. Smith
FRANCIS H. SMITH[1]

The three officers who made the trip:

Major (later Colonel) Gordon Bandy Enders, USAR
Major (later Lieutenant Colonel) Sir Benjamin Gonville Bromhead,
OBE, IA
Lieutenant (later Lieutenant Commander) Albert W. Zimmermann,
USNR

Five others mentioned in the letter:

Sir George Cunningham, GCIE, KCSI, OBE, LLD, governor, North-
West Frontier Province
Lieutenant Commander Francis H. Smith, USN
The Honorable Cornelius Van H. Engert, CBE, U.S. minister to
Afghanistan
John R. Harris, central liaison officer, Karachi
"Intelligence Bureau, Quetta"—unidentified, but perhaps a "Father
Wood"[2]

Personnel at the naval liaison office, Karachi:

Lieutenant (jg) Howard Voorhees, USNR

Two others, not mentioned in the letter, but who were involved in the planning:

> Lieutenant Colonel (later Sir) Reginald "Rex" Benson, Kt., OBE, MVO, MC
> The Honorable Clarence E. Macy, American consul at Karachi

Two more, who met the travelers during the trip:

> Field Marshal Archibald Wavell, GCB, CMG, MC, first earl of Wavell, viceroy of India
> Lieutenant Colonel (later Sir) William Rupert Hay, CBE, CSI, KCIE, commissioner, Baluchistan

Three who learned about the trip while it was under way, if not before:

> The Honorable (later Lieutenant Colonel, Office of Strategic Services) Charles Wheeler Thayer, chargé d'affaires, Kabul
> Lieutenant Curtin Winsor, USNR, Far East desk, Office of Naval Intelligence
> Captain (later Rear Admiral) Gene Markey, USNR, senior naval liaison officer, China-Burma-India Theater

Two who probably learned about the trip immediately after it was completed:

> Major General (later Ambassador) Patrick Hurley, special representative of the president
> Major Ernest F. Fox, USAR, military attaché to Kabul

And seven others, who could have learned about the trip:

> Sir Francis Verner Wylie, GCIE, KCSI, British minister to Afghanistan
> Sir Denys Pilditch, CIE, director, Delhi Intelligence Bureau
> Field Marshal Claude Auchinleck, commander in chief, India
> Colonel C. Suydam Cutting, Office of Strategic Services, head of U.S. observer group, Delhi
> Major General Sir Stewart Graham Menzies, director, Secret Intelligence Service
> Major General William Donovan, director, Office of Strategic Services
> Admiral of the Fleet Louis Mountbatten, first earl of Mountbatten, KG, commander, South East Asia Command

One
Background

You've a great game, a noble one, before you.
—Captain Arthur Conolly, in Bokhara (1842)

Go up the hill and ask. Here begins the Great Game.
—Rudyard Kipling, *Kim*

Long before the beginning of the Great Game—the contest for empire between Britain and Russia—other invaders had crossed Central Asia. As it was in the Great Game of the nineteenth century, the prize was India and access to the Indian Ocean. Darius I in 515 BCE and Alexander III of Macedon (Alexander the Great), in 326 BCE were the first whose troops crossed the Hindu Kush Range into India, but then turned back. They learned that getting there was hard enough, and staying there was even more difficult. And getting back home was deadly. Others learned the same lesson, the hard way.

Britain called this contest the "Great Game" and Russia referred to it as *bol'shaia igra* (tournament of shadows). Some in Britain thought it would lose this game if it did not control Afghanistan as a forward base to keep Russia at bay, and Russia thought it must control Afghanistan to launch its drive to the Indian Ocean. Britain also fought the expansion

1

of the Russian Empire to the west, as well as to the south. The spoils of the greater contest once included the decaying empire of Turkey, and the Crimean War was also part of this struggle.

The notion of the Great Game draws on our recollections of other games. It is exemplified by Montaigne's reference to *le jeu,* the game, in an expression paraphrased by Moorcroft, an early British explorer in Central Asia. The idea of "the game" includes both chance and skill; you have to take what you are dealt, and then play it to win. It is universally understood, because that is the game of life itself. The expression "great game" has become common. Perhaps this derives from Kipling's popular novel, *Kim,* which referred to "the Great Game," although more likely it is because the game of chance is so deeply imbedded in human activities. Kipling's words resonate with our beliefs and aspirations. The term "great game" as used by Kipling has been traced back to the origin of the game of rugby, which in 1823 arose as a great game at Rugby College. After Kipling introduced the term "Great Game," it became a metaphor for spying, or for any great contest. Winston Churchill supposedly "acquired in his adventures on the outposts of the British empire a fascination for the 'Great Game' of secret intelligence."[1]

I will use the term "Great Game" as Kipling referred to it, a game that was centered on Afghanistan's border with India that Britain attempted to keep secure. Britain originally attempted to protect India by controlling Afghanistan—Britain's so-called forward policy. But after losing two brutal wars with the Afghans (in 1839–42 and 1878–79), the British decided a better course would be to withdraw to the south and allow Afghanistan to be the buffer against Russia's advance. The new British policy was to allow the ferocious border tribes—particularly the Pashtuns, who were then called Pathans—to defend their own territory. The tribes would thereby provide insurance against a Russian advance into India. In 1893 an agreement was reached between Mortimer Durand of Britain and the emir (king) of Afghanistan to fix the border between Afghanistan and India. Passing through the Pashtun territory, the intent of the Durand Line was to divide the tribes and prevent them from rising in unison.

Geography

The area that is now called Afghanistan is a landlocked nation in Central Asia surrounded by six other countries. Its borders were vague in ancient times but gradually became defined, and then shifted to their present lines. As it is with most countries, borders are based on geography and politics. The northern border largely follows the course of the Amu Darya River, which was formerly called the Oxus. In its eastern reaches, the boundary is the tributary known as the Panj River. These rivers separate Afghanistan from Turkmenistan, Uzbekistan, and Tajikistan, which were formerly Soviet socialist republics. Russia and Britain created the eastern border in 1873 to separate the Russian Empire from British India. It extends along a narrow corridor, called the Wakhan, to the province of Xinjiang in western China. It is some 150 miles long, narrowing to only seven miles at one point. In the east, the Pamir Mountains provide a natural barrier between Afghanistan and China. Iran is on Afghanistan's western border, a boundary that has been contested in the past by both Iran and Russia. And the southern border, on which this book is focused, is with the provinces of Baluchistan and Khyber Pakhtunkhwa (formerly the North-West Frontier Province [NWFP]) of Pakistan. This border formerly extended farther to the south, but in 1893 it was fixed in its present location after an agreement was made between Russia and Britain; Afghanistan was simply told that this would be the border. The Durand Line, surveyed between 1893 and 1896, pushed the border about forty miles to the north, to the Khyber Pass. It placed Peshawar in India, and it affirmed the independence of Chitral from Afghanistan. Some in Afghanistan, especially the Pashtuns, who live on both sides of the Durand Line, have never fully accepted the southern border: they dream of uniting "Pashtunistan" and extending the border to the south again.

Afghanistan is a country of contrasts. With some 251,772 square miles, it is slightly smaller than Texas, with an average elevation of three thousand feet. The population of Afghanistan is about 28 million, slightly more than the 26 million in Texas. It is transected by the Hindu Kush Mountains, which are roughly in the center of the country, tapering down in the west. The highest mountain is Nowshak, at 24,557 feet, nearly 10,000

feet higher than the peaks of the Rockies in Colorado. Some of the area
is good cropland and very lush, and other parts are arid. Sheep and goats
graze the mountains up to ten or twelve thousand feet. One of the main
crops is the opium poppy, from which Afghanistan produces much of the
world's heroin; some estimate it as greater than 90 percent of the world's
supply. It is also the world's largest producer of hashish, the resin produced from the cannabis plants, from which marijuana is prepared. The
country is divided by ethnicity—many groups have settled here and they
have their own territories. Local government is largely based on tribal
customs, which are male dominated and hierarchical. The country is
Islamic, principally Sunni, except for the Shiites in western Afghanistan.
The principal cities are the capital Kabul, Herat in the west, Mazar-i-
Sharif in the north, and Kandahar and Jelalabad, which are principally
Pashtun cities, near the southeastern border.

Two provinces of Pakistan adjoin the south side of the poorly marked,
roughly 1,500-mile long Durand Line. They are now known as Khyber
Pakhtunkhwa and Baluchistan Provinces; each province occupies about
half of the length of the border. Formed in 1901 Khyber Pakhtunkhwa
Province was originally called the North-West Frontier Province of India,
and it retained that name after Pakistan was formed in 1947. Its present
name was given in 2010, but it will usually be referred to in this book, as
it was throughout World War II, as the NWFP. Immediately adjacent to
Afghanistan within this province are the frontier regions and federally
administered tribal areas. The trip described in this book in November–
December 1943 was largely within the NWFP, but it ended in Baluchistan.

The capital of the Khyber Pakhtunkhwa Province is Peshawar, a
town that dates back to time immemorial. The province now consists of
twenty-five districts. It includes what were formerly three semi-independent states to the north of Peshawar, that are now considered as provincially administered tribal areas: Chitral, the northernmost of the three,
that was ruled by a hereditary *mehtar* (the ruler of Chitral); Upper Dir
and Lower Dir, that were ruled by the *nawab* (the ruler of Dir) of Dir;
Malakand (which in British India was an administrative district that
included Dir and Chitral); and Swat, whose ruler was known as the *wali*
(the ruler of Swat) of Swat. There are seven federally administered tribal

areas: Bajaur, Mohmand, Khyber, Orakzai, Kurram, North Waziristan, and South Waziristan. All the provincially administered tribal areas and federally administered tribal areas were traversed by the three Anglo-American officers in the fall of 1943, and all were identified by name as the travelers passed through them, except for Bajaur and Orakzai. The principal cities of the province, in addition to Peshawar, are Dera Ismail Khan and Abbotabad (where bin Laden was killed in 2011).

Baluchistan (meaning the land of the Balochis) is the province to the south of Khyber Pakhtunkhwa. From its capital, Quetta, in the north, it extends from Afghanistan to the Indian Ocean. It is the largest of Pakistan's four provinces, with some 43 percent of its area, but because of its arid and mountainous nature, it is by far the least populous, containing only 7 percent of Pakistan's population. About 70 percent of the Balochi people live in Baluchistan Province, and the rest live in Iran, to the west. The East India Company had informally occupied western Baluchistan in 1843; its territories became a crown colony in 1858 when the East India Company was dissolved. In 1872, having little choice in the matter, the Persians agreed to the present border—the so-called Goldsmid Line. Northern Baluchistan was added in 1879 from Afghanistan, including the formidable Golan Pass and Quetta in the north, and then the border was pushed a bit farther north by the Durand Line in 1893. Britain was not interested in direct rule of most of the area, and the chief commissioner for Baluchistan oversaw only the lands on the border with Afghanistan and the environs of Quetta. Most of the country was nominally independent, under the Khanates of Kalat and Las Bela. Baluchistan has continued to be restive, and the Afghan Taliban and al Qaeda have been able to find a safe haven in Quetta.[2]

Historical Background

A vivid description of the ancient history of Afghanistan and the NWFP was given by Lowell Thomas:

> Through Waziristan on the Way to High Asia . . . the land of
> another mighty range, the Hindu Kush, south of the Oxus River

and beyond the northwest frontier of India—Afghanistan. The door is the Khyber Pass, a door that has refused to swing back to all save a few. . . . Throughout history, Afghan trails have echoed to the march of northern hosts that looked with lustful eyes on India's riches. Scythian, Persian, Greek, Seljuk, Tartar, Mongol, Durani—these and others have plundered India through the Afghan door.[3]

The Mongol leader Teumjin, later known as Genghis Khan, set out at the head of the Golden Horde in 1206 to conquer the world. His empire eventually stretched from the Pacific Ocean to the border of modern Poland. In 1219–40 the principalities of Russia fell to the Mongols, and for the next two centuries they ruled Russia. Marco Polo passed through this region on his journeys in 1269–95, along what has long been known as the Silk Road.

In 1480 Russia broke free from the Mongols, as Ivan III (Ivan the Great), grand prince of Moscow, put several envoys of the Mongol leader to death. The Russians then began advancing to the south in the adventure that eventually became known as the Great Game. Meanwhile, the British role in India began with the East India Company, a joint-stock company that was granted a Royal Charter in 1600 to trade with the East Indies, but that mainly traded with the Indian subcontinent and China. The Afghans also had their eyes on India. Nadir Shah invaded India in 1738–39. His dynasty was known as Durrani—the "Durani" mentioned above by Lowell Thomas.[4]

In the first two decades of the nineteenth century, explorers from Russia and Britain made wary contact with each other. Captain Arthur Conolly reached Bokhara, insulted the emir, and was beheaded there in 1842. Before he died, Conolly wrote to another officer, "You've a great game, a noble one, before you." Rudyard Kipling seized the phrase, some fifty years later, and immortalized it in *Kim*. Kipling was born in 1865, and he made this the birth year of the fictional boy-spy, Kim, the hero of his novel. In January 1873 Russia acknowledged that the Wakhan, on the upper Oxus, "lay within the domains of the Emir of Afghanistan" and that "Afghanistan itself lay within Britain's sphere of influence."[5] Nevertheless,

Russia quietly continued to advance, and by 1875 it appeared that Russia would soon control the passes leading to Ladakh and Kashmir. In 1888 George Nathaniel Curzon, MP, visited the Oxus, Bokhara, Samarkand, and Tashkent. As Lord Curzon, he later became viceroy of India and was perhaps the most aggressive proponent of Britain's forward policy.[6]

In 1892 a serious crisis had arisen in Chitral. The aging ruler had died and "family rivals fought for the throne," producing "five successive rulers in three years." The Durand Line was demarcated in 1893, dividing Afghanistan from India. When the British subsidy to the emir of Afghanistan was raised to 1.8 million rupees, Britain hoped it had control of the northwest frontier.[7]

However, in 1895, believing (probably correctly) that the Russians (or some others, such as the ruler of Swat or the ruler of Afghanistan) would move into Chitral if it could not be brought under stable rule, the senior British officer in Gilgit, Major George Robertson, set out for Chitral with four hundred troops. Robertson captured the citadel at Chitral, but was himself besieged. After enduring for six weeks, Robertson's small force was relieved. Two weeks later, a much larger force under Major General Sir Richard Low reached Chitral from Peshawar, having fought its way through the Malakand Pass at 3,500 feet and then the snow-covered Lowari Pass. The campaign "included one future field-marshal, at least nine future generals and a number of knights. From a career point of view, Chitral was clearly a good place to have on one's CV."[8] Winston Churchill saw action at Malakand as a young lieutenant, and wrote about it in his first book. As prime minister, he would later play the Great Game in earnest.[9]

In 1898 Curzon was appointed viceroy of India. Three years later, he created the NWFP from territory that was taken from Afghanistan when the Durand Line was drawn, and from the Punjab. In Afghanistan, Habibullah became emir; he would rule until 1919. The conflict between Russia and Britain got its name, the Great Game, in 1901 with the appearance of Rudyard Kipling's novel, *Kim*. While it is true that a Russian foreign minister called the conflict the "tournament of shadows," and Conolly had called it "a Great Game" in a letter from Bokhara in about 1842, the world would never have known the conflict as "the Great Game" except for

Kipling and *Kim*. Some say the Great Game ended with a secret agreement that was signed by Russia and Britain in 1907, and what has happened since then is a "new Great Game." Others say that Russia was
duplicitous: it did not really plan to leave the Great Game in 1907, and it
continued even after the Revolution in 1917, as Lenin threatened to "set
the East ablaze." By this calculation, the Great Game did not end until
Britain withdrew from India in 1947. A "new Great Game," if one exists,
would therefore date from 1947.[10]

Because so many people involved in this book were readers and
admirers of Kipling and *Kim,* it could be said that he was the godfather of
the trip itself. Rudyard Kipling (1865–1936) was one of the most famous
writers of his time. He had a gift for capturing the dialects of ordinary
people—those from the British Isles (as they were called in those days)
and those from the Indian subcontinent. Nearly every book about the
Great Game or India or Afghanistan in the nineteenth century (and many
since then) includes a quotation or two from Kipling. The two Americans
in this trip mentioned Kipling more than once, and all three had doubtless read *Kim*. Lord Wavell's anthology, *Other Men's Flower's,* contains
more poems by Kipling than by any other poet, and Wavell was president
of the Kipling Society in his later years. Gordon Enders admired Kipling's
famous boy hero so much that he called himself "an American Kim."
Albert Zimmermann owned a complete collection of Kipling's works.
He referred to one of Kipling's heroes, the brave, fictional Gunga Din, in
describing the Swat Valley in a letter to his wife. And Zimmermann's
British friend in India, April Swayne-Thomas, referred in her letters to
places that appear in poems written by Kipling.[11]

The boy hero of *Kim* was Kimball O'Hara, orphaned son of an Irish
man who was a sergeant in the Indian army, and his Irish wife. The boy
grew up as a preternaturally wise street urchin in Lahore, although he
was, in fact, a "sahib, and the son of a sahib," which gave him a special
place in society. The Second Afghan War took place at about the time
the events in the book took place, although it is not mentioned. At age
thirteen Kim is recruited to be a successful spy in the Great Game. And
the name of the young man, Kim, has become a metaphor for spies. That
was true not only for Gordon Enders, whose travels are described in this

book, but also for Harold A. R. Philby, known by his boyhood nickname as "Kim" Philby—the most successful spy of his generation, who played the game for the Soviet Union. It was also true for Kermit "Kim" Roosevelt Jr., grandson of the president, who played the game for America, against the Soviets. A copy of *Kim* is said to have been on the bedside of the chief American spy of his time, Allen Dulles, when he died.[12]

The viceroy, Curzon, feared that a secret treaty had been signed between Tibet and Russia. In 1904 he sent two expeditions into Tibet, and the British entered Lhasa on 3 August 1904. In 1919, desiring a greater degree of independence, Afghanistan declared war on the British in what is known as the Third Anglo-Afghan War. Zimmermann and Enders observed scenes of that war in November 1943. British military aircraft dropped bombs on Kabul and Jelalabad, and both sides then sued for peace. The war lasted only a month. The Treaty of Rawalpindi in August 1919 allowed Afghanistan to conduct its own foreign affairs.[13]

After the Russian Revolution in 1917, Lenin issued a call to set the East ablaze, hoping that the Communist Party of India would create a Socialist republic there. The British government issued stern warnings in 1922, and "the Soviets agreed to sign a declaration aimed at curbing once and for all their activities in India and elsewhere." In spite of his agreement in the Atlantic Charter, Churchill fought to keep India in the empire, but after he was voted out of office India gained independence and partition in 1947.[14]

In 1933 Zahir Shah became king of Afghanistan at the age of nineteen, although for several years the actual rulers were the king's uncles. In 1934 Afghanistan was admitted to the League of Nations, and in 1940 it proclaimed its neutrality in the war. Louis Goethe Dreyfus, envoy extraordinary and minister plenipotentiary to Iran since 1939, was given an additional appointment with the same title to Kabul. The first representative of the U.S. government to reside in Kabul was Major Gordon Enders, military attaché, who arrived in December 1941, followed by the chargé d'affaires, Charles Thayer, in June 1942. The first resident minister, Cornelius Van H. Engert, arrived in July 1942. The Americans were welcomed, for they appeared to have no territorial interests in Afghanistan, whereas the Afghans remained wary of the British, with whom they had fought three wars. By 1943, however, as the Axis appeared to be losing World War II, the Afghans saw the British and Americans as useful antagonists to Russia, their ancient enemy to the north.

At the same time that Enders, Thayer, and Engert were creating an official role for the United States in Afghanistan, the United States was also engaging officially in Tibet for the first time. Franklin Delano Roosevelt (FDR) had authorized an Office of Strategic Services (OSS) mission to Lhasa in 1942. Major Ilia Tolstoy, grandson of the famous author, and Captain Brooke Dolan II were dispatched with a framed photograph of FDR as a gift to the seven-year old Dalai Lama. They left Delhi in September 1942, assisted by the secretary of state for India, Sir Olaf Caroe, and FDR's friend Suydam Cutting (then a captain in the OSS in Delhi), and arrived in Lhasa in December. The State Department sought to demonstrate American friendship and the War Department "was interested in a possible military supply route between India and China through the Tibetan mountains." The mission was terminated in March 1943. The OSS chief in China, Milton Miles, was skeptical about the mission. Tolstoy and Dolan were operating independently, whereas he believed their mission should have been placed under his command. Perhaps because he understood China's long-term interest in the territory of Tibet, he also thought the Chinese would oppose it.[15]

As viceroy, Wavell correctly saw that India would become independent, and he attempted to ameliorate the problems that he believed would (and did) ensue. Wavell was punished for his efforts by Clement Atlee, Churchill's successor as prime minister, and was pushed into retirement. But independence could not be denied, and Lord Mountbatten presided over the final ceremonies of the handover from Britain and the partition of India on August 15, 1947. After Britain left India in 1947, "for the British, at least, the Great Game was well and truly over." Sir Olaf Caroe, the last governor of the NWFP before the independence and partition of India, concurred.[16]

Two

The Travelers, and Others
Who Were Involved in the Trip

And I am reckoned something of a player of the Game myself!
—Rudyard Kipling, *Kim*

The Adventurer: Enders

Gordon Bandy Enders was the instigator and driving force behind the trip along the border of Afghanistan and India in November–December 1943. It is very likely a journey that he had wanted to make when he was a child, growing up on the border between India and Tibet, where he imagined that he was an "American Kim."[1] He saw that the journey became a real possibility when he was appointed as the U.S. military attaché to Kabul in the fall of 1941; he began to plan for the trip at that time. Two years later he drove the jeep that took the three Anglo-American officers from Peshawar over the Lowari Pass to Chitral, and then to Quetta, in Baluchistan.

Gordon Enders was born in the little town of Essex, Iowa, 7 May 1897. He was the second of the three children of E. Allen Enders, a circuit-riding Presbyterian minister, and his wife, a Swiss Huguenot named Frances-Marie Seibert. His older sister Miriam had been born in November 1895, and his younger brother Robert was born in September 1899. In about 1901 the father was accepted as a missionary, and the young family sailed to Bombay. His father began his work as a preacher while his mother raised the family and taught school at Etawah, near the Grand Trunk Road. In 1906 they moved to the village of Almora, about 250 miles to the north, near the border of India and Tibet. Their house was about eight miles outside the village, on the top of a seven thousand–foot mountain known as Simtolah, with the great peak of Nanda Devi in the background. Gordon lived in India in his formative years, from the age of four until he was fifteen.

As a *babu* (child) his first teacher was Jowar Singh, a high-caste Hindu hillman; from him he learned to hunt and to speak Hindustani. Kipling's book *Kim* was published in 1901, and although he was young, Gordon read enough of it to recognize the experiences of the fictional Kim that were similar to his own. While he was recovering from a severe burn, he was taken into the household of Jowar's father-in-law, a Tibetan named Chanti, who he learned was a spy for the Indian government. Enders became the *chela* (student or disciple) to Chanti, his guru. This relationship was similar to that of Kim, who was *chela* to his guru, a Buddhist monk. Chanti taught him the ways of the spies, the "Kim-men," as Enders called them. Gordon's imagination was vivid: "Before Chanti left Almora he took Jowaru and me along the Pilgrim's Trail . . . [where a] bronzed priest of Nepal trudged unseeing through the human stream, a naked boy at his heels. They might have been Kim and his Lama." He learned that although the Tibetans preferred to remain in isolation, they preferred Britain to Russia.[2]

Enders' father died in 1910, and his mother accepted a post as matron of girls at Allahabad College, which was Chanti's alma mater. Gordon returned to America in 1912 to begin preparation to enter college at the College of Wooster, in Ohio. He spent five years in Wooster—two years finishing high school, and three years in college. One of his housemates was William A. Eddy, who a quarter century later was "a Princeton professor [who] had lived through so many Armenian massacres in Asia Minor that he was always getting them mixed up." Enders' friend was already famous by 1935, when Enders wrote these words, and he went on to an even more memorable career in World War II.[3]

Enders had a remarkable career in World War I. He left college the year before he was to graduate, first serving as an ambulance driver for the French in Picardy and at Verdun, and then, after completing aviation school, as an aviator for the French and American air forces. It was a grim business. Forced down more than once—perhaps three times—he was so badly wounded at one time that he was declared dead. He awoke to find a Red Cross "gray lady" named Elizabeth Crump at his side. He fell in love with her, and they were married at the Hôtel de Ville in La Rochelle on 22 April 1919.[4]

He was in New York until 1920, but he planned to return to the Orient. While he was in New York, he wrote a two-page piece, "Prohibition in Old India," that was published in the monthly journal *Asia.* The lead article in this issue of *Asia* was by Roy Chapman Andrews. It is unlikely that Enders could have known it, but Andrews had until recently been an undercover secret agent of the Office of Naval Intelligence (ONI), a fact not revealed until 2003. Lowell Thomas was then an associate editor of *Asia.* Three years later Thomas became the first private American citizen to visit Afghanistan, about nineteen years before Enders became the first American diplomat to live there.[5]

Enders took the civil service examination for clerk to trade commissioner, under the Bureau of Foreign and Domestic Commerce. He was sent to the American legation in Peking (now spelled Beijing), where he was an assistant to the commercial attaché until 1923. He then went into business, selling American cotton to Chinese and Japanese mill operators, and was the China manager for the Carnation Milk Company. He recalled spending at least nine months of each year traveling, and he returned to the United States on at least five occasions. His first book was coauthored with Edward Anthony, a professional writer, and published in 1935.[6]

Enders became aware of the disorganized nature of the Chinese government, and of the unwavering focus of Japan on the conquest of China. He sold twenty U.S. Corsair airplanes to Chiang Kai-shek, and then worked for him as technical aviation advisor for two years (1927–1929). In 1932 he met Chos'gyi Nyimo, Panchen Lama of Tashilhunpo, in Madame Chiang's living room at the Chiangs' summer home. The

Panchen appointed Enders to the Upper House of the Tibetan National Assembly. This was apparently on the basis of his *chela–guru* relationship to Chanti, his unique skills as a pilot, and his Hindustani, Tibetan, and Chinese language skills, which were remarkable for a "foreign devil." Enders' "Passport to Heaven" is on the endpapers of his book, *Foreign Devil,* and he described his plan to fly gold out of Tibet for the Panchen Lama in a story published in 1936.[7]

When Enders returned to China in 1936, he found the Panchen Lama had just nominated the boy who would become the fourteenth Dalai Lama. Soon after, Japan invaded North China, and by the first week in September it was clear that Shanghai would fall. The Panchen slowly progressed back toward Lhasa; he died at the monastery of Jyekundo, close to Lhasa, on 30 November 1937. The plan to fly the gold from Tibet collapsed. Enders escaped at night via Nanking, and sailed for home.

After Enders' return to the United States, he taught history at Purdue University from March 1937 until 29 April 1941, giving lectures there and elsewhere on his wide range of experiences. On 17 September 1941 he was commissioned as an intelligence officer in the U.S. Army, assigned to G-2 (Military Intelligence Division, or MID). He was superbly well qualified, and he probably had little trouble getting approval from the Army for appointment as a military attaché in the State Department. It appears that during the final weeks before he left for India, when he was en route to Afghanistan, he paid a visit to the British embassy. There he met the assistant military attaché, Lieutenant Colonel Reginald "Rex" Benson, who had arrived in March 1941. Copies of Enders' letters from India in November and December 1941 to his wife, Betty were forwarded by Betty Enders to Gordon's niece Trudy Enders on 9 May 1942. Betty mentioned that she had heard that Gordon's brother, Robert, who had been a professor at Swarthmore before the war, was in Washington at that time. Robert Enders later became a translator for the OSS.

The letters from India were typed by Enders over a period of several days. His wife sent excerpts to WBAA, the Purdue University radio station, but the letters have never previously been published. While en route to Delhi in late 1941, Enders wrote the following:

[Tuesday 18 November] Last night before taking the train I had dinner at the Farbos, an Italian-owned restaurant, which is considered the best in Calcutta. Its windows are covered for blackouts but it is gay and full of cooling fans inside. We saw dining two Indian sisters who are reputed to be the most beautiful in Hindustan. They had been done by famous portrait painters. I took the 9:03 train and had a very comfortable two-bunk compartment to myself, and the whole car is air-conditioned. A bearer brought coffee at 7:30. We breakfasted at 9:00—the food being wired for at headquarters was brought to the compartment on trays.

I am drinking in the Hindustan that I knew 30 years ago. The big changes so far have been turkeys. There are large flocks of them in the country tended by half-naked little boys. Of course, there are motor cars everywhere and they are new. The Grand Trunk Road is now paved, and there are Hindu, Mohammedan, and vegetarian restaurants at the big stations. But otherwise I see no marked differences.

Looking at the fields I've seen parrots, pigeons, and the big, blue cranes we call sahnus. The lentils, kaffir corn, sugar cane, and grain, the sisal and mustard are still there. The cattle are on the plains—at the kites and vultures [sic]. Little boys still herd the goats and irrigation is still done with Persian wells. There are ponds with water-buffalo and water-chestnuts in them, and the dhobis [washerman/woman (Hindi)] wash their clothes by beating them on stones, while their sway-backed little donkeys graze with hobbled forelegs near-by.

In the villages the trees are still thick, with the cleared off thrashing floors, the mud huts with the animals tied outside, and the women still making dungcakes for cooking. It is India all right!

[Wednesday 19 November] We stopped to take our lunch at Fatehpur-Haswa, where my father is buried.[8] I saw that the Grand Trunk Road was not paved, and caught a glimpse of the great Peepul Tree in the monkey temple yard where they feed the monkeys in the evening. It's quite remarkable how I seem to feel the texture of the white dust everywhere, and to know the smell of the grasses, and the sound of the trees.

At Etawah, tea was brought in.[9] The same old buck-monkeys were in the station courtyard—with the oxen and bullock carts parked by the road side, with the animals lying along side ruminating. I remembered from childhood hearing the Punjab mail going by our house in the early morning at Etawah, and I remembered where the tracks were from our house. Our bungalow wasn't visible because it sits back from the road. As the train crossed the Grand Trunk Road I was pleased to find it still unpaved, with nary a motor car in sight, but a line of camels, carts, and horse-drawn ekka [buggy], all waiting for us to pass at the same old crossing with its iron gates.

In the fields, during the day, I saw some gorgeous peacocks pecking among the lentils. When evening fell, the cooking smoke streamed out whitely among the mango trees and I could see the little dung fires with dim shapes moving around them. To me it was a kind of reincarnation.

[Saturday 22 November] In a few minutes I must dress in uniform to have dinner with General Sir Archibald Wavell whom I met the first day. It's to be kind of an American affair with General Wheeler and his party, some of whom I met in Washington and some in Honolulu. . . .[10]

[Sunday 23 November] I *greatly* enjoyed the dinner at which were about fifteen—three of us Americans. General Wavell's three pretty daughters were included. The long table stretched in front of a large fire-place, with the commander-in-chief sitting in the middle and Lady Wavell opposite. I was placed at her left. After dinner I talked with General Wavell and his very charming wife. . . .

[Saturday 29 November][11] I'm all set to cross the border into Afghanistan on Wednesday or Thursday of next week. The trip from Delhi up took its allotted 24 hours and the journey was very dusty. . . .

[Monday 1 December] . . . My today's schedule is tiffin [light mid-day meal] with the R.A.F. [RAF, or Royal Air Force] and dinner with the governor, Sir George Cunningham, to whom I carry Colonel Benson's letter of introduction. . . .[12]

[Tuesday 2 December] I have had my dinner with the Governor and am now set to go through the Khyber Pass. . . . [Y]ester-day, I lunched with the local R.A.F. acting chief, his wife and some friends. We talked a lot of shop (my host and I) up to tiffin, and, after eating, we went out to see his farm. . . . At this point a distinguished Pathan landowner from Kohat [a city in North Waziristan] drove up (by previous arrangement) and two car-loads of us went into the native city of Peshawar. The landowner was a "Rai Bahadur," the holder of a title and has two sons in the Frontier army.[13] Both of them are Oxford. . . . We went back to tea with our party because we were all late, and then back here to dress for the Governor's dinner and the dinner was most satis-factory. There were Lady and Sir George Cunningham, a Mr. and Mrs. Joyce of the Civil Service, two A.D.C.'s [aides-de-camp] and myself. The Cunninghams are delightful people and my after din-ner talk with him, most informative and helpful. . . .

[Wednesday 3 December] . . . In Delhi I sat in a conference with our General Wheeler and British G.H.Q. [general headquarters] and have received what are practically orders to drive up to Russia and into Iran and down to the Indian border again. It's about 2000 miles. . . .

[Thursday 4 December] During these busy days here, I've taken a tonga only once. The remainder of the time I walk. Perhaps I average six to eight miles a day. This morning I was trying to take in some of the details to pass on to you. There is a profusion of flowering shrubs—poinsettias, bougainvilleas and a low bush with bright henna flowers which are trumpet-like and grow in clusters. The trees are magnificent—huge peepuls with smooth whitish bark and light green and glossy leaves; pines, tamarisks and sheesham. I believe I even saw a eucalyptus tree. Then, too, there's a pepper tree which looks much like a willow. Out on the dusty plain there are real autumn tints, although no trees seem to be losing their leaves. The flowers, too, are interesting. There are roses everywhere in bloom, and considered almost a weed. They come in all colors. There are many deep red lilies in bloom in a park I pass. The big thing, however, is chrysanthemum. They are everywhere in purples, russets and yellows. The birds are very noisy, especially the grey-necked Indian crow. . . . The big hawk, called chiel, has a note of his own, and he is very bold, like the crow swooping right down on the sidewalks for tidbits. There are sparrows, of course, and minas (which you have seen in Honolulu and Hongkong). This morning I saw 6 brilliant green parrots (very noisy), with long pointed tails and (I suspect) grey-green heads.

On the roads one sees tongas, bicycles galore, not so many cars, but plenty of bullock and buffalo carts with heavy wooden wheels. Then there are the donkeys. . . . Sometimes you'll see a six-foot Pathan sitting on one and holding his foot [sic] up so they won't drag. For the most part, these donkeys go in groups of four or five, carrying wood, coal, sugar cane or anything else and in charge of an urchin who is no bigger than they. Men and boys alike, however, sit on the very end of the donkey—directly over its hind legs. I suppose this is to prevent breaking its back in case of a huge man. I have a donkey-boy friend who is very dirty and loves to stare at me out of his good eye as he passes the hotel gate.

One also sees sheep and goats being led singly through the bazaars on leashes like dogs. This morning a boy had a pet (and huge) ram which he was sicking onto his boy friends, much to their terror and delight. The timid ones ran behind a grey-bearded barber who shaved a customer squatting in the dust all unconscious of what transpired.

Last evening, after tea and writing, I walked through the crowded bazaar to see the remarkably fine fruit and vegetable stands, and to watch good Moslems drinking tea out of large and lovely brass samovars. There was what sounded like a riot down the street, but when I went over I found it was only a lot of school boys holding a silver athletic trophy aloft and celebrating at the top of their lungs. But you should see the carrots and cabbages, the grapes and pomegranates they have here. I should think they are unsurpassed anywhere. This (and Afghanistan) is real fruit and vegetable country. The other shops were interesting, too; but rather a hodge-podge of shoddy European stuff mixed in with the native brass, cloth, etc. Plenty of tailors seem to live in the bazaar, and I saw a shop where the big Singer Sewing machine had been sunk into the floor so that the pedal was out of sight, its operator appeared to be legless. Coming out (and passing the old blind beggar who asks Allah to bless you) I heard some tentative drum beating. Ahead, there was a bright light as for a celebration and presently I saw a band of bearded Pathans of the most remarkable aspect. On their heads were bright yellow hats meant to look like tam o'shanters, but managing to look more like chef's caps. They had abbreviated khaki coats on, and their baggy trousers (believe it or not) were fashioned from Scottish plaid. There were four drummers and about six pipers with bagpipes under their arms. They stood in a circle facing inward, and blocking the sidewalk. When he saw me, the No. 1 drummer exercised his English. He said, 'bon, thoo, tree!' With that, the whole crowd burst into allegedly musical action. The old blind beggar came hobbling over, calling on Allah and hoping to find a generous crowd, and I escaped.

Enders left for the Khyber Pass on the morning of Saturday 6 December for the two-day drive to Kabul. He would have arrived there on Monday 8 September, the day that Pearl Harbor was attacked (Asia time). He was the sole representative of the U.S. government in Afghanistan for the next five months. It was an area that seethed in intrigue, although the country was officially neutral in the war. The British and the Americans were on one side, facing the Germans, Italians, and Japanese on the other. The Soviets were the allies of the British and Americans against the Germans and Italians, but not against the Japanese. The fortunes of the Allies looked grim in 1941 and 1942, and Burma—and India itself—appeared to be in peril. Under Rommel the Germans and Italians drove to just outside Cairo. The Germans then turned on the Soviet Union and pushed the Russians back to Stalingrad and Moscow. The Afghans wanted to be on the winning side, and it took all of Enders' skills to persuade them that the Allies, led by America, would turn the corner. His insouciance, which irritated some of his colleagues, was just right for this mission.

Enders traveled widely in Afghanistan from the time he arrived in December 1941 until he was reassigned to New Delhi in December 1943. Most of his letters are in the archives of Military Intelligence (RG 165), but some are in the State Department archives, on microfilm. As an example, Enders, by letter of 30 March 1943, requested a Dodge carryall for the Afghan king, at the king's request, and Enders requested it be the U.S. Army Air Force's Dodge, diverted to be used by the king.[14]

Some of Enders' military intelligence reports were reviewed by one or two and sometimes three different people, using a red pencil and occasionally ink, in different handwriting. They critically, and sometimes sarcastically, reviewed Enders' comments on geography, history, and politics, with global statements like "False." They frequently corrected his spelling and distances, sometimes very sharply. I do not know if Enders ever saw these comments, but if he did he must have been furious. The reports show that Enders had many, many problems with the various Afghan factions, foreign diplomats, Axis operatives, the OSS, his counterparts in the American diplomatic service, and the British.

One of Enders' reports was dated 6 September 1943, on "Afghanistan's Strategic Geography." This report describes the area that Enders planned to visit in India in November and December 1943. It implies that he already knew what he planned to see in India. The most relevant portion is Part IV, "Attack from the South": "Tribal Complications: Any advance from India is complicated by the Tribal Areas which contain uncertain elements of riflemen, totalling some 50,000, who are well known for their warlike qualities and readiness to fight. In order to cope with this potentially dangerous threat in the rear, the sub-bases at Parachinar, Miram Shah, Wanna [corrected in red pencil to Wana] and Fort Sandeman would be necessary."[15]

Other reports in this folder show problems that Enders encountered, some of which were of his own making, and others resulted when he needed to be confrontational. For example, on 20 October 1943 Enders drove in a two-car caravan to Kabul from Peshawar with Sir Aurel Stein, who was eighty-one and in poor health. Because of Stein's advanced age and illness, Enders went on ahead with Stein and arrived in Kabul at 4:30 p.m. When the other car did not arrive by 6:00 p.m., he went back to look for it. The other car had mechanical problems, and needed assistance. His memo to the minister on 22 October gives the harrowing details of the trip to recover the other vehicle.[16] Stein died on 26 October and was buried in Kabul. Another memorandum for the minister, this one on 4 November 1943, provides details of a trip by a two-car caravan to the border with India at Torkham, where "the Afghan soldiers attempted to stop the car by hanging onto the fenders." He shook them off and drove on to Quetta.[17]

If Enders had the chance to talk about his plans for the trip, he would surely have discussed them, or even bragged about them, to Louis Dreyfus, the U.S. minister to Iran. Charles Thayer stayed with Dreyfus in Tehran on his way into Afghanistan, and Enders met him in Tehran to escort him to Kabul. Dreyfus would later be the host of the successful Tehran Conference of FDR, Churchill, and Stalin that took place while the trip to the NWFP province was under way. Dreyfus left Iran for his next post on 12 December, just before the trip ended. Dreyfus would return to Afghanistan as ambassador in April 1949.[18]

Enders arrived in Peshawar to meet the other travelers—Bromhead and Zimmermann—on 15 November 1943, a day later than expected. He was alone in his jeep, nicknamed "Ma Kabul."

The Knight: Bromhead

Sir Benjamin Denis Gonville Bromhead, Bart., OBE, IA, known as "Sir Benjy," was a hereditary knight, the fifth Baronet Bromhead.[19] He was about to make the trip on the NWFP that Enders had been waiting to take ever since he came to Peshawar in 1941. But no matter how much Enders wanted to make the trip, Bromhead's consent for it was essential.

Benjy Bromhead was born on 7 May 1900 and was educated at Wellington College, Berkshire, England. He went to India as a young man and spent his military career mainly in the NWFP. He fought in the Iraq Campaign in 1920 and in the Waziristan campaign from 1922 to 1924, where he was wounded. He fought in the NWFP in 1930, where he was mentioned in despatches. He fought in the Waziristan campaign in 1937, where he was again mentioned in despatches. He was commandant of the Zhob Militia, Baluchistan, between 1940 and 1943. He was invested as an officer, Order of the British Empire (OBE), in 1943.

Bromhead was taking on a new role as assistant public relations officer for the province, working out of the governor's office in Peshawar. He planned to take an orientation trip along the entire border at the end of November 1943, from the northernmost semi-independent principality, Chitral, to the key southern city, Quetta. The trip would include visits to all of the tribal areas. He knew most of this region already, but the leaders needed to be visited regularly, and he needed to introduce himself to them in his new capacity. He was asked to take Enders along to show him the problems that the British had with the frontier tribes, and how they dealt with them. He and the intelligence officer in Quetta discussed this, and decided that, if possible, a third person ought to be added to the mission. The person selected would be from the naval liaison office (NLO) in Karachi.

Bromhead and his wife, Lady Nancy, and their two young daughters were living at the Services Hotel on Fort Road, near the Governor's House. She was pregnant with their third child, who they expected would be born at about the time the trip ended.

The Socialite: Zimmermann

The intelligence bureau in Quetta (IB Quetta) asked Bromhead if he could also take one of the Americans from the NLO in Karachi, to be added as a third traveler. Bromhead agreed, subject to the governor's sanction "which he said he thought would certainly be forthcoming."[20] The man who was picked for this was Albert Walter Zimmermann, USNR. Zimmermann, who for the sake of simplicity is often referred to hereafter as AZ, appears to have been picked at random. However, there are good reasons to believe he was a specific choice, and the message from IB Quetta was carefully written to ensure that he, and only he, would be sent.

Al Zimmermann was the second ranking officer at the NLO in Karachi. He would ordinarily have been the executive officer, but had not been officially named to that position; he would later become the commanding officer (CO). His position as a naval liaison officer (ALUSLO) was analogous to an assistant naval attaché. Like all naval attachés, naval observers, and ALUSLOs, he was trained as an intelligence officer. And, like most of them at this point in the war, he was a reservist.[21]

Albert W. Zimmermann was born in Philadelphia, Pennsylvania, on 11 June 1902, the youngest of seven children of John Zimmermann and Eva Katherine (Kellenbenz) Zimmermann. John Zimmermann had come to America from Gussenstad in the kingdom of Württemberg in 1874 as a nearly penniless man of eighteen with no close friends. He was, however, a member of the hardworking and close-knit German community in Philadelphia, and he achieved the American Dream. As a weaver, he started by selling his own carpets from a push cart on the streets of Philadelphia, where he was spotted by the owners of the Philadelphia Tapestry Mills. They took him in as an employee, and he later rose to be their partner. His patents made it possible to weave enormous carpets, and their company, renamed Artloom Corporation, became one of the largest of its type in America. In his later years, he was a very wealthy but charitable man, and he was bishop of the reorganized Church of Latter Day Saints in the eastern United States. John Zimmermann made each of his children a gift of $1 million when they married.

Albert Zimmermann received a degree in electrical engineering when he graduated from the University of Pennsylvania in 1923, where he had been a member of Sigma Tau (Honorary Engineering Fraternity), a member of the Sphinx Honorary Senior Society, and president of the Glee Club. He entered the family carpet and fabric business and eventually became a vice president of the company. In 1926 he married the daughter of a prominent Philadelphia ophthalmologist in what was said to be the society wedding of the season. In contrast to Zimmermann's second-generation roots, his wife's went back to the fleets of William Penn and John Winthrop. After a grand honeymoon, they settled in a new home, Cotswold Corners, in Haverford. He joined the usual golf and country clubs of the Philadelphia gentry, who lived along the Main Line: the Philadelphia Country Club; Merion Cricket Club; Fourth Street Club; and a men's singing group, the Orpheus Club. With his interest in textiles, he formed a wool brokerage in partnership with another Orpheus Club member. Financially, he was very comfortable, but not ostentatious; he was a shrewd observer, but he kept his mouth shut about what he saw. When he was in the Navy, he wrote to his wife that she need not worry about spending money. He assured her that they were wealthy, although he would never have said it aloud.[22]

One of his friends before the war was a naval reservist named Jack Kane, who was the district intelligence officer for the Third Naval District, headquartered at the Philadelphia Navy Yard. AZ's wife's best friend was Kane's wife, Amelie. It may have been Kane who encouraged him to take pictures of the German Bund in Philadelphia, when the Bund turned out in uniforms with swastika armbands for the wedding of one of the Zimmermanns' household employees. AZ sent these photos to the FBI, and they were AZ's first contact with the federal intelligence service.[23]

After the war broke out in Europe in 1939, AZ's friends began making plans for what they would do when the United States entered the war. Some, like AZ's father-in-law, who had been a major, were too old to serve again, but they encouraged others to prepare. Some decided to join the reserves, or to reactivate their previous commissions. AZ was a bit too old to be a fighter, and he was color-blind, so some areas of service were closed to him. Intelligence was a consideration. Army G-2 was a possibility, but he had no connections with Army intelligence. Kane encouraged him to join the ONI. AZ also knew Captain Tom Thornton, a naval intelligence officer in the Third Naval District, and he, too, was encouraging. His good friend Joseph Freeman Lincoln and his next-door neighbor Clarence Lewis joined the OSS. But the OSS did not even exist until 13 June 1942 (it had previously been known as the coordinator of information, or COI), and AZ was already talking with the Navy by then.[24]

AZ also had a couple of other door openers for the ONI. The head of ONI in the First Naval District (New York) was Commander (later Captain) Vincent Astor, who led "the Room," a secret intelligence operation in New York City. Astor had been secretly named by FDR to vet candidates for the ONI, and AZ had at least two connections with this group. His good friend John "Jack" Thayer Jr. had survived the sinking of *Titanic* as a young man; Jack's father and Vincent Astor's father had gone down together on the ship. And AZ's friend Malcolm Aldrich, who he called "Mac," had been a member of Skull and Bones at Yale. He was a cousin of the banker, Winthrop Aldrich, who was also a member of the Room.[25]

By September 1942 AZ had decided on Navy intelligence. He tidied up his personal affairs, got a waiver for color-blindness, and on 21 September he took the oath of office as a lieutenant, I-V(P), USNR—the "P" standing for probationary. His appointment was backdated to 1 August 1942, and his appointment was effective on 8 September. He went to basic training as an officer at the Washington Navy Yard from 18 October to 14 November. He then reported to the ten-week intelligence indoctrination course at Dartmouth from 18 November to 28 January 1943. While he was at Dartmouth, the new naval intelligence officers developed a sense of camaraderie, and it was not all work: AZ noted that a singer named Paul Robeson performed there on Colgate weekend, in late November. They treated with suitable respect the director of naval intelligence (DNI), Rear Admiral Harold C. Train, and his ambitious deputy, Captain Ellis Zacharias—later called "The Man Who Wanted to Be DNI."[26] Admiral Train and Captain Zacharias both spoke at their graduation from the school. How much the students knew about the conflict between these two men is unknown, but they were smart fellows, and it was probably a good introduction to the arcane and back-biting world of intelligence. A classmate there, in another platoon, was another Philadelphia socialite, and brother of his friend in the Orpheus Club, Jim Winsor. The brother, Curtin Winsor, a somewhat younger man, went to Washington in the Far East desk of ONI. Curt Winsor later became AZ's desk officer, or handler.[27]

AZ began French language school in Washington, DC, in preparation to go to Dakar, Senegal, French West Africa, as a naval observer. He enjoyed the course in French and was doing well, but his orders were canceled after two months, and he was instead sent to the Advanced Operational Intelligence School in New York City. He began the course at the Henry

Hudson Hotel on 19 April and completed it on 28 May 1943. He was then assigned to the NLO, Karachi. He would spend nearly two years there. It would be a challenging and sometimes trying experience, but the most interesting adventure of his life.

AZ's trip to Karachi would be familiar to anyone who lived through World War II, but it seems exotic to others. After saying good-bye for what would be at least a year, and perhaps eternity, on 23 June 1943, AZ boarded a commercial airline flight from Washington, DC, for New York. From there, he flew to Botwood, Newfoundland, and on to Foynes, near Limerick, in what had recently been the Irish Free State. All his letters passed the censor, and in the next two years only a few words—the names of some of the places on commercial postcards on his route to Karachi— were ever redacted by the censor. He touched down in Port Lyautey and Casablanca, Morocco; Oran and Algiers, Algeria; Constantine and Sousse, Tunisia; Tripoli and Benghasi, Libya, and arrived in Cairo on 1 July to get in line to continue on to the east.

He stayed in Cairo in relative comfort at the famous Shepheard's Hotel, and—as was the custom with expats and intelligence officers—he made good use of the time. He saw the Sphinx and the pyramids, and visited Philadelphia physicians who were at Army General Hospital 38. They started to receive casualties from the invasion of Sicily, which began while he was in Cairo. While there, he met Edgar Snow and Tom Treanor, who were also staying at Shepheard's. They were war correspondents who had been in India and China and were on their way to cover the invasion of Sicily. Treanor gave AZ an earful of the struggle that was going on in India. Treanor wrote that Gandhi and Nehru wanted the British to leave India so the Hindus could rule it; on the other hand, there was Jinnah, who refused to bargain with the British, and intended to put three-fourths of the Muslims of India into a new country, Pakistan. All three men postured for their political constituencies, and none was willing to compromise. (AZ would see that this was also the British perception of Gandhi, Nehru, and Jinnah, and would transmit this in an intelligence report in 1944.) And "despite protestations and promises of the British that India one day is to get her independence, no apparent step is being made in this direction."[28]

On 4 July AZ took movies of a baseball game with Quentin Reynolds at bat and General Strong umpiring. Reynolds was a well-known war correspondent and Strong was doubtless the Army chief of intelligence (G-2) who detested General William Donovan of the OSS. AZ's host on several days was a naval reservist from Philadelphia, Captain Thomas Anthony "Tom" Thornton, who was now with the U.S. Forces-Cairo. He had seen Lieutenant Commander Jack Kane only the previous week. Thornton planned to take AZ and Commander Gene Markey to Alexandria to pass the time while he and Markey were waiting for a flight out of Cairo, but AZ could not make the trip because he was placed on standby for his flight to the east. On one of his last nights in Cairo, he dined with Henry Hotchkiss, the assistant naval attaché, and several other old friends from Philadelphia. He finally flew out on a Royal Air Force (RAF) B-24 Liberator bomber on 16 July via Habanniah, Iraq, and another unnamed remote airfield. He commented to his wife in a letter that "I didn't need the parachute so I didn't find out whether it worked or not. They say you can always get another if it doesn't." He arrived in Karachi at 5:00 a.m., Monday 19 July 1943.[29]

The NLO in Karachi was a spacious two-story stucco-on-stone residence at 254 Ingle Road, on a frontage of about one hundred yards, and equally deep—a typical American square block. It was surrounded on three sides by a five-foot wall, and was enclosed at the rear by the houses of the twenty or so household servants and their families. In the real estate market in India it was called a bungalow, but this hardly expresses its size and beauty. The first floor of the house had twenty-five-foot ceilings, and the table in the dining room seated eighteen people with ease, and could be expanded to hold more. The first floor was for offices for the leading petty officer and the CO, and the code room, and spaces for guests, including a lounge and library; and the dining room, with its fireplace and George Washington's portrait over the mantel. The second floor was the residence: the CO's suite, the executive officer's suite, a small library, and dormitories for the junior officers and about six enlisted men. There were social events there on many evenings, and grand parties, too, but there also was an ever-present reminder of the war; a locked gun closet was on the stairway with a dozen M-1 rifles, with slings and ammunition.

When AZ arrived there were four officers at the NLO in Karachi: the CO, Lieutenant Commander Francis H. Smith, USN; and Lieutenants Burns, Callahan, and Browning. Except for Smith, all were junior in years to AZ. Browning developed eye trouble and soon headed for home. The rest worked long days, taking their turn on duty call. It was secret work, and AZ said almost nothing about what they did during the days. The Navy's long-distance radio network provided service for the Army and the State Department, so the code room must have been very busy. Karachi was a busy seaport, located near the mouth of the great Indus River. It was the entry point for everything that passed on land into India from the west, and to the north. The State Department cables show that Afghanistan was interested in selling and transshipping wool, of which AZ had special knowledge. Karachi was the entry and exit port for Axis diplomats who traveled under safe conduct to and from Kabul.

AZ was introduced to the strange ways of the NLO almost immediately on arrival, when he received an invitation to dinner with a Madame Dubash. He soon learned that she was a "good-looking" Russian woman of about fifty who was the "girlfriend" of the CO.[30] He also believed that the NLO in Karachi was spending U.S. government funds for lavish entertainment, that they were living in a fool's paradise. He believed all of this was contrary to the instructions to naval intelligence officers, and eventually he was proved right.[31]

In the evenings and on weekends, AZ played bridge with Brigadier N. Godfray Hind and his American-born wife; and with Major D. Montgomery (Monty) Smyth and his wife Joan Smyth.[32] AZ played tennis and partied at the Sind Club, where Governor and Lady Dow held forth, and at the Boat Club. He was a frequent guest in private homes, where his ability to sing was much appreciated. He was also invited to the Karachi Club, which was for Indians (Parsi, Muslim, and Hindus), a rare invitation for an American. He was invited to dinner by his prewar Indian wool supplier, where he learned (with some difficulty) to eat Indian food, and to appreciate the customs of that part of the world. On weekends he often went to the private offshore beach known as Sandspit with members of the American commercial community. He was there on 12 September 1943 with Arlo Bond, who was with Standard Oil. The war rarely intruded;

by then it appeared that Japan would not attempt an invasion of India, and the Germans were slowly retreating. In his first three months he mentioned the war only twice in letters to his wife: the fall of Mussolini and the surrender of Italy on 10 September.

The visitors who passed through the NLO were often mentioned in language that only AZ and his wife, Barbara (hereafter BSZ), could understand. Four groups of "Freeman's friends" (sent out by Joseph Freeman Lincoln, a major in the OSS in London) were so secret that he could not mention their names, but he was able to identify some of them to BSZ because she knew them, too. Others who were named included Senator Richard Russell on 23 August, Ambassador Clarence Gauss "and his attachés" on his way to China on 15 September, and a Mr. Preston, the consul general at Lorenzo Marques, on 9 November. The new American commander, General Julian Haddon, arrived in town on 15 September.[33]

Tropical diseases were always threatening. The insect-borne diseases included dengue (which Zimmermann caught), yellow fever (hopefully protected by vaccination), and malaria (although you could take atabrine to prevent it, most people decided to use mosquito netting at night). And there was diarrheal disease, known as dysentery, which could be from amoebae (lingering and bad) or bacteria (even worse).

Through all of this, AZ was being observed by Clarence Macy, the hardboiled but wise American consul in Karachi, who AZ met for the first time on 15 August and who he saw at least twice after that, but prior to the trip to the NWFP. Macy was in frequent contact with J. R. Harris, the British intelligence officer who received the message on 26 October, asking for an American at the ALUSLO to go to the NWFP. AZ had made a lot of new friends, and he had not made any enemies. Charles Thayer in Kabul probably gave him the nod to make the trip.

AZ was sent to Colombo, Ceylon (now Sri Lanka), on a courier mission on 29 October—only three days after Harris received the message from IB Quetta. His courier mission was surely just a cover; he must have been there to be briefed by Navy intelligence on what to look for and how to comport himself on the NWFP. He stayed in Colombo for two nights and a day with a Lieutenant Commander B. W. Goldsborough. He wrote to his wife that Goldsborough was from Baltimore, and that he "knew the right people." Indeed he did; Brice Worthington Goldsborough II was the son of Phillips Lee Goldsborough, who was governor of Maryland in 1911, and later a U.S. senator. Ceylon had just been designated as the headquarters of the new South East Asia Command (SEAC), and the supreme commander of SEAC, Lord Louis Mountbatten, was moving his staff from Delhi to Kandy, in the interior of Ceylon. AZ would visit Kandy later, but this trip was just to visit Navy intelligence in Colombo. He left on Friday 29 October via Ahmedabad, Bombay, Hyderabad, to Colombo; and he retraced his route, going back to Bombay and then to Karachi, where he arrived on Tuesday 2 November. He saw another ALUSLO, Lieutenant Al Payne, presumably passing on information orally to him, on both trips through Bombay.

The purpose of the trip on the NWFP was stated in the message from IB Quetta, to make "it clear to the American Legation in Kabul what are our frontier problems and our ideas and policy in dealing with them and the Afghans."[34] This was restated with little change by AZ when he sent his typed report to his family: "The trip had been already instigated by the Military Attaché to Kabul (Maj. Enders) to give him an opportunity to see what was on the other side of the fence."[35] But there were many more things that AZ and Enders were looking for. Some of these would be details that provided depth to the main goal, but others were quite different. They may not have been told about some things to watch for, but as good intelligence officers they would be on the lookout for whatever they could see.

Zimmermann was added to balance Enders. Those who had heard Enders speak, and those who had read his books, knew he could tell a good story, but his story was often very selective. It was hard to know if Enders was telling the truth, and he often exaggerated. Zimmermann, on the other hand, though not always an interesting writer, would be inclined to tell it as he saw it, not as he wished it to be.

The Governor: Cunningham

The trip would have been impossible if the governor of the NWFP, Sir George Cunningham, had not approved it. He knew the tribes along the border were quiet at that time, in November 1943, so he was willing to allow the Americans to join Bromhead on his tour.

Sir George Cunningham was born on 23 March 1888, third son of the late James Cunningham and Anna Sandeman, at Broughty Ferry in Forfarshire, now called Angus. His parents later had another son and a daughter. His father was a friend of Robert Louis Stevenson, and received an honorary LLD from St. Andrews.[36]

Cunningham was a good student and was even better at sports at Fettes College, Edinburgh, and later at Magdalen College, Oxford. He was president of the Junior Common Room and captained the Oxford University rugby team that defeated Cambridge by a record score. He entered the Indian Civil Service and left Scotland on 26 October 1911, and except for home leaves on regular occasions, he remained in India for his entire career until he retired in 1946.[37]

Cunningham was posted to Lahore and paid his first visit to the NWFP in the winter of 1913–14; he returned to the NWFP at the end of October 1914 on appointment to the Foreign and Political Department of the government of India. He received the word of his transfer to the NWFP and immediately rode thirty-six miles on horseback to headquarters at Peshawar. He left for Kohat a few days later. It was his first assignment to the tribal territory. The so-called Durand Line of 1893 separated Afghanistan from British India, and it left a depth of tribal territory of about forty miles.

In May 1918 he took a "most memorable tour" to Malakand and Dir, and over the Lowari Pass to Chitral. In his diary, he wrote that he saw yellow crocus, hyacinth, and saxifrage, and in Chitral he had this remarkable experience:

On the left of the road the ground rises in terraces, and along the edge of each terrace were rows of the Mehtar's men, each man with his musket. There must have been three or four thousand of them. . . . We came first to an open expanse of grass where a body guard of the Scouts, Rajputs, and Bodyguard were drawn up. Then horsemen galloped past the popinjay—four little gourds hung from a pole, about 30 feet from the ground—firing their enormous jezails [rifle, Pashtun] as they passed underneath. . . . We passed between heavy iron doors and under an arched entrance

and found ourselves in the outer courtyard of the Mehtar's fort. . . .
Due north, thirty miles away, Tirich Mir, like a frosted cathedral,
towers to heaven![38]

Cunningham's two brothers were killed in service in World War I. He
was assistant commissioner in Tank, NWFP, in December 1918, and he
was involved in negotiations in the brief war with Afghanistan in 1918–19,
as he spent two months traveling between Peshawar and the Khyber Pass.
He then went home on leave, and returned in the summer of 1920, posted
to Kohat, and was in Peshawar in January to be invested with the OBE.

He was involved with the tour early in March 1921 of the Prince of
Wales, for which he was officer in charge of the press. Then the viceroy
came to visit Kohat and was to be given a picnic lunch "under the trees,"
where there were no trees, at an altitude of six thousand feet.[39] There
were other duties and complicated arrangements in the Kurram Valley
and Thal, and in North Waziristan in Bannu, Razmak, Wana, and Jandola.
He went home again on leave in the spring of 1925. When he returned,
he was for a short time stationed in Kabul as the counselor to the British
legation. He was then appointed private secretary to the viceroy, 1926–
31, Lord Irwin (later Lord Halifax), who set a good model for him in his
later postings. During this time, he met and married, in 1929, Kathleen
Mary Adair, of Tullow, County Carlow. He went home on leave again until
1932, and was a member of executive council, NWFP, from 1932 to 1936.
He was on home leave again, and returned to be governor of the NWFP
until he retired. He had accumulated more honors and was knighted just
before he took over the governorship.

His tenure was marked with many *jirgas* (councils) and much travel,
especially in the two Waziristan agencies. On the same morning he took
the oath of office he traveled to Bannu to discuss the issue of the faqir
(also spelled fakir; Muslim mendicant) of Ipi, who had "just appeared on
the scene, who would be a constant source of trouble for the next ten
years."[40] In 1939 Cunningham traveled to Kaniguram for a *jirga,* and to
Razmak, Ladha, and Wana, all of which are places that were seen by the
travelers in December 1943. In 1940 he went to Bannu and Ramzak,

and Miram Shah and Mir Ali, and Kohat—sometimes on horseback and sometimes by airplane. He frequently walked about and showed great courage.

Propaganda in support of Pakistan first came to Cunningham's attention in 1941. At that time, it "was not expected to be a separate dominion [but would be] a Northern Muslim State strong enough to claim a half share with the Hindus in a Federal Government." The northern territories were unusually peaceful, and one of the few times he mentions them was on 20 November, when he had a very friendly Mohmand *jirga* at Shabkadar. His memoirs did not mention the visit of Enders early in December, and he mentions the outbreak of war in the Pacific without additional comment on 8 December.[41] Early in 1942 he had the unusual experience of entertaining Chiang Kai-shek for two days. The generalissimo traveled to Khyber and was back in time for a banquet in Peshawar on 13 February. In March 1942 Cunningham held an Afridi *jirga* in the Khyber, and was back in the Upper Kurram again in August.[42] He received a visit from the commander in chief, General Sir Claude Auchinleck, who flew in from Karachi.

At the time of the trip by Enders, Bromhead, and Zimmermann, a visitor from Dir said that Dir state was "'more peaceful than it had been for 45 years.' . . . 1943 is remarkable so far as the War was concerned only by the extraordinary few mentions of it which he felt the need to make." "But on the whole the shadow of the war seems to have been removed."[43] In April the viceroy went into Waziristan and landed at Miram Shah, then flew over Razmak and got back in time for Peshawar to shoot snipe. On 25 October Cunningham commented on the ministers in his cabinet, and on 20 November he was at a governors' conference in Delhi with the new viceroy—Wavell having become viceroy in October. Cunningham mentions there was a "bad affair" at Razmak on 14 December, when two Gurkha battalions suffered many casualties during an "ordinary exercise."[44] This was only days after the travelers passed through Razmak on their way to Quetta, and it was on the day before AZ reached Karachi.

Cunningham believed the British were a benevolent presence in the NWFP, because they kept peace between the warring tribes. This benefited

Britain and the empire, and it was also the humane thing to do. He quoted Kipling: "At any price that I can pay, let me own myself."[45]

It is remarkable that there is so little about World War II in Cunningham's memoir. In fact, while there is much about the problems with the tribal areas, especially in the Waziristans, and about politics in Peshawar and Delhi, there is much that is not here—either because it did not appear in the diary, or, more likely, because it was not included by Norval Mitchell in his book.

The Commanding Officer: Smith

The CO at the NLO in Karachi had to agree to send someone on the trip, and he would also have had to decide whether to send himself or to designate someone else. The trip would take at least a month, and in the event it took longer. What good would this trip do for the Navy, and could he spare a man for it? We do not know the answers to the questions, but there are indications for the reasons that he said yes, and sent Zimmermann. He would be glad to get AZ out of Karachi for a while, for although Zimmermann was properly obedient, it was obvious that he did not enjoy Smith's company. He was, as the saying goes, upstaging Smith, and Smith would have been hard-pressed to find a reason to say no.

Lieutenant Commander Francis Howard Smith, USN, known at that time as Howard Smith, was a regular Navy officer who came originally from Akron, Ohio. He was born 27 August 1892, and he had worked in India for the past thirteen years as an employee of the Firestone Corporation, which was headquartered in Akron. He was said to be fluent in Hindustani His regular Navy commission and his work in intelligence suggest that he had been under cover for a long time. He was well connected in the local community. As Zimmermann relates it, his girlfriend was a Russian émigrée, Nadia, who had been (or was still) married to an Indian. Madame Nadia Dubash and a man named Sheikh were employed in some sort of counterespionage activity. The ONI in Washington was wary of this, but had not (yet) put an end to it. Smith threw a birthday party for himself at the NLO in Karachi on 27 August 1943, shortly before the request came to send someone to the NWFP.[46]

Smith was apparently a bit of a martinet to those who worked for him. AZ called him "Com Smith" and wrote to his wife that Smith was "short—quick-witted and cocky—. . . . He knows a lot about this country, having lived here a number of years—can speak Urdu and loves to bask in his importance."[47] On the other hand, he was appreciated by his superiors, or at least by one who had flag rank. Commodore (later Vice Admiral) Milton E. Miles wrote, "'Smitty' didn't fluster. . . . So we requisitioned [him] from the Office of Naval Liaison, Karachi where most of his work had been for SACO [Sino-American Cooperation Organization]."[48]

Kiss up and kick down, the saying goes, so it is not surprising to have two different views of his ability. Smith finished the war in Calcutta, doing cumshaw work for Miles, and then left the Navy. He probably returned to his native Ohio. A "Francis Smith," born on 27 August 1892, died in Akron in January 1975.

The Minister Plenipotentiary: Engert

The message on 26 October 1943 from IB Quetta to J. R. Harris said that it "would be up to Smith to explain the presence of a Naval Liaison Officer to Enders and Engert."[49] Cornelius Engert was the U.S. minister to Afghanistan.

We do not know if Lieutenant Commander Smith, head of the NLO in Karachi, ever contacted Engert or Enders about this message, but after the trip was over Enders wrote to AZ asking him to "remember me to Commander Smith," and it is possible that Smith also contacted Engert. The trip, however, is never mentioned in Engert's personal papers or his official correspondence, nor did his son, Roderick, know about the trip. There is a coded message in Engert's papers that could (and I think probably does) relate to the trip after it was over, which we will see later. There was a lot else going on in Afghanistan that was of concern to Engert, and he and his wife and daughter were in India, two of them sick with typhoid, just before the trip began. He would not have wanted to admit that the trip happened without his knowing it, and he was good at bluffing his way through things. In fact, his entire life as a diplomat was never quite what it seemed to be, but it was, nevertheless, a remarkable career. It was only after he died that his granddaughter pieced together the facts of his life.[50]

The Honorable Cornelius Van Hemert Engert (1887–1985), CBE, was the first U.S. diplomat to serve as a resident chief of mission in Afghanistan. Engert was the envoy extraordinary and minister plenipotentiary in Kabul in November to December 1943, at the time the Enders-Bromhead-Zimmermann mission was proceeding in the NWFP.

Engert was born in Vienna, 31 December 1887, the son of John Cornelius Engert, who was of Dutch origin but a Russian citizen, and Irma Babetz, a Hungarian Jewish physician. Jane Engert says that her grandfather, Cornelius Engert, falsely claimed that he was a great-nephew of Alexander Francis Charles Engert, who was from Hamburg, Germany, and that the Dutch and German Engerts were separate lines from the seventeenth century on. Furthermore, although Cornelius claimed California as his boyhood home, he did not grow up there. His birth name was Adolf Cornelius Van Hemert-Engert. His father had immigrated to St. Petersburg and married for the second time in 1881; he adopted Russian citizenship and died a year later. His wife, Cornelius' mother, went back to her native Hungary, although she also may have returned from time to time to St. Petersburg. After many attempts to have the first name, Adolf, deleted from the official record, he apparently had succeeded by about 1924.

He had gone to school at the K. K. Oberrealschule in Gorz (then Austria-Hungary, now a town divided between Italy [Gorizia] and Slovenia [Nova Gorica]). He traveled to America with his mother in 1904, attended high school in California, and became a naturalized citizen. He received a bachelor's degree in 1908 and a master's degree in 1909 from the University of California, Berkeley, and he was a law student there from 1909 to 1911. He was a Le Conte Memorial Fellow at Harvard in 1911–12, with a scholarship awarded by UC Berkley. He did not matriculate at Harvard, but he nevertheless struck up a friendship with President A. Lawrence Lowell and they continued to correspond for many years. His granddaughter said that from his perspective, "the more times he and Harvard were mentioned in the same sentence, the better."[51]

Engert started working for the U.S. Foreign Service as a student interpreter in Constantinople in 1912, and he was American vice-counsel in

Chanak in 1914. He was vice-consul at Constantinople, February 1915; vice-consul and interpreter at Baghdad, August 1915; on detail at Constantinople, September 1915 to December 1916; and on detail in Syria and Palestine, December 1916 to April 1917. He was attached to Viscount Ishii's mission to the United States from Japan in San Francisco. Engert then served as assistant to and secretary to the American legation at The Hague from August 1917 to September 1919. He served as second secretary to the legation in Tehran from 1920 to 1922.

In May 1922, when he was chargé d'affaires in Iran, he became the first American diplomatic officer to visit Afghanistan. His letter to Robert Woods Bliss on 2 September 1921 requesting the trip included the comment that he had made to the Afghan minister to Persia, suggesting "that it would be a good thing for this country if some American oil experts could be allowed to sniff around a bit and see if there was anything in Afghanistan." Bliss replied on 12 December 1921 that Engert could make an "entirely informal and unofficial" visit to Afghanistan on his way home, at which time he "would doubtless be able to gather much information which would be useful to this and other Departments of the Government."[52]

To reach Afghanistan, Engert traveled to Kabul via ship from Persia through the Persian Gulf to Karachi, by train from Karachi to Peshawar, and by car through the Khyber Pass from Peshawar to Kabul. He was received with great courtesy, and was told that only two Americans had ever been there before him. While he was in Kabul, he heard that Lowell Thomas needed help securing a visa, and he nudged the emir to offer a visa to Thomas. Engert submitted a "Report on Afghanistan" to the State Department in 1923, more than two hundred pages long, which became the department's unofficial guide to the country. Engert then served at the State Department in Washington, DC, from October 1922 to September 1923. During this time, he worked on a deal securing oil concessions from the Iranian government for American oil companies. He was, however, always somewhat controversial. Jane Engert called him a "social climber." She said his efficiency reports commented, "Engert had never been taught in his youth the enormity of false and inaccurate statement."[53]

Engert met his future wife, Sara Cunningham, in San Francisco. She
was from a wealthy and well-connected family and had been a nurse in
Europe in World War I, for which she received the French Médaille de la
Reconnaissance. In September 1923 Engert began eight years of service
in Latin American countries, beginning with Cuba, San Salvador, and
finally Venezuela. Their first child was born on 10 December 1924; the
little boy died at ten hours of a cerebral hemorrhage. Sara had two more
children: Roderick (who was interviewed for this book), born in 1925 in
El Salvador; and Sheila, born in 1929 in Venezuela.[54]

Engert served as first secretary to the American Embassy in Peiping
(now spelled Beijing), China, from June 1930 to June 1933. After serving
in Cairo from June 1933 to July 1935, Engert was named consul general
and resident minister at the American legation in Addis Ababa, Ethiopia.
Engert and his wife were instrumental in saving the personnel of the U.S.
mission from rioters during the collapse of Ethiopia as it fell to Italy, and
he and Sara were commended by FDR. As a result, he developed a personal relationship with the president, which he utilized outside of State
Department channels.[55]

In January 1937 Engert was named consul for the legations in Tehran
and Kabul, and in August 1940 he was posted as consul general in Beirut
and Damascus, where he served during the invasion of France. The minister to Iran, Louis Dreyfus, was accredited by Washington to represent
the interests of the United States in Afghanistan. On 28 January 1941
Dreyfus was directed to visit Kabul, and he was expected to make the
trip when the weather was good enough in the spring. He was told that
"an American diplomatic mission had not been established [because]
our interests in Afghanistan continue to be slight." Dreyfus reported to
Washington on 27 June 1941 that "the Afghans have a sincere and deep
rooted desire in the absence of a friend or neighbor to whom they can
turn to have a disinterested third-power friend to assist and advise them
and they have always hoped that the United States would be willing to fill
such a role."[56]

Over the next several months, the Afghans and Americans negotiated over what the senior U.S. diplomat would be called. It was difficult,
because travel and message traffic was slowed by the war. The break in

negotiations was made by FDR personally, who wrote on 16 March 1942, "Why not name the regular Minister to Afghanistan now and get it over with." Nine days later, Sumner Welles recommended Cornelius Engert. Charles Thayer was given approval by the Afghans to move to Kabul on 22 April, and he opened the U.S. legation on 6 June 1942. Engert presented his credentials to the king on 25 July 1942.[57]

At the same time, the India issue was a problem. It would always be there in connection with Afghanistan, whether India was unified or divided. At the time, it appeared that India would be unified after independence, but as we will see below, Engert was considering a "Pakistan" solution. FDR was concerned about India, too. He wrote to John G. Winant, who was ambassador to England, on 25 February 1942: "In the greatest confidence could you or Harriman [W. Averell] or both let me have a slant on what the Prime Minister thinks about new relationships between Britain and India?"[58]

On 2 August 1942 Enders sent a warning telegram from Peshawar to Engert in Kabul. It shows the ease with which Enders moved across the border, and that he worked for G-2 in New Delhi as well as in Kabul. Enders visited the Valley of Tochi in Waziristan, and he would visit it again on the trip to the NWFP.[59]

There is nothing in the trip reports that suggest that Donovan or the OSS had any role in the initiation of the Enders-Zimmermann trip, or that Engert recorded anything about the trip in his notes, or that he made a definite statement about it after it was over. There was, however, in Engert's correspondence an indication that something was going on at this time that was too sensitive to write about. Engert's telegrams from September 1942 to November 1942 include several exchanges with Donovan and Charles Thayer. This correspondence shows that Engert's communications with Donovan were intact, and Thayer later worked for the OSS, but neither man mentioned the NWFP trip specifically.[60]

Completely out of context, but of interest because it involves the NLO in Karachi, on 2 December 1942 the NLO in Karachi requested permission to send a U.S. Navy lieutenant on a special mission to Kabul. Engert wrote a long response in which he did not actually refuse the request, but gave many reasons to show that it would not be a good idea, and he actively discouraged it. That was apparently the end of the matter, but the question is, Why did the NLO in Karachi request it, and what was the "special mission" the NLO had in mind? It is very likely that Enders had by this time become acquainted with the CO of the NLO in Karachi. However, there is no indication of why Smith or Enders would have initiated this request.[61]

The letters from Engert to Enders and others in India show his knowledge of the people involved in intelligence, if not the actual events of the trip. In a letter of 13 January 1943, Engert mentions Brigadier General (later Lieutenant General) Raymond Albert Wheeler, then commander, U.S. Forces Services of Supply in the China-Burma-India (CBI) theater; and Major General Clayton Bissell, G-2. Bissell later became head of G-2 in Washington in February 1944; he continued in that position until January 1946.

MAJOR GORDON B. ENDERS, U.S. ARMY, HQ REAR ECHELON,
U.S. FORCES, CBI, NEW DELHI.

Dear Major,
    We are all looking forward to your return to Kabul. . . .

P.S. Please give my best regards to Generals Wheeler and Bissell, Colonel Ferris, and my old friend from Peking, Colonel Wyman. Also my salaams to everybody at the Diplomatic Mission.[62]

It is clear that Engert saw Afghanistan as a linchpin in the war effort. He commented to the State Department on 27 January 1943, "Any weakening of the present regime [here] would react unfavorably upon the Allied war effort in the Middle East and in India." And on 14 February, he said that when the Axis attacked Russia, "it looked as if the traditional menace from the north were eliminated or at least postponed."[63]

A mysterious visit was proposed in April 1943 at a very high level by an "officer of the United States Army handling Afghan matters." It was then just as mysteriously dropped. It was understood that this officer would "enter Afghanistan openly as an Army officer and would travel in uniform" for about two weeks. It was probably General Patrick Hurley, who was then circulating in the Middle East as a personal representative of the president. The request was from Secretary of State Cordell Hull to Engert on 28 April. Two days later, Engert replied coolly, "I would suggest that a high ranking officer, nothing less than a brigadier or major general be sent out or perhaps detailed from India. . . . Quite frankly, I do not believe he could possibly collect any information which the Military Attaché or I could not obtain." Engert is territorial enough to be on the defensive; regardless of how he felt about Enders, he protected Enders, too. Hurley was determined to get to Afghanistan, however, and he finally got there in 1944, following the trip to the NWFP that is the subject of this book.[64]

On 29 April 1943 Engert stated more explicitly the Russian threat, as the Afghans perceived it: "The Afghans are convinced that when the war is over Russia will demand substantial territorial concessions of her neighbors and that neither the US nor Great Britain will be able to stop her."[65] This led to a remarkable series of meetings in Kabul, that Engert reported on 16 May 1943, of Cunningham, governor of the NWFP; Sir Olaf Caroe, secretary to the government of India (only the second foreign secretary of India to visit Kabul); Sir Denys Pilditch, director of intelligence, Delhi; the political agent at Khyber; and the director of IB Quetta. They were in Kabul "entirely unofficially [but were] very much interested in ascertaining Afghanistan's attitude toward India but more especially in her attitude toward Russia."[66]

Presumably because he met Pilditch at this time, Engert wrote a letter to him the next day, 17 May 1943. It is a most interesting letter because Engert introduces the word "Pakistan" into the dialogue, yet the existence of Pakistan was more than four years away. The letter was sent to Pilditch, a shadowy figure if ever there was one:

> I have for some time been trying to collect a little information regarding "Pakistan," but not had much success. I am therefore wondering if you could help me, either by referring me to some published material, or perhaps by lending me some Memoranda or Reports which I could return to you. . . .
>
> The reason I want to study the question a little is that the Afghans are—albeit cautiously and quietly—following its develop-

ment and trying to figure out just how it may ultimately affect them. . . . Quite a number of officials, including the Prime Minister, have already asked me what I thought of Pakistan, but I have always answered evasively. . . . However it occurs to me that I could perhaps be helpful to you and Caroe if I expressed myself in a sense that would be in harmony with the views and hopes of the Government of India and with the interest of a post-war world such as you and we are fighting for.[67]

On 20 July 1943, at the end of his first year in Afghanistan, Engert submitted a report noting that "there is little room for doubt left in the minds of the majority of thinking Afghans that the Axis is losing the war."[68] The "hinge of fate," as Churchill put it, had turned.

In the summer of 1943 Engert was in India, where his daughter had typhoid; his wife was taking care of her, and he was sick, too. Thayer was in charge of the American mission in Kabul. Thayer transmitted a memo to the secretary of state on 31 August 1943 regarding the safe conduct via Karachi of the members of the Axis legations who were returning to Europe. Within a month the situation had changed, and Hull sent messages to Thayer on 14 and 16 September, encouraging him to establish contact with the Italians on an informal basis—Italy having surrendered on 8 September. Enrico Anzillotti, secretary of the Italian legation, and Pietro Quaroni, the Italian minister, remained in Kabul. Thayer said that, with regard to the tribes, "Quaroni said Axis operations have been very much hampered by inept German management. Less than a million Afghanis (80,000 dollars) have been delivered to the Faqir of Ipi. He himself succeeded in sending the Faquir only one Lewis gun and several thousand rounds of ammunition." He continued, "Military Attache requests pertinent portions of above be communicated to G-2."[69]

Engert got back to Kabul on 1 October 1943 and sent a telegram at 4:00 p.m. to the State Department: "Returned and resumed charge today. Owing to the serious illness of my daughter in Simla I was unable to fix any definite date for my return until a few days ago. I myself was ill between August 8 and 24."[70] On his return to Kabul, he immediately was involved

in the events of the day, including brigands on the border, and the desire
of Sir Aurel Stein to visit Afghanistan. He wired the State Department via
Peshawar:

OCTOBER 9, 1943

Secret. I learn indirectly from the Prime Minister that four widely
separated bands of robbers have during the past week held up
and killed a number of Afghan travelers. One of these bands operating this side of the Khyber area had already held up several
trucks when I passed through there last week; some bandits are
operating near the Shibar Pass, and two bands are reported active
in the provinces of the North.[71]

Stein had a long relationship with Engert, which had begun with correspondence in June 1922. He was attempting to complete his travels to the
highlands of Asia with a visit to Afghanistan in 1943, but because he was
English he was having trouble getting a visa. Stein wrote to Cunningham
in Peshawar on 5 April 1943, and to Caroe on 16 July, but it was apparently from Engert's help, not the British, that he finally got permission
to enter Afghanistan. Engert wrote to the State Department: "October
9, 1943, 8 p.m. I suggest the Department inform Harvard University that
Sir Aurel Stein, the distinguished archeologist, has just received permission from the Afghan Government to make a reconnaissance trip to
Afghanistan."[72]

Stein wrote to Engert four days later, just before he left in a U.S. legation car for Kabul:

OCTOBER 13, 1943
GOVERNMENT HOUSE, PESHAWAR, N.W.F.P.

Dear Mr. Engert,
    Your very kind letter of the 6th inst and telegram, apparently
of the 7th, greeted me on my arrival here this morning. . . . The
departure on October 18th will be most convenient for me and

give me a little more time for various tasks I shall be glad to dispose of before the start. I shall, of course, follow closely your kind advice about the halt at Jelalabad, etc.

I am delighted to know that you could welcome your son at Karachi and then bring your family from Simla to Kabul, fully reassured of the health of your daughter. It must be a great comfort to you and Mrs. Engert to find yourselves reunited with your children.[73]

We see from this letter that Engert passed through Karachi in October 1943. He probably met with the consul, Clarence E. Macy, and perhaps the CO of the NLO, but there is no written record that confirms this.

Stein arrived in Kabul on 19 October. He developed a slight cold a few days after he arrived. His condition worsened, his heart failed, and he had a stroke. He died at Engert's residence on 24 October 1943. His last written words were but a scrawl, giving a London address; these words are preserved in the Engert Papers.

There are eighteen pieces of correspondence in October, November, and December 1943 in the Engert Papers. One shows that direct personal communications were often utilized, rather than trusting anything to a written document. On 12 October 1943 a vague "same activity" is not given any additional description by either Lieutenant Colonel Edward O. Hunter of the rear echelon, Headquarters U.S. Army Forces, CBI, or by Engert. Hunter wrote,

I am most anxious to meet you and discuss several matters, so would appreciate it very much if you would let me know the next time you are in Delhi, so that I may call.

For your information I am engaged in the same activity as Col. Fleming with whom you have been in touch.[74]

Engert replied to this letter twelve days later, and it was also uninformative. It was apparently too sensitive a matter to discuss in a letter, no matter how guarded the wording. On 24 October Engert wrote to Hunter:

Thank you very much for your letter of the 12th instant.

I am afraid I shall not be in Delhi in the *near* future [emphasis in original], although I try to go there once in three or four months. The next time I am down I shall, of course, be glad to let you know in advance.

In the meantime, I believe it to be quite safe for you to communicate with me through Colonel Fleming on the subject that interests you. Be sure to let me know if I can help. The opportunities here are considerable.[75]

This Lieutenant Colonel Hunter was known after the war as Edward Hunter. He had an interesting career in the OSS in China, and later in the CIA, and he was also a journalist. He is noted for coining the word "brainwashed." Whether he knew of AZ and the trip to the NWFP is unknown, but he surely must have known, or known of, Gordon Enders, who came to Delhi in December, and at other times before then.

In the meantime, as the memo from IB Quetta to Harris was being formulated, Assistant Secretary of State Adolph Berle had a conference with the Afghan minister. Berle reported this memo for the record on 22 October 1943. The minister told Berle that the Afghan government had tried hard to keep the arrests of Axis sympathizers in Afghanistan a secret, "but the British Government has decided to take advantage of the situation to put a stop to Axis intrigues also on the Indian Border." The faqir of Ipi was reputed to be behind all of this.[76]

There was another interesting point raised that "relates to the northwest frontier and to territory on the Indian side of the present frontier claimed by Afghanistan," in which "by agreement with the British," the Afghans "reserved their right to re-open the question should India gain her independence."[77] This point resonates to the present day.

Engert wrote another long letter to the State Department on 4 November 1943, describing the many bands of "brigands" operating in the south of Afghanistan, with details of their numbers, provinces in which they operated, and depredations they had caused, including deaths and robberies. It is clear that the southern border was a dangerous place, at the very time Enders and Zimmermann were planning to go there.[78]

Two items are in Engert's papers during the dates of the trip, from 11 November to 15 December 1943, and neither of them mentions the trip.

HULL TO KABUL
23 NOVEMBER 1943
TELEGRAM

113. November 23, 9 p.m. The Navy Department requests (with reference to your 215 of November 5) that you convey to the Department by telegraph any additional information available regarding the possible manner and method of routing materials overland to Germany from Japan.
Hull / File No. 711.9[79]

The second telegram, however, shows Engert and Thayer had a good relationship, not the just barely speaking relationship that Engert had with Enders at this time.

ENGERT TO DEPARTMENT VIA PESHAWAR TELEGRAM
4 DECEMBER 1943. NO. 235. 5 P.M. URGENT.

With my dispatch 329, November 18, I transmitted Thayer's request for home leave. As he has not been in the United States for nearly five years he would appreciate it very much if he could be permitted to proceed to London via Washington and be granted a few weeks leave unless urgency precludes it.[80]

Roderick Engert was Cornelius Van H. Engert's son. I spoke with him by phone at his home in Washington, DC, on 13 August 2009. He was born in 1925, and he was in the American mission in Kabul when the trip took place November to December 1943. He later joined the OSS, and was a translator of Hindustani documents. He was with the OSS in Kandy, Ceylon, where he knew Julia McWilliams (later Julia Child). He later went to Yale in the class of 1950, and retired after a career as a civil servant.

I asked Roderick Engert if he had any knowledge of the trip AZ, Bromhead, and Enders took. He replied, "No, that would have been kept very secret. It was the sort of thing that my father would have discussed with Cunningham—they were in frequent communication—and he would have been careful not to let any word about it get out." Then he asked me, "What do you know about the purpose of the trip?" I said I thought it was all about the Great Game, and he agreed. The message from IB Quetta said that it was to give the Americans a chance to see what problems the British had with the frontier tribes and how they were dealing with them, and that a Navy man was to be added to the trip for reasons that were not very clear to me. I thought maybe it was to provide some balance to the report that Enders would be making. Roderick Engert said, "Yes, I think that would be a good reason to put someone else on the trip, such as Zimmermann." I speculated that these were the first Americans ever to make this long trip along the border, and they were probably the only ones ever to do it, and he replied, "Yes. That must be true."

Roderick Engert said Pietro Quaroni, the Italian minister, might have provoked unrest along the border. "Quaroni was the best the Axis had in Kabul. He organized the Axis operations there, and did a very good job of it. In September of '43 he made a clean breast of it to my father and the British minister, and my father gave him a great write up, said he was the ablest diplomat he had ever known. They became good friends after the war, and my father always looked him up when he traveled."[81]

The Intelligence Officer: Harris

John R. Harris, esquire, central liaison officer, Karachi, was the British intelligence officer in Karachi. He is usually referred to as J. R. Harris. He probably knew AZ before the trip, and he certainly knew him well thereafter. He was first mentioned in the caption of a photo on 21 August 1943, at which time AZ had to forgo dinner with an incoming American general because he was, at the same time, hosting the U.S. ambassador to China, Clarence Gauss, for dinner. He was photographed with AZ on 28 December 1943, and he is mentioned on that date in AZ's letter to BSZ.

The Staff Officer: Voorhees

Lieutenant (jg) Howard Voorhees arrived at the NLO in Karachi on 24 October 1943, bringing a personal letter to AZ from Curt Winsor, the desk officer for the Far East Section of the Office of Naval Intelligence (ONI/FE). Voorhees is one of several relatively low-ranking officers and enlisted men who were aware of the plans for Zimmermann's trip. How much AZ told them about the trip is unknown, but it was probably just enough for him to get what he needed—a sleeping bag, warm clothing, a pistol and ammunition, and so forth. They had no reason to know any-thing more than his plan to "proceed to Peshawar and other such places." What he was to look for was none of their business. All of their letters that might have mentioned the trip were censored at the time, and are now lost. We know the name of only one enlisted man, a chief yeoman named Frank R. Leavitt, although there were as many as six enlisted men at the NLO in Karachi at one time. Voorhees is mentioned by name at this point because he had the longest connection of any of these men with AZ, and would have learned more about AZ's trip than any of them.

In addition to AZ and the CO, Lieutenant Commander F. Howard Smith, two other Navy officers were at NLO in Karachi in the fall of 1943. They were Lieutenant Harmon Burns Jr., who had arrived on 13 September 1942 and would depart on 28 November 1943, while AZ was on the trip; and Lieutenant Frank J. Callahan, who arrived on 3 October 1942 and would depart on 5 January 1944, three weeks after AZ returned from his trip to the NWFP. Lieutenants Burns and Callahan would certainly have known about the trip, if not the details.

Two other Navy officers arrived at NLO in Karachi in December 1943, and would soon have learned that AZ was away on a confidential mission. They were Lieutenant (jg) Walter G. Hebford, who arrived on 3 December (while AZ was in Waziristan), and Lieutenant (jg) Paul M. Baker, who arrived on 26 December 1943, less than two weeks after AZ returned. Lieutenant (jg) Philip Halla, USCG, arrived later in 1944, and would surely have learned of the trip, too.[82]

Comments in AZ's letters to his family, and in Winsor's letters, sug-gest that Howard Voorhees may have been known to AZ personally before he came to Karachi. After Smith departed and AZ became CO at NLO in Karachi, his right-hand man—his executive officer, in fact, if not in name—was Lieutenant Howard Voorhees. (The "jg" was dropped in conversation.) He was tall and suave, a gentleman, well liked by other Americans and

British military and civilians. He and AZ were often invited out as guests. All else that was known about him was that he was a Roman Catholic, and that he had no middle initial. None of the official records shows a middle initial or name, and the Navy is precise about this. He and AZ worked well together, without ever a problem that deserved mention in AZ's letters. Every CO should have such an executive officer. He signed AZ's orders and remained at Karachi for at least a few days after AZ returned to the United States in 1945. He then departed from Karachi for parts unknown. He remains a mystery, however, and he has since disappeared.

The Spy: Benson

Lieutenant Colonel Reginald Lindsay "Rex" Benson, MVO, DSO, MC, was military attaché of Great Britain in Washington in 1941. Gordon Enders presented Benson's card of introduction to Sir George Cunningham, governor of the NWFP, when he was on his way to Kabul in December 1941. Cunningham's warm welcome included dinners on two nights at Government House. Enders and the governor must have enjoyed recalling their many years spent in the high mountains of Asia, and Enders may have broached the notion of a trip along the border with him at that time. Enders was the sort of man who would have found a way to meet Cunningham anyway, but there was no one who could do it better than Benson. Benson knew India well. He had personally been to the border, and had served in Kabul. He was the right person to vouch for Enders.

Like many intelligence officers, Rex Benson led two separate lives, and because of the Official Secrets Act in Britain, it is especially difficult to get the details of the secret side of his life. The service for which he worked, the Secret Intelligence Service (SIS, or MI6), was not officially acknowledged even to exist until recently—although it has appeared in fiction and fact for many years. Now that the official history of MI6 has been published, one might think that much about Benson and his work would be there, but he is not mentioned by name in the index, and I cannot find him in the text.[83] In order to find out about Benson and what he did for British intelligence, one has to turn to other sources. The Freedom of Information Act (FOIA) has revealed American sources, and those sources in turn have enabled an unofficial history of MI6 to be written. Some of those in Washington probably knew that Benson was a very rich man, married to an American heiress, and head of one of the largest banks in England—and that he was a relative of the head of the MI6. Whether they would have told Enders about this is uncertain, for in intelligence you only tell someone what he or she needs to know. Here is the story of Rex Benson, assembled from various sources.[84]

Reginald Benson, known as "Rex," was born 20 August 1889 at 16 South Street, Mayfair, London, second of the three sons of Robert Henry "Robin" Benson and his wife, Evelyn Mary Holford, daughter of Robert Stayner Holford. The Benson name goes back for many generations. In business, Benson first appeared as Rathbone and Benson, who worked with Alsop & Hicks in New York in 1795. The Benson family had extensive interests in America, being a major owner of, among others, the Illinois Central Railway and the Westinghouse Company.[85]

The Benson family was happy; although they had problems with finances from time to time, their connections were such that they survived and prospered. The children were very fond of each other; the older, Guy, was awarded the DSO at twenty-two and was in military intelligence; and the youngest, Constantine, was called "Con." Rex's uncle, the fabulously wealthy George Holford, was having an affair with the mother of Stewart Menzies. She was married to a wealthy but dissolute man, who eventually died. After she and Holford were married, Rex and Stuart became step-cousins. But they were chums already, and Rex was very supportive of Stuart, one year younger than him. As president of Pop, the most important social club at Eton, Rex intervened when Menzies was blackballed, and ensured that Menzies, too, would be elected. Benson was always considered as Menzies' best friend. Rex went on to Balliol College, Oxford, in 1908, but he soon decided to become a soldier. Menzies, too, became a soldier, and they joined the service at the same time.[86]

Rex left Oxford in 1909 and was initially attached to the Life Guards. He was made a subaltern in the 9th Queen's Royal Lancers in 1910, and he paid for his journey to join the regiment in South Africa "by working as a stoker on a Union Castle steamer."[87] In 1913 he was appointed aide-de-camp to the viceroy of India, Sir Charles Hardinge, and he moved into the viceregal lodge. Rex and his fellow aide-de-camp, the Honorable J. J.

Astor, of the First Life Guards and future owner of *The Times,* won the Calcutta Cup in polo in 1913. In July 1914 Benson toured the northwest frontier, entering Afghanistan through the Khyber Pass to call upon the emir, Habibullah Khan, in the hope of inducing the Afghan army to march with the British Indian army if there was war with Germany. The emir showed him much courtesy, but declined to answer the question.

Benson joined his regiment in France in August 1914, survived the battle of Aisne, and was awarded the MC for service at the First Battle of Ypres. In May 1915 he was badly gassed and severely wounded in the right arm at the Second Battle of Ypres. While recuperating, he was sent to Paris as liaison officer and was unofficially the head of the secret service there. He did some curious work with the French secret police. He then served in Ireland during the 1916 uprising, and again in France as liaison officer with Marshal Philippe Petain at French headquarters. After the armistice he became chief of the British mission and was on the staff of Sir Henry Wilson. He received the DSO and was mentioned four times in despatches in France. The French made him a member of the Légion d'Honneur and awarded him the Croix de Guerre.

Meanwhile, Menzies, too, served in the same regiment, and he, too, was wounded at the Second Battle of Ypres. Menzies also was awarded the MC and DSO, and was also in military intelligence. They both were on the British staff at the Paris Peace Conference. Menzies then made intelligence a career, and Benson was one of his closest collaborators, even though it was totally secret. Menzies rose to become head ("C") of the MI6. He was said to have been Ian Fleming's model for "M" in the James Bond "007"novels.[88]

In 1920 Benson was on his second tour in India. He was appointed military secretary to the governor of Bombay, Sir George Lloyd, and in this capacity, he traveled extensively in the NWFP. In 1922 he helped to organize the tour for the Prince of Wales, for which he became MVO. He then resigned his commission and was sent on a covert mission to Russia by Prime Minister Lloyd George, under the cover of attempting to reopen trade with postrevolutionary Russia. After some close calls, he returned to England, and had succeeded in selling goods worth £10,000; no details are known about his intelligence mission. His father then insisted that he enter the family bank, and Benson brought it through the Depression and back into good shape by 1935. He made many business trips to North America, and in 1932 he married Leslie (Foster) Nast, daughter of a wealthy banker of Lake Forest, Illinois, Albert Volney Foster. She was the second wife of Condé Nast, the magazine publisher; they were married in 1928 and divorced in 1932. With Nast, she had one child, a daughter, Leslie. Benson and Leslie spent their honeymoon in India—it was his third trip there—as guests of his uncle, the viceroy, marquess of Willingdon. They raised her daughter by Nast and had two sons of their own.[89]

On New Year's Day 1936 Benson gave a dinner at his house in Belgravia. His guests included the Prince of Wales and Mrs. Wallis Simpson. The king died on 20 January, and the prince became King Edward VIII. On 10 December 1936 Edward abdicated the throne, and a few days later he went into exile as the Duke of Windsor. His security had been the responsibility of the Security Service (MI5), but it now became the province of MI6. Benson suddenly abandoned an expensive duck-and-goose-shooting expedition in Hungary and returned to Vienna, arriving there on the eve of the Duke of Windsor's arrival from London. Benson appears to have met the duke and may have arranged with the Austrians to guard him. In the course of the year 1936, he also succeeded his older brother as chairman of Robert Benson & Co. He was at Blenheim Palace, meeting with Churchill, on New Year's Day 1938.

In September 1939 Benson was called to active duty, and served as liaison officer to the French First Army until the British army was evacuated at Dunkirk. When he returned to England, Menzies, who was now the head of MI6, sent Rex to London to keep watch on the duke. The Windsors soon left London for Spain, and then Portugal, and finally sailed for the Bahamas on 1 August 1940. They were then safely away from Europe and their dalliance with Hitler. Meanwhile, William Donovan had returned to London as FDR's envoy on 17 December 1940. Churchill gave him lunch and handed him off to Menzies, who said he would like to send Rex Benson to Washington as liaison officer at the War Department. Donovan had met Benson in 1936 at Waterloo Station, and they had seen much of each other thereafter. After Donovan left England on 24 December 1940, his wife wrote in her diary, "Bill has British Empire for breakfast." Those present included William S. Stephenson, Rex Benson, David Bowes-Lyon (brother of Queen Elizabeth), and Colonel Charles H. Ellis—who reported to Menzies directly about what went on in Stephenson's New York office. Stephenson was the head of British intelligence in the United States during World War II.[90]

Donovan approved Benson's appointment, and Menzies spoke with Churchill. Churchill agreed that Benson would go as assistant military attaché. He sailed on a tramp steamer on 26 February 1941, carrying intelligence that was very secret and of great importance to the United States. Benson's orders were to serve as a military attaché in Washington, and at nine other capitals in the Western Hemisphere. He was one of the most popular diplomats in Washington at the time, for he was able to play the piano by ear for hours. In spite of his severe wound in World War I—his brachial artery and the nerves to one arm were destroyed—he became a champion polo player and sailor. He was said to have been disarmingly friendly when he introduced himself: "Hello, I'm Rex Benson."

Privately, he soon became engaged in political and military intelligence on a very large scale. On 1 April 1941 the British military attaché, Major General F. G. "Paddy" Beaumont-Nesbitt and Benson met with representatives of the U.S. Army and Navy intelligence services, and the British began the transfer of Ultra and Enigma to the United States. At the same time, Benson began to receive Magic, the American decrypts of Japanese diplomatic and military traffic. On 13 May General Sherman Miles, the U.S. Army's chief of G-2, told Benson that the Japanese were aware that their cipher was being read by the Americans, and that he blamed Beaumont-Nesbitt for this. Benson succeeded Beaumont-Nesbitt when the latter was recalled, and he was warned on 21 October that the War and Navy Departments' antipathy to Donovan was so severe that "we should not deal with [Donovan] until U.S. Services say OK."[91]

Sometime in the summer or early fall of 1941, he met with Gordon Enders and gave him a card of introduction to Sir George Cunningham, governor of the NWFP. Enders presented the card to Cunningham on 1 December in Peshawar. Anthony Cave Brown suggests that Churchill, Benson, and the other British readers of Magic became convinced that the Japanese were going to attack at multiple locations on the weekend of 7–8 December, and that they even suspected that one of the targets might be Pearl Harbor. Benson left Washington for Cairo on 6 December with William C. Bullitt in a B-24 Liberator. On landing at Miami, Benson left the aircraft, and Bullitt—who was a special assistant to the secretary of the Navy—flew on to Cairo alone. Benson stayed with friends in Miami and learned of the attack while in a Miami drugstore. He then went off to play golf. Benson returned to Washington and wrote in his diary that he was astonished to learn that "in spite of plenty of warnings, everything was caught completely unprepared."[92]

Benson met frequently with Secretary of War Henry Stimson and his assistants Harvey H. Bundy and Robert Lovett, and with Washington insiders Harry Hopkins, Bernard Baruch, Walter Lippmann, Arthur Krock, and, of course, Donovan. Benson began with a good relationship with Miles in U.S. G-2, but—perhaps because of his friendship with Donovan—he had very poor relations with his successor, General George V. Strong, and with General Leslie J. McNair, chief of Army ground forces. Benson had recommended Luke Asquith to General William Donovan, to serve as Donovan's ghost writer.

Benson learned that Strong alleged that in September 1943 Benson had leaked information from Ultra to his wife about a German missile threat, and had warned her to leave London. Benson denied it, but the long knives were out, the damage was done, and Benson was recalled. He stayed with William Stephenson in New York on 5 December 1943, and he arrived in England just as the "little Blitz" began in January 1944.

The Consul General: Macy

The Honorable Clarence E. Macy, usually referred to as C. E., was officially consul for the United States in Karachi, but because the consulate was large and relatively independent, he was often referred to as the consul general. He supervised a large staff of junior consuls. He was well acquainted with AZ before the request was made to send an ALUSLO to Peshawar. Macy and Harris were in frequent communication with each other, and they were often guests for dinner at the NLO. AZ said that Macy's spouse was a "2 ton French wife" who was "quite opinionated," when he met her on 15 August, and when he joined them for dancing on 21 August 1943.[93] He took the consul and his wife to mess aboard a U.S. Navy ship on 2 September, when he experienced being piped over the side for the first time.

Clarence Edward Macy was born in St. Joseph, Buchanan County, Missouri, 9 November 1886. He was a railway mail clerk before World War I, when he served in the U.S. Army. He then joined the Foreign Service and was vice-consul in Coblenz, 1921–25; Dakar, 1925–27; and Monrovia, 1927–28, which he left just before it was revealed that Liberian governmental officials were involved in slavery. He was promoted to consul in Port Elizabeth, 1928–30; Tampico, 1932; Kabul, 1938 (although he did not have an office in Kabul); and was also appointed as consul in Karachi in 1938.[94]

The Viceroy: Wavell

Field Marshal Archibald P. Lord Wavell spent sixteen years, on three separate occasions, in India. He twice went to the NWFP on military expeditions. On both occasions, he went into Chitral, and he wrote an account of his harrowing traverse of the Lowari Pass on horseback. Thirty-three years later, he went back to India to serve as commander in chief, and then as viceroy.[95]

Wavell was born 5 May 1883 at Colchester, England, the only son of Major (later Major General) Archibald Graham Wavell, who was with the Black Watch Regiment. From the age of five until he was eight he lived in an Army cantonment in India and went back to England as a student in 1893. In October 1900 Wavell entered Sandhurst and he, too, was commissioned into the Black Watch in May 1901. In September 1901 he was sent to South Africa, where he saw action during the Boer War. In February 1903 he rejoined the regiment at Ambala, in the Punjab, near Simla. His next five years were spent in India.

Wavell "never enjoyed three years more . . . a sharp crisp winter; a brief, lyrical, flower-strewn and tingling spring; and an intense but short hot summer." He "found the Pathans 'attractive, with a sense of humour, and obviously men; though they often justified their reputation for cruelty and treachery.'"[96]

In 1906 Wavell went on a transport course, and in the autumn had himself attached to the Chitral Relief Column, "only a morning's ride from Chitral itself, but through wild and precipitous mountain country. With another officer from the Guides named Campbell, Wavell hired a couple of local ponies and set out to see Chitral."[97] Wavell wrote,

> The path was narrow with a rock wall on one side and a sheer drop into the river on the other. The ponies would insist on walking or trotting on the extreme edge of the precipice. . . . Campbell and I found it rather nerve-testing to be continually on the edge looking over a straight drop and proceeded delicately, till a mile or two short of Chitral we were overtaken by an officer who turned out to be the commander of the Chitral Scouts, named Sawyer. . . . Suddenly round a bend our guide's pony stumbled and both disappeared over the edge. We dismounted and looked over for the corpses; the accident had happened, fortunately for them, where there was only a comparatively short drop of about 15 or 20 feet, but both were lying apparently knocked out.[98]

It was therefore hardly a surprise that Wavell would be interested in hearing from Enders of the crossing of the Lowari in a jeep.

Wavell was introduced to the Great Game while he was in India during World War I. As "conflict seemed imminent between Britain and Russia, the N.W. Frontier threat looked like [it was] becoming an urgent reality. . . . [N]ine divisions were speedily deployed along two main axes which met at Peshawar . . . [and] The Black Watch moved up from Ambala to join the Gordons in Peshawar itself." In February 1908 Wavell was in Rawalpindi preparing to be examined for the Staff College when "there was trouble on—and beyond—the Frontier." Wavell attached himself to the Seaforths, which "fought a stiff little engagement at the northeastern end of the Bazar Valley and lost some officers." The Khyber Scouts then "came across from the Khyber in a swift outflanking movement, and the fighting was over." He was awarded another campaign medal, and enjoyed his first independent command. On 1 April 1908 he went home on leave, not to return to India for more than thirty-three years. Wavell "knew by heart Kipling's 1890 poem 'The Young British Soldier,' . . . 'Jest roll to your rifle and blow out your brains.'" He later wrote, "I owe much to India, where I have spent more than thirteen years of my life."[99]

In World War I Wavell was wounded and lost his left eye from a frag-ment that hit it on 16 June 1915 near Ypres. For this action he was men-tioned in despatches and was awarded the MC. About six months later he was assigned to general headquarters and was there from December 1915 until 16 October 1916, when he was ordered to go to Russia as a tempo-rary lieutenant colonel. He was at general headquarters when Benson and Menzies were also there. Two years later, on 8 January 1918, Wavell was appointed AA & QMG, Supreme War Council, Versailles. Benson and Menzies were also there.

During the interwar years, his career moved forward slowly and irregu-larly, as it did for all senior officers. He was known for his "taciturnity, and remained tongue-tied except with close friends." He had "the most expressionless poker face," which was alarming to those who tried to read his mind or to have a conversation with him. The king, who had his own problems with stuttering, was unable to get Wavell to speak; he called him "the oyster."[100]

Wavell married and had four children, three daughters and a son. His boy, Archie John, was in the service; he was badly injured by a landmine in Palestine in the spring of 1938, and his hand was so badly damaged in action in Burma on 12 June 1944 that it was amputated. He was awarded the MC for this, and continued to serve. His three daughters—Pamela, Felicity "Fizzie," and Joan—eventually married well. They were at home with him when Enders had dinner with the Wavell family on his way to Afghanistan in November 1941.

On 24 July 1932 he was named to the newly created post of general officer commanding in chief, Middle East, with the rank of full general, and he was knighted in 1939. His sphere of responsibility in the early years of the war was very great, and although he initially had considerable success in Africa, Churchill faulted him for losses in Greece, the Balkans, and the Middle East. He was relieved in the Middle East and was sent to India as commander in chief on 20 June 1941, replacing General Claude Auchinleck, who took over his command. He arrived in India as com-mander in chief on 11 July. He then flew back to England in September, via Baghdad, Cairo, Malta, and Gibraltar, arriving on 8 September 1941. He was sent to Tehran and Tiflis to sound out the Russians, who remained generous with vodka, but were otherwise opaque. He returned to Delhi on 23 October 1941. There is nothing in his diary from 13 November–12 December when a group of American officers, including Enders, visited him in Delhi.[101]

Surprise attacks by the Japanese on 8 December 1941 local time in Malaya and the Philippines, and at Pearl Harbor on 7 December, suddenly put the British Empire in jeopardy. Secretary of War Henry Stimson was unimpressed with Wavell's skills, and Churchill continued to find fault with him throughout 1942. Wavell returned for consultation in London in April 1943, and on 14 June he was given the opportunity to become viceroy. He then upset the War Cabinet by proposing to negotiate with Gandhi and Nehru as part of his plan to retain India in the empire. He was, however, given the position anyway, and he arrived at the viceroy's house in New Delhi on Monday 18 October 1943. In his first six months as viceroy, he visited all eleven provinces, usually accompanied by Lady Wavell. He had been in office for less than two months when he visited Peshawar and met Enders and Zimmermann at the governor's garden party. Meanwhile, Auchinleck had been fired from his position in North Africa, and had been transferred to India as commander in chief, replacing Wavell. Mountbatten had just been named supreme commander of SEAC. These three strong-willed men were forced to work together. Wavell's last diary entry in 1943 was on 1 December, when he met with Mountbatten on Mountbatten's return from the Cairo conference. Wavell wrote, "He was more tired and depressed than I have seen him. He had a difficult time at Cairo with P.M. [Churchill] and with the Generalissimo and they had not got much settled."[102]

Throughout all of this, Wavell remained outwardly unperturbed. While he was in Delhi he completed work on his anthology of poetry, which included no fewer than twenty-nine of Kipling's poems—more than any other poet. His selections from Kipling include the well-known inspirational poem "If," and "The Sea and the Hills," selections from which appear in the epigraphs of two chapters in *Kim*.[103]

The Chief Commissioner: Hay

The chief commissioner of Baluchistan, Lieutenant Colonel William Hay, whose office was so independent that he was sometimes referred to as "His Excellency (or H. E.), the governor," met the travelers at the end of their journey. He and his staff debriefed them, gave them a dinner and a picnic lunch, and sent them on their way.

Lieutenant Colonel (later Sir) William Rupert Hay was born on 16 December 1893. He was educated at University College, Oxford, and commissioned on entry into military service in 1915. He was promoted to lieutenant in 1918, and after the armistice, as a captain, he was posted to Mandali, Mesopotamia, a small town on the border with Iran. He wrote a book about his experiences there as a captain, entitled *Two Years in Kurdistan: Experiences of a Political Officer, 1918–1920.*[104]

He entered the political department, government of India, in 1929 and was promoted to major in 1933. In that year he was appointed a Commander of the Order of the British Empire (CBE). He was political agent and resident in the Persian Gulf from 1941 to 1942; in 1942 he was appointed lieutenant colonel and was made a Companion of the Order of the Star of India. He was revenue and judicial commissioner, Baluchistan, 1942–43. He was appointed resident and chief commissioner in Baluchistan in 1943 and was in that position when the travelers arrived. He continued as chief commissioner of Baluchistan until 1946. He retired in 1953 and died 3 April 1962.

The Chargé d'Affaires: Thayer

Charles Thayer is mentioned in AZ's letter to BSZ on 25 November 1943 as the brother of AZ's good friend George Thayer of Philadelphia. I thought he was probably the person who identified AZ as the ALUSLO to go on the trip, and Roderick Engert, who knew Thayer well, agreed.[105]

On 9 February 1920 Charles Wheeler Thayer was born in Villanova, Pennsylvania, four towns away on the Main Line of the Pennsylvania Railroad from Haverford, where the Zimmermanns lived. Charles and George also had a sister, Avis Howard Thayer, who married the future Ambassador Charles E. "Chip" Bohlen in 1935. AZ did not know Charles or Avis before the trip, or at least did not know them well enough for their children to have known about them. However, George Thayer and his children were well known to AZ, his wife, and their children.

Charles Thayer took an unusual career path, and thus veered away from his brother George, who was a rather typical young Philadelphia gentleman. Charles attended St. Paul's School in Concord, New Hampshire, and then went to West Point, from which he graduated in 1933. He was in the cavalry for a brief period, but in 1934 he became a Foreign Service officer. He served in Russia, where he roomed with his future brother-in-law, Charles Bohlen, and in Germany and Persia. He then went to Afghanistan, and it was there that he was involved with the trip that is the subject of this book. His official correspondence in Afghanistan is summarized along with Engert's.

In December 1941 or January 1942 Thayer was named chargé d'affaires to Afghanistan, but he was not allowed in the country by the Afghans, and he remained in Tehran for nearly six months, until May 1942. The Afghans would not let him into the country until someone was given the rank and title that they deemed appropriate. Enders had been allowed (or had simply come into the country) as military attaché, but they would not allow anyone else to open a U.S. legation. Cornelius Van H. Engert was named as minister in May 1942, and the door was then open for Thayer to come in to get the legation open and ready for business.

When he was ready to go and looking for a way to get to Kabul, "a jeep rolled into Teheran from India with Major Gordon Enders who announced he was the new Military Attaché for the Kabul Legation." Thayer hired a thirty-passenger Chevrolet bus to take his group and his equipment to Kabul, escorted by Enders, who had a machine gun mounted on his jeep. They spent two and a half days to get to the border of Afghanistan, during which they were shot at and got a bullet hole through the gas tank.[106]

Thayer provides interesting insights into the thinking of Afghans regarding the Great Game, and current events. On the Great Game, from the Afghan point of view: "The Afghan Emir, Abdur Rahman (1880–1906), has written in his autobiography some candid comments on the Russian diplomatic method during the latter half of the nineteenth century. During that period Afghanistan was a bone of contention between the British, who looked upon it as an outpost on the mountain passes between Russian Central Asia and their Indian empire, and the Russians, who regarded it as a legitimate field for expansion."[107]

Thayer was one of the first to foresee a new Great Game, with the Soviet Union and China as players. The Afghan king, Abdurrahman Khan,

who ruled until 1901, "had some advice for his British and Russian neighbors, the gist of which was they'd better be friendly to Afghanistan, or
else. Specifically he told the British that if they'd keep the Russians in
order in Europe he'd take care of them in Asia. But that was long before
Lenin, Stalin or even Mao Tse-Tung were even thought of."[108]

On 20 February 1943 Thayer sent a letter to the secretary of state
on the subject of "Some Observations regarding Motor Roads through
Afghanistan and Central Asia to Eastern China." The letter was received
on 2 April 1943 by the Division of Near Eastern Affairs and went to the
War Department and other unknown addressees. In that letter, Thayer
wrote, "certain agencies of the United States Government appear to be
interested in possible motor roads to China via Afghanistan and Central
Asia." In other words, roads to by-pass "the Hump," the dangerous air
route from India to China.[109]

In August 1943 Thayer wrote to the secretary of state regarding "Afghan
Reactions to Recent Developments in Sicily, Italy." Thayer observed that
the Afghan government "is constrained to a type of savage tribal democracy which has, in fact, little in common with modern democratic ideals."
Thayer also correctly anticipated Russian expansion into the affairs of
Afghanistan, and believed that this should be countered by what we would
now call humanitarian assistance, supplying teachers and engineers, and
"scrupulously living up to all the engagements we undertake." He recommended that we avoid being drawn by Afghanistan into a conflict with
Russia in that part of the world. Thayer said that the faqir of Ipi was troublesome, but not particularly effective. "The tribes never actually rose,
but I got the impression that the Faqir and the Mullah [religious leader]
turned a pretty penny at German expense."[110]

Thayer tells many stories about Sir Francis Wylie, British minister in
Kabul. He apparently got along better with Wylie than with Engert. On
the recommendation of Wylie, Thayer bought a mare called Nur Jehan
that came from Peshawar with her Pathan groom, who was from "that
Northwest tribe which has kept things hot for several centuries along
the Indian-Afghan frontier."[111] The Cairo Conference of FDR, Churchill,
Chiang Kai-shek, and others got under way at about the time the trip by
Enders and others was starting. And although the details of the conference

were generally unknown at the time, Thayer was aware of it. His former chief in Tehran, Louis Dreyfus, was responsible for the Americans at the Tehran Conference, which followed directly after Cairo.[112]

Thayer offers a somewhat different view than Engert did of the side-switcher, Pietro Quaroni. Just at this time, the Italians surrendered. Engert was very much taken with Quaroni, but not Thayer, although he acknowledged his skill and his cooperation after the Italian surrender. He later recalled, "When Italy switched sides in 1942, the Italian minister in Kabul, who had up to then been on the enemy side, showed me a photo-stat of a handwritten message [that was] a penciled draft of a top-secret telegram I had sent some months before, in my own handwriting. He then explained that the German minister in Kabul had given it to him."[113]

Thayer's contemporaneous communication to the State Department regarding Quaroni was, however, somewhat more appreciative. On 30 November 1943 Thayer wrote a memorandum entitled "Observations of the Italian Minister, Mr. Quaroni, on Afghan-Axis-Allied Relations, 1939–1943." This memorandum was prepared while the travelers were completing their trip in the NWFP. The memo was written in the last month that Thayer was in Afghanistan. It represents a unique opportunity to see how the war was being conducted by the Axis and the Allied powers, as seen from the Afghan perspective. It was related by Quaroni, who told Thayer

> The Axis aim in its war time policy in Central Asia was obviously to foment as much trouble for the Russians and the British as possible, thus forcing them to maintain the maximum number of troops in Turkestan and on the North-West Frontier. . . .
>
> Fortunately for the Axis, every blunder it made was balanced by another made by the British. "Every night I went to bed," Quaroni said, "I thanked God for Sir Francis Wylie." The British habit of warning the Afghans of every petty intrigue among their own subjects, and the unceasing worry of the Government of India over the possibilities of tribal uprisings constantly irritated the Afghan government. . . .
>
> Quaroni . . . said he believed it would be efficient for the time being for the British and Americans to finally but definitely assure

the Afghans that the Russians had *not* been given a free hand in Central Asia at the Moscow Conference. [emphasis added][114]

Thayer offers several miscellaneous thoughts that are specific to Afghanistan, and some that are memorable because they relate to the mission that is the subject of this book. He commented, "Contrary to myth, [State Department] couriers are seldom overtly attacked and they never carry guns." This was something that AZ never talked about with his wife, but he did, indeed, carry a side arm when he traveled in the NWFP. Thayer also refers to his skills in making do with very little in Afghanistan: "A typewriter we borrowed; for an official seal I used my thumbprint; for the rest we did without."[115]

Thayer was thoroughly unimpressed in 1943 with the men that the OSS sent to Afghanistan. He later had a change of heart; in 1944 he transferred from the State Department to the OSS. He describes the state of mind known as "localitis," which means the place you are is the most important post in the world. It was a term that he used to describe Afghanistan and the NWFP of India in those days—although this area is now one of great importance to the United States. And he mentions a "Kipling-lover" in Washington, DC, who "got himself confused with Gunga Din" and sent a water-cooler to Kabul. This is something that rarely happens now; referring to Kipling or Gunga Din is no longer au courant.[116]

Thayer was high in the Hindu Kush in December 1943, probably not far from where the travelers were on the other side of the border. He tried to get to a 23,000-foot mountain in the Hindu Kush, which he did not name, to hunt ibex, and perhaps the Russian "bear" too, without success. A "few days" after he returned to Kabul, "a telegram from Washington" (signed by Hull) ordered him "to go to London with all possible speed to be Secretary to the European Advisory Commission. The chief of the U.S. delegation to the commission was George Kennan. It didn't sound like a very imposing job," and indeed, he found an interesting way out of it, as we will later see.[117]

Someone who knew him well summarized his skills as follows: "Despite his West Point training and his distinguished service as a career diplomat, he possesses, among other attributes, the sort of mind which makes a man a natural guerrilla."[118]

The Desk Officer: Winsor

Lieutenant Curtin Winsor, USNR, was Zimmermann's desk officer, or handler, at the ONI. He certainly knew of the trip as it was under way, because he visited Karachi early in December 1943 and learned that AZ was in the NWFP. Very likely, he was aware of it from soon after AZ was picked to go on the trip, on about 26 October. He may have been aware of—or even authorized—the courier mission as a cover for AZ's orientation trip to Ceylon.[119]

Curtin (Curt) Winsor was the son of James D. Winsor and Marion Harding Curtin. He was born 5 December 1905 in Ardmore, Pennsylvania. He was at Princeton University from 1925 to 1929, where he was secretary of the Class of '27 and a member of the editorial board of the *Daily Princetonian* and of the Quadrangle Club. He went to the University of Pennsylvania Law School, graduating LLB in 1930. He served in the National Recovery Administration, but returned to Philadelphia and graduated from the Curtis Institute of Music in 1942 with a degree in composition and criticism.

He married (first) in 1937, as her second husband, the former Elizabeth Browning Donner, who was born 12 May 1911. Elizabeth Donner had married (first), in 1932, Elliott Roosevelt (1910–1990), the son of FDR. They had a son, William Donner Roosevelt (1932–2003), and then the marriage was annulled in 1933. Winsor and Elizabeth Donner were divorced in 1943, and he married (second) in 1943, Margaretta Rowland, in Washington, DC. Curtin Winsor and Elizabeth Donner had two children: Curtin Winsor Jr. (born 1939) and Joseph Donner Winsor (born 1941).

Winsor joined the Navy at about the same time that AZ did, and they went to the Navy Intelligence School at Dartmouth at the same time. The school was large, so they may not have known each other there; they certainly did not see much of each other, because most of their time was scheduled for study. AZ, a full lieutenant, was in the Fourth Company, Platoon 1; and Winsor was a lieutenant, junior grade, in Platoon 6 of the same company. Winsor was promoted to lieutenant when he got his job in Washington. He was junior in grade to AZ, but was his handler nevertheless; that sort of thing rankles in the Navy, even to reservists. His brother, James D. "Jim" Winsor Jr., was a member of the Orpheus Club, and had been a close friend of the Zimmermanns before the war. He entered the Army after Curt and AZ joined the Navy; Curt kept AZ closely informed in his letters of Jim's progress in training and subsequent service.

Winsor wrote to AZ on 15 September 1943, referring to two mutual friends—Morris Duane, who temporarily moved near Winsor's home on Massachusetts Avenue near Wisconsin Avenue; and Henry Pemberton, who planned to board with him.[120] Winsor lived in a beautiful house about six blocks from the Washington National Cathedral. It is near Observatory Circle, where the vice president now lives. Winsor's wife had already left him, and the children would soon leave to live with her. She was fabulously wealthy, and the children would not suffer financially. He also mentioned that his brother, Jim, was at Air Transportation Training School and believed it would lead to a real job after the war. He continued, "ONI staggers along. I could write much about JICA [Joint Intelligence Collection Agency], JANIS [Joint Army Navy Intelligence Studies] and other alphabetical improvements but I guess it's not my cue to do so." He added, "I did phone Barbara as soon as I heard of your arrival."[121]

Winsor's next letter to AZ, written on 15 October 1943, was carried to Karachi by Lieutenant Howard Voorhees, when Voorhees arrived to replace a departing officer. Winsor thanked AZ for his letter, and said that he was waiting for AZ's port summary report in order to include it a larger ONI report. This is one of the very few instances where we have an idea about what AZ did during his working days. Winsor said that he would be making a trip as a courier next month, and expected to visit AZ in Karachi.

In a third letter, written from Delhi while the trip was under way, Winsor wrote to AZ, "Sorry to have missed you coming in. Barbara and your kids are fine and send their love. You're going to kill me when you read that she gave me some letters for you and I forgot them! However, I've sent a dispatch to Washington asking that they be forwarded to you by the next pouch." He adds that he expected to reach Karachi on the way back on 7 January, and wants to "talk to you then about many things concerning you and others."[122] In fact, he spent only an hour or so at the NLO, leaving AZ puzzled and discouraged.

AZ was wary of Curt Winsor, and he became increasingly convinced that Winsor was playing a game of his own, with AZ as the pawn. What the game was all about was never clear, but AZ wrote to his wife that "skull-duggery" was involved. AZ believed that for some unknown reason Winsor wanted AZ to remain in Karachi long after he was due to rotate home.

The Producer: Markey

No records have been preserved to show when Captain Gene Markey, the senior ALUSLO in the CBI theater, first knew of the trip by Zimmermann, Enders, and Bromhead in the NWFP.[123] In October 1943 Lieutenant Commander Howard Smith, ALUSLO in Karachi, was preparing to order one of his subordinate officers—Zimmermann—to proceed to Peshawar "and such other places" for an indefinite period of temporary additional duty.[124] As Zimmermann's CO, Smith had the authority to detach Zimmermann for this duty, and there was probably no requirement for the senior ALUSLO in the theater to give concurrence for these orders. (A copy of the orders went to the Bureau of Naval Personnel [BuPers] but this was simply a file copy that was inserted into Zimmermann's record jacket.)

Given the sensitive and unusual nature of the trip, however, under ordinary circumstances, Smith would not have ordered Zimmermann to perform this duty without notifying the senior ALUSLO in New Delhi of his plans. He could have done this by a phone call, and no permanent record of the call would have been preserved. But Smith was a regular USN officer, and had been in India for many years, whereas Markey was a USNR officer, newly arrived, and far away in New Delhi. Smith played an independent game in Karachi, and he may have tested the waters by not informing Markey in advance of Zimmermann's assignment.

Shortly before he went to Peshawar, AZ was sent on a courier mission to naval headquarters in Colombo, doubtless to learn what he should be prepared for on his trip to the NWFP. While he was in Colombo, plans for the trip to the NWFP surely became known to other ALUSLOs in the CBI theater—including Markey, the senior ALSULO. Markey was responsible for the ALUSLOs in Bombay, Calcutta, and Karachi. He was a very smooth operator who got what he wanted, and (unlike Smith) rarely offended.[125]

Zimmermann had previously met Markey as he passed through Cairo on his way to India. Markey was then already in Cairo, visiting (and presumably being oriented by) Zimmermann's friend Captain Tom Thornton, a naval reservist from Philadelphia. Thornton was Markey's counterpart in the Middle East—the Navy representative on Joint Intelligence Collection Agency Middle East (JICA-ME). Thornton had planned to take AZ and Markey on a day's drive to Alexandria on 10 July 1943. Expecting the letter describing this trip to be censored, AZ did not name the city until his next letter, when he said that the trip to Alexandria had been canceled because he was expected to fly on toward Karachi on 10 July. His letter only mentioned a "Com. Markey," without further details. No further identification was necessary; there was only one man that this could be. Markey's name was so well known at that time that BSZ must have been dying to know what this fabulous ladies' man was like, and what he had to say.

Gene Markey, at age forty-seven in the fall of 1943, was one of the notable characters in what is called the Golden Age of Hollywood. He was truly a "fabulous" person, a "raconteur," and a "man about town," as he was called in the gossip columns. In her biography of Myrna Loy, Markey's third wife, Emily Leider, wrote, "Gene Markey had the gift of gab. Well educated, droll, and socially polished, he shone in company. Catnip to women and a collector of beauties, he had dated Gloria Swanson and Ina Claire; he would later add Lucille Ball's name to his list of conquests."[126]

The story of Markey's life could have been the script for a movie. Born 11 December 1895, in Jackson, Michigan, Eugene "Gene" Willford Markey was the only child of Eugene Lawrence and Alice (White) Markey. His father had been a colonel in the U.S. Army who became wealthy in the sale of printing presses; he died in Los Angeles in 1940. His uncle, Daniel P. Markey, had been speaker of the Michigan House of Representatives. The Markeys were Irish; Gene's great-grandparents are said to have been born in Ireland and to have immigrated to Michigan. By 1943, Gene Markey had become a successful author, Hollywood producer, and screenwriter. He was also a skilled artist who studied at the Art Institute of Chicago (1919–20). Markey illustrated several of his own books, including *Literary Lights* (Knopf, 1923) in which he sketched each of fifty important American authors, and *Men About Town* (1924), with fifty-eight of his own illustrations. He also collaborated on *Actorviews* (1923), *Erasmus in*

Praise of Folly (1925), and *The Dark Island* (1928). His novels of the
Jazz Age included *Amabel, Stepping High* (1929), *The Road to Rouen*
(1930), and *His Majesty's Pyjamas* (1934). His screen credits as writer or
producer included twenty-four films between 1929 and 1941, with titles
such as *As You Desire Me, The Great Lover,* and *Lucky in Love.* Many of
Hollywood's most memorable actors were in these films.

Markey was most famous as a film producer for *Wee Willie Winkie*
(1937), a Darryl Zanuck film starring Shirley Temple in one of her earliest
films, and the Academy Award–winning Victor McLagen. It was based on
the story of the same name by Rudyard Kipling (1897). The movie was
directed by Markey's close friend, John Ford, who—like Markey—later
became a Navy captain and retired as a rear admiral. Filmed in southern
California, it depicted the NWFP of India. The film was nominated for an
Academy Award in art direction. It is not beyond imagination for Markey
to have been curious about the NWFP, and he might have wondered if
Zimmermann would find scenes there that were similar to those in *Wee
Willie Winkie.* The scene in which Shirley Temple acquires the nickname
"Wee Willie Winkie" on the parade ground was indeed eerily similar to the
British children scampering about on parade grounds in movies taken by
Albert Zimmermann on the trip, and elsewhere in India in 1943–44.[127]

All of this would have made Markey famous enough, but by the time
AZ first met him in 1943, there was more: he had been married to two of
the most beautiful women in the world: Joan Bennett (1932 to 1937) and
Hedy Lamarr (1939 to 1941). He was the second of Joan Bennett's three
husbands, and father of one of her four children. Their daughter, Melinda,
who later became an actress, was devoted to Markey. He was also the second of Hedy Lamarr's six husbands. After they were separated and then
divorced, Hedy continued to use his surname (Markey) when she adopted a little boy. And when she recorded patents for electronic devices with
her co-inventor, the composer George Antheil, she used the name H. K.
(for Hedwig Kiesler, her full maiden name) Markey.[128] Markey's divorces
from Bennett and Lamarr were generally amicable, by Hollywood's stan-
dards. After he separated from Lamarr in 1941, Markey again became one
of the most eligible bachelors in Hollywood, and speculations about his
affairs were in scores of gossip columns.

But there was still more: By the fall of 1943 Markey was already a highly decorated officer of the U.S. Navy Reserve (USNR), wearing medals earned in both world wars. After graduating from Dartmouth, where he was a member of Delta Kappa Epsilon and Sphinx (AZ's fraternity at the University of Pennsylvania), he was on active duty in 1918 as a second lieutenant in the Army. He was at the Battles of Belleau Wood and Second Marne, and he was awarded the Legion of Honor from France and the Star of Solidarity from Italy. He was promoted to first lieutenant in November 1918 and continued in the Army until 1919. He transferred to the Navy in 1920, and worked his way up to lieutenant commander by 1941. He was ordered to active duty prior to Pearl Harbor, and he was an intelligence officer on Admiral William Halsey's staff in the Battle of Guadalcanal and the Solomon Islands in 1942. He was awarded the Bronze Star with V device for leading a reconnaissance mission in the Solomons, and he also was awarded the Navy Commendation Medal. He was attached to the USS *Jamestown* (PG-55), a PT boat tender, which was awarded the Presidential Unit Citation for its support of the 1st Marine Division on Guadalcanal—another ribbon for Markey. Halsey regarded Markey as a friend and valuable staff member, and their friendship continued after the war was over.

It is not clear when Markey left the South Pacific, but given the direction of his route to India (through Cairo), it appears likely that he had been detached from Halsey's staff in late 1942 or early 1943 and traveled east via the continental United States. He would surely have been briefed on his new duties at the ONI. He proceeded to New Delhi, where he was promoted to captain. He became the senior ALUSLO for the CBI theater in about July 1943. He was also the Navy's senior officer on the JICA, and the reports of all of the subordinate NLOs would pass across his desk to Joint Intelligence Collection Agency Far East (JICA/FE; also known as JICA/CBI). And when the SEAC was established in October 1943, with Admiral Lord Mountbatten as supreme commander, Markey was assigned as naval liaison to the SEAC staff. Mountbatten soon moved SEAC headquarters to Kandy, Ceylon, and Markey must have then divided his time between New Delhi and Kandy. In his official position, and with his panache, he could, as the saying goes, write his own orders. It should be no surprise to learn that he became a personal friend of Mountbatten. He would later write a memoir of Mountbatten, and their friendship would continue after the war.

The Major General: Hurley

Major General Patrick J. Hurley, as President Roosevelt's personal representative, traveled to Karachi, Peshawar, and Kabul at the end of December 1943 into early January 1944. He was met in Kabul by Gordon Enders, who dashed back from his new position in Delhi, wiring that he would arrive on 8 January, and "Tell Hurley." They had many things to talk about, and one of them must have been the trip in the NWFP that Enders had completed less than a month earlier. But we have no direct evidence for this discussion.

Patrick Jay Hurley was born 8 January 1883, third of the eight children of an Irish-born coal miner, Pierce and Mary Hurley. He was born in a log cabin in Indian Country, near the town of Lehigh in what is now Coal County, Oklahoma. His father lived on land owned by Benjamin Smallwood, who later became a chief of the Choctaws. Patrick became responsible for his brothers and sisters after his mother died in 1896, and Smallwood became his mentor.[129]

Hurley was a scrappy young man with an explosive temper, which served him well in later life. He enrolled at Indian University in 1900, and received a bachelor of arts in 1905, and then became a clerk in the Indian Service. He read law with James H. Huckleberry in Muskogee, Oklahoma, and he attended law school at National University Law School, Washington, DC, from 1907 to 1908, when he received his law degree (LLB). In 1911 he was inducted as an honorary member of the Choctaws, and from 1911 to 1917 he divided his time between Washington and Oklahoma. He had enlisted as a private in the Oklahoma Territorial Militia in 1904 when he was a student at Indian University, and soon became a lieutenant and then a captain. He returned to the military in 1914 as a captain in the Oklahoma National Guard. He was called to active duty in 1916 as part of the effort to capture Pancho Villa, and in 1917 he joined the regular army as a major. He arrived in France in April 1918 and was in various staff positions in the First Army, and then promoted to lieutenant colonel. On

the eve of the Armistice, 11 November 1918, he was involved in reconnaissance under fire, for which he was awarded the Silver Star. Hurley
learned to pilot his own plane and continued to do this until he was ordered
to use a professional pilot.[130]

Hurley married Ruth Wilson, daughter of Admiral Henry B. Wilson,
who was commander of the Atlantic Fleet, on 5 December 1919. By 1929
he had accumulated more than $1 million from his law practice and work
for the Choctaws. A staunch Republican, he was appointed assistant secretary of war by Hoover, and then became secretary of war in November
1929 upon the death of Secretary James Good. He held this position at
the time of the Bonus Expeditionary Force's ejection from Washington by
the Army, under General Douglas MacArthur, in July 1932.

His wealth increased as he conducted negotiations with the Mexican
government on behalf of American oil companies, especially Sinclair.
Mexico later awarded Hurley the Order of the Aztec Eagle. He received
$1 million from Consolidated Oil for this work, and in 1940 he was con-
sidered a possible candidate for the Republican presidential nomination.
He applied for a commission after Pearl Harbor, and after he was rejected
by the Army, he appealed to President Roosevelt, who sent him to the
Southwest Pacific in 1942 as a brigadier general and U.S. minister to New
Zealand. He flew to Australia and began to negotiate for transport ships to
go to the Philippines to provide supplies for the Americans on Bataan.

Hurley met General Douglas McArthur at Alice Springs when he
landed after escaping from the Philippines. Hurley was sworn in as minister to New Zealand on 1 April 1942. He accompanied the prime minister
of New Zealand on a visit to FDR in July 1942, and then FDR asked him to
return by way of the Soviet Union to discuss the war objectives (Europe
first) with Stalin. Hurley arrived in Moscow via Tehran on 4 November
1942. Stalin allowed him to visit the front at two places—near Stalingrad,
where the Soviets were completing the encirclement of the besieging
Nazi armies, and at Alagir in the Caucasus Mountains. Lohbeck says that
Hurley and his aides were "the only non-Russian military officers permitted to view actual combat operations of the Soviet Armies." Hurley
believed (and told FDR) "that Stalin was a useful and trustworthy ally,"
although FDR's chief of staff, Admiral William D. Leahy, "believed Hurley

may have been duped." Hurley was asked by [George] Marshall to go
to Russia, and from Russia "to the port near Colombo—without seeing
Wavell—and from there proceed by ship to New Zealand." He returned
from the southwest Pacific to Washington, arriving in the capital on 14
January 1943.[131]

For his work in Iran, meeting with the shah and giving recommenda-
tions to the United States, he was awarded an Oak Leaf Cluster for the
Distinguished Service Medal on his return to the United States. He was
then sent back to the Pacific on 3 March 1943 as FDR's "personal representative to the Middle East—to report to Roosevelt personally. . . . You
should likewise be prepared to extend the field of your observations and
reports to me as far as Karachi." He arrived in the Middle East in April
1943. Hurley traveled from Iran to Riyadh and had an audience with King
Ibn Saud, was made an honorary member of the nobility of Hejaz and
Nejd, and returned to Cairo, where he was awarded the Distinguished
Flying Cross. Hurley espoused the Saudi position opposing a Zionist state
in Palestine, and became persona non grata with American Jews. He was
thus in opposition to Sumner Welles and Drew Pearson, as well as many
prominent American politicians. Hurley was accused (quite rightly, of
course) of being "interested in oil," based on his good relationships with
Saudi Arabia and Sinclair, and was not sent back to the Middle East,
because FDR "feared the animus his appointment would engender with
U.S. Jews." During the summer of 1943 the United States tried to gain
control of the California-Arabian Standard Oil Company, but at the end
of 1943 these negotiations were suspended.[132]

In September 1943 Hurley was in Washington "meeting regularly
with the President." FDR planned to send Hurley to Iran, but the president
first sent him to Afghanistan, India, and China "for a variety of reasons"
including supply matters, sites for new air fields, disputes between British
and U.S. military officials, and to "seek Chiang's concurrence to attend a
conference in Cairo in November."[133]

On 14 October 1943 Hurley left Washington via Scotland, Casablanca,
and Algiers, arriving in Cairo on 17 October, to remain in the Middle East
for two weeks. On 31 October Hurley left Cairo for China, stopping at
Baghdad, then Abadan, Karachi, and New Delhi, where he was met by Major
General George Stratemeyer, American air commander in India. He spent

a day or so in New Delhi, meeting with Mountbatten, Wavell, Auchinleck, and American generals. On 7 November he flew to Assam and over the Himalayas to Kunming, China, where he boarded General Stilwell's plane. He flew to Chungking (now spelled Chongqing) and was met by Stilwell and General Claire Chennault and had the first of several meetings with Chiang Kai-shek. On his arrival in Chungking, he received a message from Marshall stating that the president needed him to remain in or near Cairo. He therefore left Chungking on 10 November to return to Cairo via New Delhi.

Hurley arrived in Cairo on 16 November. He learned there that he had been recommended for promotion to the temporary rank of major general and was given the title of "special representative of the president of the United States with the rank of ambassador." FDR and his party arrived at Cairo on the morning of 22 November. Lohbeck says that Hurley told FDR that "neither Britain nor the Soviet Union was any longer willing to be bound by the Atlantic Charter as a statement of their war objectives."[134]

Hurley left Cairo for Tehran on 24 November, and FDR arrived in Tehran on the morning of 27 November to begin the Tehran Conference. The signed document of agreement by Churchill, Stalin, and FDR regarding the conclusion of the Tehran Conference was taken by Hurley and Minister Dreyfus to the Iranian foreign office "just a few minutes before midnight" on 1 December 1943.[135] The banquet was that evening and the following morning—2 December—FDR and Hurley talked privately before Roosevelt returned to Cairo by plane. After he left FDR on 2 December, Hurley conferred with the shah, cabinet officers, and others, and visited several areas of Iran. FDR held a second conference with Churchill in Cairo from 2–4 December, and then returned to Washington. Hurley wrote a long memo to FDR on 21 December 1943, proposing a six-part plan for Iran. The record of his visit to Afghanistan in January 1944 appears below, in Chapter 4.[136]

Hurley was ambassador to China from 17 November 1944, in the administration of FDR, until 26 November 1945, when he submitted a scathing letter of resignation to Truman. He believed that Roosevelt had seriously erred in a secret agreement with the Soviet Union at Yalta, granting concessions that enabled the Communists to take over China, and that Truman had failed to rectify Roosevelt's mistakes. He continued to fume at the State Department. Hurley was the Republican candidate for the U.S. Senate from New Mexico in 1946, 1948, and 1952, but lost all three times. He died in 1963.

Patrick Hurley was sui generis. With his erect posture, bright eyes, and well-trimmed moustache, he always attracted attention, whether in a smartly tailored suit or in a uniform bedecked with medals. He was irrepressible; he would let out a war whoop on a solemn occasion. Roderick Engert, son of the minister to Afghanistan, met him in Kabul when he was a young man, about eighteen years old, before he joined the OSS. "Hurley was even more flamboyant than Enders. I met General Hurley, thought he was a bit of a blowhard, but I decided later that he was really a genuine article, after I learned that he parachuted out of a plane somewhere in the east—India or China—when it got into trouble. And at his age, that was really something. When I came back to Washington, I met his daughter, Mary Hurley, a very nice person, very self-effacing."[137]

The Military Attaché: Fox

Major Ernest F. Fox was appointed in 1944 as the new U.S. military attaché in Kabul. Fox replaced Gordon Enders, who was transferred to U.S. Army headquarters in Delhi soon after he finished the trip to the NWFP. The record shows that Enders drove back from Delhi to Kabul twice in the first three months after he completed the trip. He first dashed back on 8 January 1944 to meet with General Patrick Hurley, and he returned on 19 February 1944 with Fox. Fox was a captain in the U.S. Army when he was first mentioned in cables from the Department of State, and he was promoted to major before he arrived in Afghanistan. His appointment as a diplomat was effective 11 January 1944.[138]

Ernest F. Fox was born on a farm in Wood River, Illinois, on 31 October 1902. Wood River was on the east side of the Mississippi River adjacent to Alton; it is now a northern suburb of St. Louis, which is just across the border to the southwest. A review of one of his books says that his career was "extraordinarily diverse," and indeed it was.[139] He received a bachelor of arts from the University of Illinois and later a master of science from Harvard. Between receiving those degrees, he was a student at the

University of Arizona and the University of Iowa, and worked as a geologist and explorer. He was an accomplished rider, and could shoe his own horses. He also was, at one time or another, a mining engineer, a surveyor, a writer, and a college professor. In World War II he was a soldier, a diplomat, and a member of the Army's G-2. His travels before and after the war took him to Peru, Canada, Rhodesia (now Zimbabwe), the Congo (now the Democratic Republic of the Congo), Greenland, South Africa, Afghanistan, Alaska, Iran, Pakistan, India, and Nepal. He was a member of the Harvard Travellers Club and the Explorers Club. His many honors included a listing in *Who's Who in Engineering*. The Geological Society of America and the Geological Society of South Africa published technical accounts of his explorations.

Fox's international travels are documented on ship arrivals: in New York on the *Santa Ana* from Callao, Peru, on 6 February 1928; in Boston on the *Scythia* from Liverpool, on 11 September 1933; and in New York on the *Westernland* from Southampton, England, on 2 August 1938. In 1938, Fox was on his way back to America from a trip to Afghanistan, where he and two other geologists had been sent by the Inland Exploration Company. This company was a consortium of Seaboard Oil of Delaware and Texaco, which in May 1937 had acquired a concession to all oil and mineral rights in Afghanistan for seventy-five years. As a member of the Explorers Club, he carried Flag No. 76 on this trip, and he produced a report on his travels in Afghanistan for the club. It was later published as a book.[140]

Fox was a mineral specialist, and he and his colleagues, Howie Kirk and a man named Buie, were looking for signs of oil in Afghanistan. For most of his time there, from September 1937 till June 1938, Fox was separated from the others, usually traveling on foot or on horseback with an interpreter and men he hired along the way. His travels took him to the northeastern part of the country, a few miles away from the Soviet Union at the Oxus River. He was warned away from the border because local residents said "the Russians" frequently crossed the river into Afghanistan and were liable to shoot at him. He also explored the mountains in the southwest, where the Helmand River originated. In that area, he encountered nomads who crossed the border and were supposedly involved in the unrest in Waziristan at that time. Fox was an intrepid explorer, traveling over high passes in winter, often going ahead alone, and with hardly a margin of safety.

His account is filled with instances of his Afghan employees' duplicity, lying, theft, and laziness. He wrote that "the foreign engineer in Afghanistan who accomplishes the most work will always be the one who takes most fully into account local custom and arranges his schedule accordingly, without any interference."[141] But in fact he was more often than not impatient, and he endangered himself and his mission by his failure to be tolerant and by his insistence on moving ahead and upward when his employees fell behind or deserted him.

He entered the country from Peshawar at the Khyber Pass on 17 September 1937, and he flew out on a Lufthansa flight to Berlin from Kabul after he returned there on horseback in June 1938. In the end he found few deposits of minerals, and none that was new; presumably the other geologists found no traces of oil, either. The consortium then relinquished the concession, much to the dismay of the Afghan government, which had "great hope of easy wealth from oil and mines."[142] Fox's trip to Afghanistan was the subject of his first book, *Travels in Afghanistan,* which he published in May 1943. It was reviewed in the *New York Times* in that same month and year, and mentioned in his letter of appointment as military attaché.

As the incoming military attaché, he had the opportunity to speak with Gordon Enders for several days. They first met in Delhi on 7 February 1944 and proceeded from there to Kabul, where they arrived on 19 February. Enders stayed in Kabul until sometime after 26 March, when he met with Fox and an Afghan general, Daoud; he then returned to New Delhi. It is inconceivable that Enders would not have told Fox about his trip on the NWFP. It would have been especially important for Enders to have given Fox the names of key people on the British side of the Durand Line, and he may have even introduced him to some of them as they passed through Peshawar.

After World War II Fox published *By Compass Alone,* the story of his trip with two other geologists in Rhodesia in 1929–1932. On the dust jacket, he is referred to as "Colonel Fox." He married Merle Miller, who had been a WAVES (Women Accepted for Volunteer Emergency Service) and later was with the United Nations diplomatic service. They raised horses in Tucson, Arizona. He died in 1975 and she died in 2009.[143]

He Probably Knew: Wylie

It is hard to believe that the British ambassador to Afghanistan would not have learned of the trip, either before it started or after it was over. Sir Francis Wylie, who became the British minister in Kabul in 1941, was in frequent communication with Sir George Cunningham and the American minister, Cornelius Van H. Engert. He had an especially friendly relationship with the American chargé, Charles Thayer. All of them knew of the trip. His name appears in the letters and reports of Gordon Enders, who was never one to hide his triumphs. Wylie left Kabul in December 1945 to become governor of the United Provinces of India.[144]

He Probably Knew: Pilditch

Sir Denys Pilditch, CIE, was head of the Delhi intelligence bureau (IB Delhi) at the time of the trip in the NWFP that is the subject of this book. In the novel *Kim,* the position of head of British secret service in India was held by "Colonel Creighton," who Peter Hopkirk believes was modeled on Colonel (then Captain) Thomas Montgomerie, FRS, of the Survey of India. Montgomerie's commander in chief was never named, but Hopkirk convincingly argues that he was modeled on Field Marshal Lord Roberts of Kandahar, VC, who was commander in chief of the Indian army between 1885 and 1893. In *Kim* the head of the secret service in India worked closely with the commander in chief, and we can be sure that this relationship persisted in 1943 with Pilditch and his commander in chief, Field Marshal Claude Auchinleck.

Throughout the nineteenth century and up to the time of Indian independence in 1947, the Indian Police Department and its intelligence service, known as the intelligence bureau (IB) or IB Delhi, was responsible for both domestic and international surveillance in India. The Security Service (MI5), responsible for domestic intelligence in Britain, and the MI6, responsible for foreign intelligence, long had an interest in India, and thus a relationship with IB Delhi. During World War II, to the relationship of MI5, MI6, and IB Quetta was added the American intelligence services (G-2, the OSS, and the ONI). Liaison was never perfect, because of turf battles and the need to keep sources secret, and even now the history of these organizations is incompletely written. It is clear, however, that IB Delhi was a major intelligence force in India in 1943, and it had primary responsibility for domestic and border intelligence in the subcontinent. The head of IB Delhi in 1943 was a little-known individual named Denys Pilditch, Esquire, CIE.

The official history of MI5 is silent on the subject of its activities in India from 1939 to 1947, and the official history of MI6 says little more. In 1919 it was Curzon, who had been involved in the Great Game on the North-West Frontier, who oriented the Secret Service Committee to the "Red menace." In the 1920s the most active imperial liaison of MI5 was with the IB Delhi, whose small London office was situated inside MI5's headquarters. But the relationship apparently deteriorated, and by 1941 it had collapsed. Some activity persisted, however, because it was officially (though secretly) agreed that MI5 would have a security liaison officer stationed in New Delhi after the end of British rule. "For almost a quarter of a century, relations between the Security Service and its Indian counterpart, the Delhi Intelligence Branch (DIB or IB), were closer and more confident than those between any other departments of the British and Indian Government." After 1948 it was agreed that MI5 would be responsible for British intelligence in the former colonies—the commonwealth—and MI5 thus continued to work with IB Delhi. During the Cold War the relationship between MI5 and IB Delhi, which was now run by India, was an uneasy one. Soviet intelligence presence in India grew to be greater than in any other country in the developing world, confirming the fears of Kipling, Curzon, and Pilditch.[145]

Denys Pilditch spent a long career in India, but it was largely in the shadows. In 1933 he was assistant to the deputy inspector general of police, Criminal Investigation Department, when he was awarded the King's Police Medal. Sometime after that, but surely before 1943, he rose to become director of the IB. He was on the New Year's Honors List for 1944, and he received his knighthood from Wavell on 12 February 1944 at the viceroy's house in New Delhi.[146]

After he retired, he was married in England, with his son, a major in the Royal Engineers, as his best man, to a woman with a son and daughter from her previous marriage. They moved to Australia, where Sir Denys and Lady Pilditch led a grand social life that bore little resemblance to the intrigues he had known in India.[147]

He Probably Knew: Auchinleck

Field Marshal Sir Claude J. E. Auchinleck, called "the Auk," was commander in chief, India, during the trip that Enders and Zimmermann took with Bromhead on the NWFP. There is no direct evidence that he heard of the trip, either while it was being planned or after it was over, but there are reasons to believe that he would have heard of it eventually.

In the first place, he had a personal interest in the NWFP, having been in battles there on two occasions. You never forget the terrain where you have dodged bullets. Zimmermann mentioned Auchinleck's previous engagements when he and Enders were in the tribal area north of Peshawar, and again in North Waziristan, and he took photos of both of those scenes.

And in the second place, it was Auchinleck's business to be aware of what was going on in India. The commander in chief and the viceroy have often been at odds. Field Marshal Horatio Herbert Kitchener and Curzon fought over control of the Army in India in 1905, and Kitchener won. Wavell's diaries show that he barely tolerated Auchinleck, who favored military action over political negotiation to control the restless tribal people in the NWFP. It was in Auchinleck's interest to be aware of the trip; his intelligence officers would have told him about it, if Enders (who was in Delhi for the rest of the war) did not mention it first.

One additional fact suggesting that Zimmermann may have met Auchinleck: a loose snapshot in the AZ Wartime Papers shows "the Auck [sic] showing a sepoy how to hold a gun," with the caption written in Zimmermann's handwriting. The photo is not dated, and we do not even know if AZ took it. But he went to Delhi, and he could have met Auchinleck at the time. Zimmermann was a good conversationalist and not easily intimidated, as we will see below. He could have opened the conversation with a comment about the NWFP, mentioning Auchinleck's adventures and the photos that he took of those sites, and then the traverse of the Lowari Pass.

He Probably Knew: Cutting

Colonel Charles Suydam Cutting, known as Suydam, was one of the few Americans who had experiences in the Himalayas before World War II. His record of Tibetan exploration rivals that of Enders, though it was not as long-lasting. A Harvard graduate, he was independently wealthy. Shortly before the war, he and many others of the East Coast elite (including his step-son James Cox Brady Jr.) were active in Vincent Astor's secret intelligence operation called the Room that Astor operated on behalf of FDR. Cutting had gone to Harvard with FDR and they had been friends for many years. While he was in the OSS, he was instrumental in getting Sir Olaf Caroe, secretary of state of the Indian government, to allow Ilia Tolstoy and Brooke Dolan to go on the OSS mission to Tibet in 1942, a mission personally initiated by FDR.[148]

Cutting's prewar experiences in Asia include a hunt for the rare and elusive Marco Polo sheep for the American Museum of Natural History in an expedition with Kermit and Theodore Roosevelt Jr., sons of President Theodore Roosevelt, and explorations later on his own and with his wife. His position in Delhi at the beginning of the war was as a captain; as a major, he was head of the U.S. Observer Group in New Delhi. He later wrote an article on "Cheetah Hunting" and signed himself as a colonel.[149] His intelligence services before the war are documented in publications on the Roosevelt-Astor espionage ring, and his services during the war are documented in Meyer and Brysac's *Tournament of Shadows: The Great Game*. Unfortunately, none of his papers has been found, and apparently they were discarded.

As an OSS officer in New Delhi, he would have been in a position to hear of the trip from Enders, who was stationed there after mid-December 1943. Both men apparently enjoyed talking, although they were in different branches of the American intelligence establishment.

He Could Have Known: Menzies

Major General Sir Stewart Graham Menzies was head of the Secret Intelligence Service, also known as SIS or MI6. We saw previously that he was a close friend of Rex Benson, and, by marriage, a member of the Benson family. As a result of the second marriage of his mother to Benson's uncle, they became step-cousins. Menzies and Benson had been at Eton at the same time, and they both served in World War I. Each was wounded and was awarded the MC and DSO, and they spent the last part of the war in military intelligence. Benson then went into the family banking business, although he continued to do intelligence work under cover. Menzies remained in service, and rose to become the head of MI6. Stewart Menzies became "C" (Head) of MI6 in November 1939, in the third month of World War II. Menzies was a brigadier at the time of his appointment, and he was later promoted to major general; he was knighted in 1943. At the time of the trip to the NWFP that is described in this book, his diverse activities included the responsibility for monitoring and directing the activities of MI6 in India.[150]

MI6 had been monitoring Soviet activities in the Far East since the 1920s. The intelligence operations in India at the time of the trip were complex, and no one was truly in charge of all intelligence gathering and secret operations. MI6 was responsible for gathering foreign intelligence, but its operational arm, the Secret Operations Executive (SOE) was often unwilling to cooperate with the intelligence gathering component. There was also the Indian police intelligence unit, headed by Sir Denys Pilditch, with responsibility for security and monitoring of subversive activities within India. Pilditch headed the IB Delhi, and IB Quetta and IB Karachi reported to him.[151]

By 1943 the war with Japan was slowly turning around, but it was still the most pressing concern for the Allied intelligence services in the Far East. The Chinese were unwilling to accept the presence of British intelligence officers, so MI6 was stymied in what was "an extremely hostile environment."[152] In order to achieve coordination of intelligence for the armed forces within India (and the CBI theater), an Inter-Services Liaison Department (ISLD) was formed in Delhi. It was similar to the ISLD in

Cairo, on which representatives of the OSS, G-2, ONI, and MI6 were represented. MI6 was represented in the Delhi ISLD by Colonel Reginald Heath. Heath would have been in a position to learn about the NWFP trip from Enders, who was transferred to G-2 in Delhi immediately after the trip ended, and to report it to Menzies. At about the same time, in August 1943, Admiral Lord Louis Mountbatten was appointed supreme Allied commander, South East Asia Theatre (SAC SEAT). He moved the headquarters of SEAT to Kandy, Ceylon, and MI6 appointed Brigadier Philip Bowden-Smith to head MI6 activities in the Far East. This appointment was also confirmed by MI5. Bowden-Smith arrived in India in February 1944. His assistant was Captain G. A. Garnons-Williams, RN, who was in charge of all clandestine operations (including MI6 and OSS) in SEAC. He left England for India in December 1943 and arrived in January 1944. Neither Bowden-Smith nor Garnons-Williams would have known of the NWFP trip before it took place, but they were in a position to learn about it when Zimmermann went to Ceylon immediately after the trip concluded.

Menzies monitored the situation in India closely, requiring Bowden-Smith to keep him frequently informed on his activities. However, the interests of ISLD and MI6 were focused on the campaign in Burma, Malaya, and China, because of the pressure of active war and the limitation of personnel. Nothing is known about their interest in the NWFP or the Soviet Union, but there is no indication that they were particularly concerned about threats to the empire from that direction. And Menzies was so disinterested in the Soviet threat that some wonder if he was actually a mole for the Soviets. There is no evidence for this, but it was on his watch that Philby and his friends who were Soviet spies were kept on board, promoted, and on his watch that those spies gave away the secrets of state. We must presume that although Menzies had access to information about the trip by Enders and Zimmermann, it was probably not reported to him. The Great Game that Menzies played in World War II was not the Great Game of Kipling and *Kim*.[153]

He Could Have Known: Donovan

I originally suspected that William J. Donovan, the charismatic chief of the OSS, was involved in the trip, and perhaps even authorized it, but I now believe that he was not. There were plenty of reasons to suspect his involvement, but they all appear to be coincidences. Donovan may have learned of the trip after it was over, but there is no direct evidence even for this. The main reason to reject him as a participant in planning the trip—or even as the chief planner—is that he and General George V. Strong, head of the Army's G-2, had a profound dislike for each other. And Gordon Enders, who instigated the trip, was in G-2, not the OSS.[154]

William J. Donovan (1883–1959) was born in Buffalo, New York, of Irish immigrant ancestors. He attended schools there and then went to Columbia University where he received his bachelor's degree in 1905. While at Columbia his performance on the football team led to his nickname "Wild Bill," which stayed with him for life. After graduating from Columbia's law school, he became a rising star as a Wall Street lawyer. In 1912 he raised a troop of New York cavalry that went to the Mexican border campaign against Pancho Villa in 1916. As a major, he raised a battalion of the 165th Infantry Regiment, 69th Division, which fought in Europe as part of the federalized 42nd Division. He was awarded the Distinguished Service Cross and two Purple Hearts and was promoted to colonel. He later received the Medal of Honor for his service near Landres-et-Saint Georges, France, on 14 and 15 October 1917. Between the wars his success as a lawyer continued and he served as the U.S. attorney for western New York. He also ran unsuccessfully as the Republican candidate for lieutenant governor in 1922 and for governor of New York in 1932.

He traveled widely in Europe and became convinced that another war would break out, and that the United States should prepare for it. FDR, who knew Donovan as a lawyer and politician, respected his advice—although they were from opposite political parties. On the recommendation of his secretary of the Navy, Frank Knox, also a Republican, FDR asked Donovan to be an informal emissary on his trips to Europe, where he reported on intelligence matters. William Stephenson, who was the head of British secret intelligence in New York, requested that Donovan head a similar organization for the United States; Admiral John Godfrey, head of British naval intelligence, spoke to FDR, saying, "Make Donovan intelligence master of the United States." On 11 July 1941 FDR appointed Donovan as COI, with secret, wide-ranging duties that involved the gathering of intelligence and clandestine operations, reporting directly to FDR.

The mission of the COI was to include "supplementary activities" that were understood to include "espionage, sabotage, economic and diplomatic warfare, deception, and 'special means.'" This brought him into conflict with the existing intelligence agencies in the Department of State, the FBI, the ONI, and the U.S. Army's G-2.[155]

Donovan's competitors in the American intelligence community eventually prevailed. The office of the COI was split into two parts on 13 June 1942, and placed under the Joint Chiefs of Staff. One part was renamed the Office of War information. The part that remained for Donovan to lead was called the Office of Strategic Services (OSS), which was particularly active in Europe, and, to a lesser extent, in China. General Douglas MacArthur succeeded in keeping the OSS out of his area of responsibility in the Pacific. Donovan was promoted to brigadier general and then to major general by the end of the war, and, writing his own orders, he traveled almost anywhere in the world that he was interested in, no matter how dangerous. With regard to the SEAC, he mainly wanted to have a good relationship with Mountbatten (because Mountbatten was ultimately responsible for China). Donovan's desire for a good relationship was tempered by the belief held by Donovan and many other Americans—especially Irish Americans—who saw the principal role of SEAC as being self-serving, to "save England's Asia colonies." Donovan had no personal background in the Great Game, and he never displayed any interest in Afghanistan or its border with India.

The OSS eventually grew to some 24,000 employees before President Harry S. Truman abolished it soon after the war ended. The executive order disestablishing the OSS was signed on 20 September 1945, effective 1 October. After an awkward interim, the CIA was created on 18 September 1947 out of the remains of the OSS.

Nevertheless, some of the coincidences that appear to link Donovan with the trip are rather astounding. In addition, as a practitioner of the world of intelligence, he was always watching what others were doing. He was very close to several members of Roosevelt's secret intelligence committee known as "the Room," and to Britons who were connected with it. The Room included David K. E. Bruce (who later was OSS chief in London when Charles Thayer joined the OSS there), and Suydam Cutting (who later facilitated the OSS mission of Ilia Tolstoy and Brooke Dolan that went to Tibet). The Britons who were connected with it included Rex Benson and William Stephenson (who was head of MI6 in New York City, and who thus reported to Stewart Menzies); and Admiral John Godfrey, with whom AZ was invited to dine in 1944, after Godfrey became admiral commanding the Indian navy. AZ missed having dinner with Admiral Godfrey, because he had to leave that day to fly to Kandy, Ceylon.

Donovan was crisscrossing Asia at the time of Enders' and Zimmermann's NWFP trip, and he returned to the United States when it was over. He arrived in Cairo on 13 September 1943 and was there for the Cairo Conference on 22 November; he then went with FDR to Tehran on 25 November. In Cairo, Chiang Kai-shek gave him permission to visit China, and in Tehran, Stalin told him he could visit the USSR. On 2 December, while Enders and Zimmermann were in Miram Shah, Donovan arrived in Chungking, and on 5 December he confirmed in writing what he had told Commodore Milton Miles on 9 November: Miles was fired as the head of OSS in China.

Donovan left China on 6 December 1943 for India, stopping on 7 December to visit Detachment 101 in the Burmese jungle. He then flew on to Delhi to meet with Mountbatten and the regional OSS commander in India, just as Zimmermann arrived back in Karachi and Enders arrived in Kabul. Their paths were close, but did not cross. Donovan went from Delhi to Moscow on 14 December and was there until he flew to Cairo in W. Averill Harriman's B-24. He was in Naples on 14 January to organize secret operations in Italy. He returned to Cairo and was there until 5 February 1944, when he flew to London; he went from there to the United States. The Joint Chiefs are said to have given him verbal permission to begin secret operations against the USSR at about this time, in anticipation of postwar espionage by the NKVD (Stalin's secret police) against the United States. But these trips were for other good reasons—because he had business in all of those places, not because he was monitoring the trip on the NWFP.[156]

He Could Have Known: Mountbatten

Mountbatten's name appears frequently in this book. Many people who knew of the trip by Enders and Zimmermann would have been able to talk with him about it, if they had chosen to do so. He was a bon vivant, and a good listener. But whether anyone talked about the trip is unknown.

Lord Louis Mountbatten, was "a Royal," as they say in Britain. He was an uncommonly debonair and handsome man, and not afraid of controversy. Born in 1900, he was a second cousin once removed of the princess who later became Queen Elizabeth II, and uncle of her husband, Prince Philip. He was a career officer in the Royal Navy, with service that began as a midshipman near the end of World War I. He was a captain by 1937 and was commodore of a fleet of destroyers when World War II broke out. He was in heavy combat early in the war, and received the DSO in January 1941. He survived when his flagship, the *Kelly,* was torpedoed in 1940, and again when *Kelly* was bombed and sunk in 1941. He bore most of the responsibility for the controversial, and disastrous, raid on Dieppe in 1942. In October 1943, with the rank of acting full admiral, he was appointed supreme Allied commander (SAC SEAT, sometimes abbreviated SEAC, for Southeast Asia Command). He was thus the overall officer-in-charge in India when plans were made in that month for an Anglo-American intelligence mission on the northwestern border of that country.

Mountbatten worked closely, though not always effectively, with the viceroy, Wavell, and the commander in chief in India, Auchinleck. As will be seen, Wavell met the travelers while they were on the trip, and Auchinleck probably met Zimmermann at a later date. A photo of SEAC headquarters at Kandy, Ceylon, was taken by Zimmermann when he visited OSS headquarters there. The chief U.S. Navy liaison officer in India, Gene Markey, to whom Zimmermann reported, was also a liaison officer to SEAC staff. Markey became a personal friend of Mountbatten. Both men loved to gossip, but it is unknown if the trip on the NWFP would have been interesting enough for them to talk about.

Mountbatten's postwar career was interesting and controversial: He returned to India as the last viceroy, where he presided over both the independence and the partition of the subcontinent—which many believed was done too quickly. He then became chief of the defense staff, with the rank of admiral of the fleet, and succeeded in uniting the British armed forces. The Provisional Irish Republican Army assassinated him in 1979.[157]

They Might Have Known: FDR, Dreyfus, Churchill, Others

It is tempting to think that FDR himself might have known of the NWFP trip, and for a time I thought the trip was his idea—after I learned that in 1942 FDR had asked the OSS to conduct a similar trip to Tibet. However, I have found no indication that FDR even knew of the existence of the NWFP trip. The Tolstoy-Dolan OSS mission that FDR requested was to visit the Dalai Lama, and thus to create an opening for the United States in Tibet. Although it was in Central Asia, this trip had nothing to do with Afghanistan or the NWFP. FDR also knew Engert, and had probably personally selected him for the Afghan post, but Engert did not communicate about the NWFP trip to FDR.

Gordon Enders could have bragged about the trip to the NWFP in Tehran to Louis Dreyfus, U.S. minister there, or to others in Delhi, where he moved after the trip. There were many OSS officers in Delhi at that time. His brother Robert Enders was in the OSS, and although the record is not clear, he was probably in Delhi, too. He probably learned about the trip, but we have no indication that he spoke to anyone about it. Roderick Engert says that he and Robert Enders both were translators of Urdu for the OSS. Headquarters in Delhi was a small world, and as Zimmermann said, "modesty was not one of [Gordon Enders'] virtues."[158]

Winston Churchill would have been very interested to hear about the trip, because he had an intimate, personal, knowledge of the NWFP, and he was a consummate player of the Great Game. But he was not feeling well during the Cairo Conference, and his condition worsened while in Tehran, and deteriorated when he returned to Cairo. He had to stay in North Africa to recuperate from pneumonia until he was well enough to return to England. No one would have bothered him about the Enders-Zimmermann-Bromhead trip.

Zimmermann, too, had many friends in the OSS, including a dozen or so who passed through his residence in the NLO in Karachi. They included his next-door neighbor and close friend Clarence Lewis, who was in the Marines and the OSS. About a year after the trip to the NWFP, Zimmermann visited OSS headquarters at SEAC in Kandy, Ceylon, where his friend Lieutenant Colonel Joseph Freeman Lincoln (in the OSS) and Virginia "Peachy" Durand, the daughter of "Bitz" Durand, a family friend, were working.

Three

The Trip

The letter from IB Quetta to J. R. Harris in Karachi dated 26 October 1943 is found in the Key Documents and Players at the start of this book; it appears that Albert Zimmermann was immediately told to get ready for the trip. In his next letter home, however, he said nothing about it. He said only that he had just completed a trip as a courier to his regional headquarters in Ceylon. He mentioned his trip to Colombo, where he spent two nights and a day in the office of the senior liaison officer for the region, in a letter that he began on Sunday 30 October, and that he completed after he returned via Bombay on 3 November. The letter was filled with personal items and descriptions of the terrain; it said nothing about the real purpose of the courier mission.[1]

And then a week later, on 10 November 1943, AZ casually mentioned at the end of his usual weekly letter home, "Day after tomorrow I leave for the North West Frontier by Indian train 48 hrs to be away about a month so you can look for some delay in my letters [and this] means I won't get any from you which will be pretty tuff."[2] And so the trip began. AZ wrote two letters to BSZ about the NWFP trip. The first letter was written in Peshawar on 25 November. He started the second letter in Wana on 6 December, added to it in Ft. Sandeman on 9 December, and completed it after he returned to Karachi on 15 December. I have reconstructed the story of the trip from the letters and notes AZ made as he bounced along on the road, from his trip reports and photographs, and from his captions on photos.

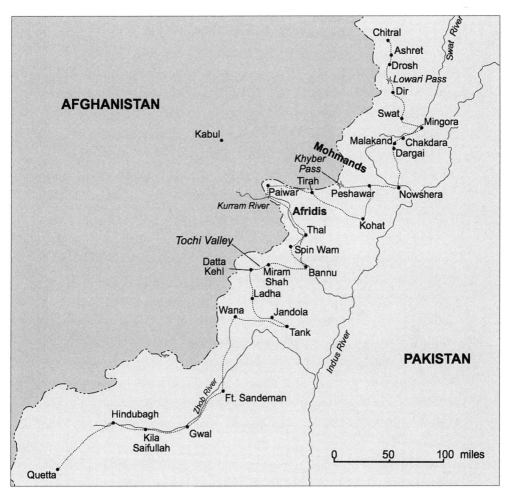

AFGHANISTAN

PAKISTAN

Chitral
Ashret
Drosh
Lowari Pass
Dir
Swat
Mingora
Malakand
Chakdara
Dargai
Kabul
Mohmands
Khyber
Pass
Tirah
Paiwar
Peshawar
Nowshera
Kurram River
Afridis
Thal
Kohat
Tochi Valley
Spin Wam
Datta
Kehl
Miram
Shah
Bannu
Ladha
Wana
Jandola
Tank
Indus River
Zhob River
Ft. Sandeman
Hindubagh
Kila
Saifullah
Gwal
Quetta

0   50   100 miles

Charles D. Grear

Part 1: To Peshawar and the Mohmand Tribal Territory

Day 1 through Day 4 (12 November–15 November)

**The tribes have never really been conquered and the present
set up seems to be the best solution of a bad situation.**
—Zimmermann, in Peshawar, November 1943

AZ recorded the trip, but as far as we know none of the other participants
made a record. Bromhead certainly did not need a journal because he
knew most of the area already, and Enders did not have time to create one,
because he was driving. We therefore see the trip through AZ's eyes.

AZ boarded the train at 3:40 p.m. on Friday 12 November, and spent
the next forty-eight hours in transit. He crossed the Sind desert in an air
conditioned train car. This first part was luxurious, with double windows
to keep the air fresh and clothing clean. His traveling companions were
interesting: he shared a compartment with a British Army officer, a Major
Lyon, who had been a prisoner of war for four years in World War I; and
an American Army officer named Major Sharp. And there was a mysterious Colonel Fagin, said to be a West Point graduate, who was wearing old
clothes of India—not his dress uniform. Fagin knew AZ's friend General
John H. "Nonnie" Hunter 2nd quite well, said Hunter was pretty pam-
pered, and could understand why the general hated Karachi.[3] AZ learned
to accommodate to the Indian mode of travel on trains, getting off at a
station to enter the dining car, and then waiting for another station to get
back into his own coach again. All in all, that part of the trip was quite
pleasant.

At Lahore he switched to a less comfortable train car for the second
part of the trip. Lahore was capital of the state of Punjab, and second only
to Karachi in population in western India. They were moving north now,
and there would be no luxuries on this train, not even a dining car. AZ
had to fight his way onto the train, even though he had a reservation. He
decided that requiring a tip to get back on was just another way of getting
baksheesh. During the night, there was a lot of commotion, people getting
off and coming on. It was more like third class, although it was supposed

to be first class. His compartment, however, was again filled with interesting people. He started off traveling with two Sikhs and ended his trip
with a "London limey" who had been in India for ten years, interviewing
musical candidates for Trinity College London. The music teacher's bearer
(porter) sat on the floor all night. AZ got off the train at Rawalpindi in an
overcoat and pajamas, apparently to look around and stretch, and had to
wait for the doors to be opened again to get back on again, which he found
confusing. There was also a British colonel and his wife. He commented
wryly, "Too bad the colonel's wife wasn't a bit younger and more attractive.
It would have added a bit more zest to the intimacy of our bed room."

The second night was similar to the first: Those who had a bed roll
unrolled it (or the bearer did it for them); they hopefully had "less chance
of picking up small traveling companions" [bedbugs] that way. AZ wrote
that you could get a bedroll from Cook's although he borrowed his from
Lieutenant Commander Smith. A Major Ellis and his wife got on the train
in the middle of the night, en route to their home in Nowshera. This
was probably Major A. J. Ellis, whose first wife was captured and killed
in Kohat on 14 April 1923, shortly after Lowell Thomas passed through
on his way to the Khyber Pass, and who had since remarried. Kohat
would be visited by AZ and the other travelers when they went south
from Peshawar toward Quetta. Nowshera, in Swat, where Ellis was then
stationed, was on the way from Peshawar to what would be the AZ's first
important stop on the trip.[4]

By this time, or shortly thereafter, AZ was in possession of three maps,
and the course of his travels can be followed on these maps. He actually
had several copies of one map that shows the entire trip, one of which
was doubtless used by him, for it is quite bedraggled; the other copies
of this map are better preserved. The other two maps are aeronautical
quadrangles. One shows the way north from Peshawar to Chitral and
south toward Waziristan; the other continues farther south to Quetta.
These maps were folded and were studied as the travelers would have
turned them to get their bearings.

AZ passed through all four of Pakistan's provinces on his trip: He went
through Sind, Punjab, and the NWFP on the way to Peshawar. He returned
to Karachi through Baluchistan, and he was probably the first U.S. naval

officer to visit all four provinces. He crossed the Indus River at Attock, the strategic point that has been used since time immemorial as the gateway onto the plains, and took the first of his 130 photos on the trip. He had borrowed a camera, and he was unfamiliar with it. He never knew until the trip was over that almost every photo was a "keeper."

He was met by Major Sir Benjamin Bromhead on 14 November and was taken immediately to the Peshawar Club for a festive Sunday lunch. "The English colony was out in full force, drinks and lunch being served to the accompaniment of a grand Indian orchestra playing most of the good modern tunes." Bromhead gave him a briefing on the local customs and politics. Bromhead had been to Sandhurst and had lived in India for many years. He had married an English woman in Buenos Aires in 1938. They had two children, and she was about to have another one. From Bromhead AZ heard,

> The city is divided into two sections—the native and the cantonement. The cantonement is surrounded by a barbed wire fence with gates on the entrance roads. This is a protection against the plundering tribes that inhabit this part of the world.
>
> The Northwest Frontier Provinces have a peculiar set-up for government. The Administered Area is governed with Indian laws. A boundary extends thru the provinces that separates the administered from the non-administered area or tribal area and then comes the boundary between India & Afghanistan known as the Durand Line, more or less arbitrary one set up around the turn of the century. The Tribal Area has its own local governments ruled by mehtars, nawabs, Walis or mullahs [religious leader] according to where you are in the Provinces.
>
> The tribes have never really been conquered and the present set up seems to be the best solution of a bad situation. The terrain is practically all mountainous and lends itself very well to guerilla warfare, necessitating a large force & enormous expenditures to beat unwilling tribesmen to submission. The tribes have their own laws, with offenses against property taking precedence over [offenses against] lives.

The various sections have scouts or militia oftentimes officered by the British to defend the frontier and help preserve peace. They also have Political Agents who try to advise the local rulers but otherwise the local rule is undisturbed.

Peshawar is on the edge of Tribal Territory, and is the house of H. E. the governor of the Provinces. It is the Indian end of the Khyber Pass—quite primitive in many ways—ox-carts, goats, water buffaloes all over the place.[5]

Bromhead appeared to be about forty-five, rather large, with a dry English sense of humor. He had been an officer in one of the scout outposts and had recently joined the public relations department at provincial headquarters. They had drinks and dinner at the Services Hotel with Sir Benjamin and Lady Nancy Bromhead. It was a nice way to start the trip. AZ does not say where he stayed; the Bromheads' hotel (Services Hotel) was reserved for full-time service personnel. He probably stayed at Dean's Hotel, where Enders had stayed on his first visit to Peshawar. It was reputed to be the finest hotel in the city.

AZ must also have been aware of the significance of Peshawar in history, but in any event he would surely have heard more about it in the conversations that he had while waiting to depart.

Peshawar is one of the oldest cities in Asia. AZ's friend and bridge partner in Karachi, April Swayne-Thomas, whose husband was stationed in the NWFP, wrote a letter from Peshawar, describing the city and its environs. April and her husband Geoffrey, a lieutenant colonel in the Engineers, had been stationed in Quetta early in the war, but she stayed in Karachi as her husband traveled throughout western India. She recalled going from Agra to Peshawar, through the Khyber Pass, and to the Swat Valley and Malakand—all of which would also be visited by AZ and his fellow travelers. In her letter, she recalled Kipling's poem, "East Is East," and she mentioned ruins that remained from Alexander and the Greek invaders at Nowshera. Even in winter, when AZ was in Peshawar, she saw

beauty there. At Christmas she wrote, "The Vale of Peshawar is quite the
most fertile valley imaginable and between the bright green rows of winter wheat were lines of fruit trees, leafless and bare, making a beautiful
tracery against the far distant blue ranges that surround the plain like the
rim of a bowl."[6]

The viceroy, Lord Wavell, who met the travelers at the governor's
home in Peshawar on 27 November 1943, had visited Peshawar several
times. Five years in India as a young officer "had a deeply formative effect
on Wavell's life and outlook." In February 1903 Wavell sailed for India, and
joined his regiment at Ambala, in the Punjab, near Simla. Ambala is about
three hundred miles from Etawah, where Enders lived as a young man,
and at about the same time (1903). Though Enders was much younger,
their coincident experiences would have given them something else to
talk about at the garden party. In October 1904, during Wavell's second
tour in India, "conflict seemed imminent between Britain and Russia,
and the N.W. Frontier threat looked like becoming an urgent reality."[7]

Wavell's most recent trip to Peshawar began just as the travelers were
returning to Peshawar, and before they set off on their second part of
their journey to the south. On 21 November 1943 he finished a two-day
conference with the eleven governors, and on 23–30 November he visited
Punjab and the NWFP. "I enjoyed visit to N.W.F.P., I have always liked
Peshawar since I was stationed there nearly 40 years ago."[8]

In his letters to BSZ, AZ mentioned Kipling, Auchinleck, and Churchill, all of whom visited Peshawar. Kipling made only one trip to Peshawar,
but it had a profound influence on him. He is said to have stayed at Dean's
Hotel. Churchill, too, stayed at Dean's Hotel in Peshawar. Churchill mentioned the city several times, as a city and as a jumping-off point for
adventures to the north. He reportedly said "it was impossible to garrison
Chitral without keeping up the road from Peshawar." In the *Malakand
Field Force*, Churchill opined, "Nothing in life is so exhilarating as to be
shot at without result," a statement that has become one of his most
famous expressions. Churchill recalled that Alexander had been there
too, on his march to the Indus River in 356 BCE. After the British destroyed
most of the villages in the Mamund Valley in retaliation for the attacks by
the Mamund tribesmen, Churchill said that Alexander's difficulties began

in the same valley: "Thus history repeats itself, and the people of Bajaur their tactics."[9]

George Nathaniel (later Lord) Curzon visited Peshawar in 1887 on his first trip around the world. After reaching Agra, he proceeded to Delhi, Peshawar, Khyber, and then through the Bolan Pass by railroad to Quetta. He, too, is supposed to have stayed at Dean's Hotel in Peshawar. Lord Curzon's son-in-law, Edward "Fruity" Metcalfe, was the host for the Prince of Wales (later Edward VIII) when he visited India in 1921. He was rewarded with the title of equerry and moved into high society. The prince reportedly told Metcalfe, "Be careful of that little bitch [unnamed] from Peshawar."[10]

Cornelius Van H. Engert is a key person in the background for this trip, and he was one of the first American officials to visit Peshawar. He was perhaps the first American to travel by car across the Khyber Pass from Peshawar, and Lowell Thomas was probably the first nonofficial American to travel by car across the Khyber Pass. After waiting some time for approval, which was granted through intervention by Engert in August 1923, Thomas began at Peshawar and entered the pass at its southern extremity. The fort of Jamrud, commanded by a British general, is located about two-thirds of the way through the twenty-seven mile-long pass. Many officers on his staff were married, and "most of their wives live at Dean's Hotel, in Peshawar." Thomas's return trip through the Khyber took place via Jelalabad, Landi Khana, and "back into British India. . . . In the chief commissioner's garden, a fox-terrier romped with a well-washed goat; over them flapped lazily the Union Jack." AZ was in that same garden twenty years later.[11]

Ernest F. Fox passed through Peshawar in September 1937 as a geologist and explorer. He would return again as Major Ernest Fox, military attaché to Kabul in January 1944. As he saw it in 1937, Peshawar "was once the residence of Afghan kings, and the Afghans say that they will occupy the town again one day. . . . Tonight we will rest in Dean's Hotel."[12]

Unknown to AZ, but probably not to Enders—who seems to have been on to everything—a well-known explorer who had been in Peshawar was at that time with the OSS in Delhi. Suydam Cutting had been in Peshawar six years earlier. Cutting said it was the perfect time of the year to vacation in Peshawar. It was six years later, in the same month, that AZ and Enders were there.[13]

Walter Reeve, a young son of an officer in the Royal Indian Army, arrived in Peshawar in December 1935 and left Pakistan in 1949. Reeve later described the Services Hotel on Fort Road, where the Bromheads lived: "[It was] the biggest and most well appointed in Peshawar . . . located in a pleasant district fairly close to Government House and opposite a large recreational ground or maidan." He described the "grandstand view of the hotel gardens, Fort Road and the playing field beyond."[14]

Lutz Kleveman, who traveled to Peshawar in 2002, said that "Only by obtaining special permission and an armed escort of the Afridi clan, am I allowed to travel through the 'Khyber Agency' to Peshawar, on the last leg of the Great Trunk Road from Kabul." Kleveman wrote that many Pashtuns envisage a 'Great Pastunistan' [sic] stretched across the Durand Line," a hope that persists to this day.[15]

Early on Monday 15 November 1943, Bromhead and AZ crossed into the Mohmand tribal territory near Peshawar. Enders was supposed to be with them, but he was delayed and did not arrive until evening.

They picked up Subhardar Sarwar Khan, intelligence liaison officer to the governor, to go with them. "At the entrances to all Tribal Territory there is a gate for proper identification both ways and a place to park your shootin-irons [sic] when you are entering the land of law and order. Caravans of donkeys, mules and camels pass thru taking grains, poultry, etc., to the towns, bringing back piece goods, and other supplies. They would never think of traveling thru most of the Tribal Territory without a gun." AZ noticed a "man carrying a baby camel on his back" and others bringing wheat into town to be exchanged for quilts and cloth. He learned that the community produced a surplus, and exported its products to India.

They first stopped at Shabkadar, where AZ took several pictures, and there they added Mohammed Isaac, assistant political officer under the deputy commissioner for Peshawar. "At Shabkadar is an old fort with lists of dead more from disease, sunstroke and drowning than from fighting."

Peshawar train station [officer not identified].
Albert Zimmermann photos, 14 November 1943.

Kasai Munidi. Reception Committee.
Albert Zimmermann photos, 15 November 1943.

Albert Zimmermann photos are contained within the *Albert Zimmermann Papers* at the United States Naval Institute. The captions are Zimmermann's own.

The malik of Kasai Munidi. His beard is red, showing he's been to Mecca.
Albert Zimmermann photos, 15 November 1943.

Typical Pathan head dress. Lunch – roast chicken (very tuff) hard boiled eggs,
many varieties of cuke (gourd), chapattis. All done with the right hand.
Albert Zimmermann photos, 15 November 1943.

Shazada the malik of Yusef Kheyl and his right hand man.
Albert Zimmermann photos, 15 November 1943.

Saidu—Palace of Wali of Swat. Major Bramhead, Sect. to Wali, P.A. Packman,
[Waliahad], Wali of Swat. *Albert Zimmermann photos, 16 November 1943.*

Saidu—Band that greeted us. *Albert Zimmermann photos, 16 November 1943.*

Headworks Malakand Hydroelectric—gates to Swat River Canal.
Albert Zimmermann photos, 16 November 1943.

Jeep "Ma Kabul" ready to start for Dir State. Maj. Enders at wheel.
P.A. Kenneth Packman, Bengie [Bramhead],
Mrs. P. *Albert Zimmermann photos, 17 November 1943.*

Punjkara River Valley. Camel caravan on way to Dir.
Albert Zimmermann photos, 17 November 1943.

Dir to Gujar. *Albert Zimmermann photos, 18 November 1943.*

Top of Lowari Pass. Hgt. 12,000' [sic]. Chitral Scout, me, Benjie.
Hindu Kush Mountains in background.
Albert Zimmermann photos, 18 November 1943.

Going down. Getting out to see what's ahead.
Albert Zimmermann photos, 18 November 1943.

"Tirichmir" at dawn. Height 25,000' [sic] Land of Fairies.
Albert Zimmermann photos, 20 November 1943.

Kohat—Enders, Deputy Commissioner Sheiku, his brother, Mir Ali.
Albert Zimmermann photos, 29 November 1943.

Peiwar Khotal, with Afghanistan's highest mountain (16,000') [sic] in background.
Albert Zimmermann photos, 30 November 1943.

Peiwar Khotal. Tommy [Sgt. Nicholson], Col. Francis, Benjie.
Political Agent Knneth Donald, myself.
Albert Zimmermann photos, 30 November 1943.

Parachinar Plain from Peiwar Khotal. Height 10,000'.
It was through this valley the Afghans tried to invade India in 1919.
Albert Zimmermann photos, 30 November 1943.

Miram Shah. This is headquarters of Tochi Scouts and the Political Agent.
Albert Zimmermann photos, 1 December 1943.

South Waziristan Khadassars.
Albert Zimmermann photos, 5 December 1943.

Copy of pen and ink drawing of Zimmermann by United States
Coast Guard Combat Artist Joseph Di Gemma, 1945.
Albert Zimmermann photos.

Roasting mutton for lunch—Gov's youngest child.
Albert Zimmermann photos, 12 December 1943.

Lunch on the chickor shoot. Enders, Gov. Hays, A.A. Woods-Ballard,
Mrs. Hays, Benjie on right. Gov. children in middle.
Albert Zimmermann photos, 12 December 1943.

Leaving Quetta for Karachi. Maj. Alston, Mrs. Woods, Benjie, Tommy, Enders.
Albert Zimmermann photos, 12 December 1943.

Albert Zimmermann,
in about 1924.
*Albert Zimmermann
photos.*

Barbara Shoemaker, in about
1924. She married Albert
Zimmermann in 1926.
Albert Zimmermann photos.

Lt. Zimmermann.
Albert Zimmermann photos.

Albert Zimmerman on the left; Lt. Howard Voorhees, center;
Lt. Phil Halla (USCG), right.
Albert Zimmerman photos.

Al and Barbara Zimmermann at home after the war.
Albert Zimmerman photos.

Lt. Zimmermann, on the bank of the Indus River near Karachi, spring, 1945.
Albert Zimmerman photos.

At Shabkadar they met a *malik* (king or tribal chieftain, Arabic) who was the enemy of the *malik* of the Yusef Kheyl tribe. "Yusef Kheyls are a portion of the Lower Mohmand Tribe whose protection was guaranteed by the British. The Mohmands, however, misused this protection by taxing the Upper Mohmands who passed through their territory." In order to stop the fighting, *khassadars* patrolled the roads, working alternate months; these *khassadars* were immune from *badis* (blood feuds) while they were on duty. The British stopped illegal taxation, on threat of withdrawal of British protection. However, all villages were fortified and there were no schools, to avoid *badis*. The nearby *maliks* were still feuding, with *badi* being widespread.[16]

They visited Hali Gandao, a town in tribal territory, and Kasai Mundi, where the *malik* allowed himself to be photographed. He was proud of his red beard, "showing he's been [on a pilgrimage] to Mecca." They saw Hill 19408, where Auchinleck had fought in 1935. They went to Yusef Kheyl for lunch with Shazada, *malik* of the lower Mohmand tribe—"one of the peaceful ones," in spite of his enemy, the *malik* of the upper Mohmand tribe. AZ was amazed at the lack of utensils at lunch. "We started off having our hands washed by pouring water over them as we sat at the table. Everything was picked up by hand and you weren't supposed to use your left hand." He spoke of eating chapattis, which every reader of Kipling's *Kim* remembers. And we "had roast chicken (pretty tuff), native bread (large doughy pancakes) and lots of hard-boiled eggs, cooked just right and very good. For dessert there was fruit (casawba melon) and cookies. . . . An interesting time was had by all. I was more or less a curiosity being American and in the Navy."

They returned in time for drinks at Mrs. Licpur's—"one of the few [Western] women who can talk Pushtu"—and Mrs. Cole, wife of the political agent of Khyber. Enders arrived in time for dinner at the Bromhead's hotel. AZ notes that "the secretary to the minister at Kabul is Charley Thayer from Phila, brother of George Thayer." As the secretary and chargé d'affaires, Thayer knew Enders well.[17]

Enders had been to Peshawar at least once before, and perhaps more than once. His routes and travels in Afghanistan and Pakistan were the despair of his chief, the U.S. minister, Cornelius Van H. Engert, who tried without success to keep an eye on him. Enders may not have told the minister, Cornelius Van H. Engert, about the trip until it was over. There is nothing about the trip in the Engert papers and nothing is recalled about it by his son, who was a teenager at the time. It would be consistent with the way he (and other intelligence officers) would act, saying only what was necessary. In addition, this trip was entirely in India, which he could rightly say was in the other sphere that he operated in, reporting to G-2 in India, not via the State Department in Kabul.

Part 2: The Northern Portion
Day 5 through Day 12 (16 November–23 November)

In Dir, Swat or Bajaur, range after range is seen . . . and in the distance some glittering snow peak suggests a white-crested roller, higher than the rest.
—Sir Winston Churchill, *The Story of the Malakand Field Force: An Episode of Frontier War*, 11.

The trip to the north began on 16 November with an introduction to the first of the exotic rulers and the territories of the northern three states. Along the way, they would meet the *wali* of Swat, the *nawab* of Dir, and the *mehtar* of Chitral. They would visit the famous area of Malakand on the way to Dir, and they would go almost to the Wakhan, the narrow strip of Afghanistan between India and Russia. The first morning they passed through Nowshera on the way to Swat, and on the same morning through Mingora, which is not on the map but is now regarded as the principal town of Swat.

The scenes that they must have seen were incredibly beautiful, although there is very little about them in the trip reports and in AZ's letter of 25 November, which was written after he had returned to Peshawar. And there is little there, too, about the interesting history of the area, which had been settled first by Buddhists and later by the Sufi sect of Islam. I will therefore turn to others for a description of the area.

They picked up Major Kenneth Packman, political agent for Malakand, and he was their guide on this part of the trip. The trip to Swat went through country that is much like the Lower Mohmand country, except that they went up the Swat River valley. They went by a fort where they were told that the British garrison was imprisoned, and where the fictional Gunga Din came down to the Swat River to get water for the troops. Only a heliograph could be used in those days to communicate between the forts.[18]

Lunch on the first day was just beyond Mingora, at Saidu, the palace of the ruler of Swat, Wali Bashah Sahib. They also met the *waliahad* (crown prince), who succeeded to the throne when his father retired in about 1949; his name was Miangul Abdul Haq Jahanezeb Khan. They were greeted with saluting soldiers—the levies—who lined the streets, and a blare of trumpets at the palace gate. They were met by "the old Wali himself at the door," the *waliahad* (whose short name was Jehan Zeb); and Attaullah, secretary to the *wali,* who functioned as the prime minister. Photos were taken of the *wali,* the *waliahad,* and Attaullah, with the British and Americans.[19]

The palace was beautiful, with Persian rugs, modern furniture, modern plumbing—all surrounded by mud huts and buffaloes. AZ says it they had a very good lunch, with many courses and all the trimmings; it was his first try at *poulow* (a mild curry). This part of India being "95% Mohammedan and meat eating," they enjoyed having meat in their food for a change. They learned that Swat was one of the newest states, having been established in 1926. "And they were told privately by their British hosts that the *wali,* a venerable man, was said to have pushed his brother over a cliff."[20]

Returning to the main road after lunch, they heard that Churchill, as a sub-lieutenant, fought in these mountains, and that Auchinleck had been stationed near here in 1935. As they continued up the Swat River, they inspected the head works of the Malakand hydroelectric system, and took photos of it. The hydroplant looked fine to the prime minister of Swat, but they observed that "there is no evidence to show there is electricity in the Swat River."[21] They saw many Buddhist towers along the road, and a school—called a college, which was really more like a high school. AZ observed that education appeared to be the only way to bring the people under peaceful government.[22]

Sir Benjamin told them that the Axis was conspiring with Hindus and Sikhs to boost the black markets throughout India. He said that educated Sikhs were of "a higher type," and were used in the Army, although Sikh merchants were lined up with Hindus and the Congress Party.[23]

They dined and spent the night with Major and Mrs. Packman. As the political agent for Malakand, he was in charge of Dir, Swat, and Chitral. The Packmans lived at the fort of Malakand with their two daughters in what AZ described as a "very nice house," overlooking the Swat Valley. However, AZ observed that as "with the other P.A.'s [political agents], they live a rather lonely existence, living so far from civilization and seeing very few white people for months. They have a baby ibex as a pet," named Bix.

Malakand and the Swat Valley

Churchill described the Swat Valley and the Lowari Pass to Chitral in the introduction to *Malakand Field Force*. The prose is flowery; it was, after all, written by a man who later was awarded the Nobel Prize for literature:

> After crossing the Malakand Pass the first turning to the right leads to the Swat valley. . . . In every direction the view is restricted or terminated by walls of rock. The valley itself is broad, level and fertile. The river flows swiftly through the middle. . . . It is a beautiful scene. . . . The reputation which its present inhabitants enjoy is evil. . . . Among Pathans it is a common saying: 'Swat is heaven, but the swatis are hell-fiends.' . . . Beyond Dir camels cannot proceed, and here begins the third section—a path practicable only for mules, and about sixty miles long. From Dir the road is a triumph of engineering. In many places it is carried on wooden galleries perched on the faces of steep and tremendous cliffs, and at others it works round spurs by astounding zig-zags, or is scraped from the mountain side. At the end of the road is Fort Chitral.[24]

AZ's friend April Swayne-Thomas visited the Swat valley in peaceful times: "Malakand and Swat. Then we left the valley and started to wind up and up and up, on a perilously twisting but well kept road, until we reached Malakand. . . . After a few days of sketching and motoring, we packed up again and went on to the Swat Valley—a lovely place that reminded me of the Lake District on a misty day. The Kabul river came, icy and green, leaping over boulders and across the valley."[25]

The travelers departed early in the morning of 17 November and entered the Dir tribal territory at Chakdarra. They stopped at the village of Bat Kheyl to buy a length of rope to pull the jeep back on the road in case it slid off, or needed a boost over rocks. (They would need this rope the next day.) They negotiated their way into the tribal territory but declined an escort of *khassadars*. Sir Benjamin said, "We were American guests and what would we think if khassadars would not let us through."[26]

They drove up the Punjkara River valley to the foot of the Lowari Pass, passing terraced paddies on which wheat was grown in winter and rice in summer. The hillside views were spectacular. They also saw sugar cane growing in Lower Dir and Swat, and passed a sugar refinery at Takht-i-Bhai. They passed groups of Kazakhs, who were on the move back to their homeland in Outer Mongolia. In Dir City, they saw a collecting point for antimony ore that was coming down from Chitral (and they would learn more about that in Chitral). Dir City, they learned, had hydroelectric power.

From Bromhead they heard that Dir and Swat were jealous of each other, Swat being partly taken out of Dir State. In the tribal territory the scouts and militia were sometimes officered by British, sometimes by natives. The Waziri Scouts, Tochi Scouts, and Kurram Militia numbered three thousand each; the Zhob Militia numbered two thousand; and the Chitral Militia numbered one thousand. All of these militias were south of Peshawar, except Chitral. Sir Benjamin believed it was better to use locals rather than to bring in outsiders, which would foment trouble. In Chitral and Kurram the scouts were mostly locals, but others were made up of both locals and neighboring tribes. The Chitrali Scouts were officered mostly by British, although the British allowed relatives of the ruler to become officers, too.

Sir Benjamin said that the *nawab* of Dir used to collect levies from the British government for allowing troops to pass through his territories. To make it appear to be worthwhile, the *nawab* occasionally shot up British troops. (This story also appears in Churchill's account, so it has been repeated for a long time.) In tribal territory, there is no written record of land ownership, so there were many *badis* regarding ownership. Sir Benjamin mentioned an episode in South Waziristan where coal was found on tribal land and was being used by the scouts. Five men laid claim to the land and a bad *badi* resulted. The American officers learned about the distinction between a *mullah* and a *malik*. The faqir of Ipi, who was active in Waziristan and Baluchistan, combined both offices in himself.[27]

On the afternoon of 17 November, they paused for tea and dinner and spent the night at the residence of the *nawab* of Dir. His name was most impressive: Khan Bahadur Nawab Sir Shah Jahan, Khan, KBE.

He was officially known as chief of Dir, Dir State, and AZ addressed him in writing as "Dear Nawab Sahib." They were joined by the *waliahad,* who they found to be rather childish because he did not smoke in front of his father, and an unnamed captain, who was a doctor, apparently watching over the sickly *nawab.* The *waliahad* had been married for about two years and had one daughter.

This was truly historic country. In the first European expedition to this area, Alexander of Macedon in 327–326 BCE saw much of the same scenery, although the report of his trip places more emphasis on the army and the tactics, rather than on the countryside:

> Alexander moved on north, into the rich forest-clad mountain region below Chitral. One night the column pitched came in a wood. It was so bitterly cold that they gathered fuel and built a number of campfires. The flames spread, and engulfed what turned out to be cedar-wood coffins hanging among the trees. These went up like tinder. . . . It used to be thought that this whole episode was pure fantasy, put out as propaganda either by Alexander himself, or else (in the view of more puritanical scholars) by his enemies. Yet the mountains south of Chitral— abounding in wild game, lush with vines and ivy, walnut and

plane, mulberry and apricot—exactly match the description given by our ancient sources.[28]

As the Chitral River flows south, it becomes the Kunar, then bends west and flows down the Durand Line for about ten miles, before turning into Afghanistan then flowing into the Kabul River at Jelalabad. The river does not flow through the Khyber Pass, but instead flows back across the border a few miles north of the Khyber. The Kunar Pass is probably the route that Alexander took, and because he avoided the usual route, the Khyber, he caught his enemies by surprise.[29]

Thursday 18 November was the most important day of the trip. The urgency of the day was increased by the need to make the journey in a jeep for political and military reasons. A new ruler known as the *mehtar* had come into office in Chitral, and he had not yet been visited by anyone from the provincial capital in Peshawar. The problem of the Lowari Pass, however, was uppermost in their minds. They wondered if it could be crossed in a motor vehicle, and especially at that time of year. They had been warned against the attempt by British officers on both sides of the pass. They were due to meet with Haji Shahazada Muzaffar-ul-Mulk, *mehtar* of Chitral. He was addressed later by AZ as "Dear Friend."

Chitral had become a nominal part of the British Empire in 1892 when the king of Chitral asked to join the empire instead of becoming part of Afghanistan, and the British in turn agreed to a financial tribute and annual payments to the ruler of Chitral and his successors. The modern history of Chitral is said to have begun in 1854 with the alliance of the maharaja of Kashmir and Shah Afzal, *mehtar* of Chitral (1840–56). Over the next 116 years, nine men in seven generations of descent from Shah Afzal seized or were awarded the title of *mehtar* of Chitral. Some *mehtars* were deposed, but fratricide and regicide were also pathways to power in Chitral. The third in succession from Shah Afzal, Aman ul-Mulk (1857–1892) was called the great *mehtar,* and chaos followed his death. The *mehtar* in early 1943 was Honorary Major Sir Nasir-ul Mulk (b. 1898). He had no sons, so upon his death on 29 June 1943 the title passed to his brother, Muzaffar-ul-Mulk, who was *mehtar* from 1943 until he died in 1948. Sir Benjamin may have been given the task of bringing tribute to the new *mehtar* on this trip, although nothing about this appears in Zimmermann's notes or letters. Bromhead may have performed his "bag man" duties quietly, without telling the Americans, or they may have decided not to make a written record of this delicate piece of business.[30]

AZ began to take movies at this point in the trip to supplement his still photos, and Bromhead also took photos of the historic journey. The grainy images in AZ's movies, starting near the summit of the Lowari Pass and continuing down the north slope into Chitral, show the difficulty that they encountered. You can feel the urgency, and wonder as you watch the pictures if it will end successfully. It finally does, however.[31]

They were accompanied on this part of the trip by a Captain Behts of the Chitrali Scouts, which meant that the jeep was fully loaded with four people. He spoke Chitrali, which was the only language the local people knew. Pushtu, which Sir Benjamin was familiar with, was no longer useful here, and Urdu was not understood at all in this part of India. About twenty men and a half dozen horses accompanied them, to carry their baggage and to pull the jeep back onto the road if need be. The trail was nothing more than a donkey caravan route. The jeep did slide off at least once, and the men and horses pulled it back on to the road.

On 18 November they pushed off at 9:00 a.m. from Dir. Going up, on the south side of the pass, turned out to be relatively easy.[32] They arrived at the Gujar Levy Post at 7,800 feet at 11:00 a.m.; they were encouraged because they had not encountered any snow. With continuous switchbacks, they inched their way upward, on a road that was narrow in spots, with rocks at the upper end, but it was passable without assistance from the animals. They paused when they reached the 10,240 foot summit of the Lowari Pass at 12:30 p.m.

Going down, on the north side, was another matter: "Snow on top [of the Lowari pass] only; none on way up. Road narrow in spots, rough with rocks at upper end. On descent, ice and snow found in patches. Descent much steeper than ascent, with many awkward zig-zags."[33] The travelers left Enders to manage the jeep while they got out and walked, inching their way down the pass. The descent was much steeper than the ascent. They squeezed between a cliff face on one side and the edge of the trail on the other, which sometimes dropped several hundred feet to the valley below. They crept carefully over ice and snow, coaxing the jeep around the many zig-zags, and simply picking it up and lifting it from time to time. They were grateful for the first sign of habitation, at Ziarat, 7,500 feet, where they paused for tea at 2:30. The road was still a challenge—in fact, it does not look like a road at all in the pictures. They pushed on to Ashret, almost nine miles from the summit, which was the road head on the Chitral side, reaching there at 4:30 p.m. From there the route was better and they reached their stopping point for the night at Drosh, thirteen miles from Ashret, at 6:30 p.m. They estimated that the running time was seven and a half hours, with stops totaling about two hours. They traveled on that one day 35.8 miles. They had gone from 4,000 feet on one side to over 10,000 feet, and back to about 4,000 feet on the other side of the pass.[34]

They were met at Drosh by Major M. W. H. White, MBE, commandant of the Chitrali Scouts in Drosh, who was also commandant of the mess; and a Captain Hemming. They looked across a swaying extension bridge to the airfield at Drosh. The airfield was marked with a white circle in the center, in order to be visible from the air, 1,500 feet below the fort, and it was on the opposite side (right bank) of the Chitral River. It was very small, L-shaped, and only 1,500 yards by 200 yards. The prevailing winds were up and down the river valley, and they thought it would be dangerous in cross-winds. In fact, the *mehtar* was later killed on the summit of the Lowari Pass; it is unknown whether he was attempting a landing here, or was by-passing this dangerous field. AZ's movies show the way up the Lowari, the top of the pass, and the way down to Ziarat. AZ then changed film, took movies of the donkeys having a break by walking around in a circle, and a supporting bridge at Ziarat. He had thirty feet of film left to take movies in Drosh. With great relief, they paused for dinner at the mess, and spent the night at Drosh.

The three travelers and their Chitrali Scout guide had breakfast and enjoyed the morning at Drosh, and left after lunch to descend to the village of Chitral, some twenty-six miles away. On the way, they passed a group of Kazakhs who were on their way home. The Soviets had chased them out; they left with twenty thousand head of cattle, but they were down to five thousand head by the time they reached Kashmir. They lost more, and returned empty handed.

AZ's movies were the first taken by an American in Chitral, and were perhaps the first movies ever taken in Chitral. The movies show the south face of Tirich Mir very well. Tirich Mir is the highest mountain in the Hindu Kush range, and the thirty-third highest in the world, at 25,289 feet (7,708 meters). AZ wrote, "Chitral is surrounded by snow-capped mountains, the highest being Tirichmir. We were very fortunate to see its top as it is usually in the clouds. But the two days we were there, the weather was perfectly clear, giving us wonderful mountain scenery to look at all the time."[35]

They reached Chitral Village at 4:30 p.m. and were greeted with great fanfare: blaring trumpets, bands playing, much saluting, and an honor guard to welcome them to the palace. They were met on horseback by Gazi ud-Din, brother of the *mehtar,* who escorted them to the palace. They had tea with the *mehtar,* Muzaffar-ul-Mulk, and then went to a polo match held in their honor; they were told that polo originated in Chitral.[36] After the game, they went for drinks to the residence of Mr. and Mrs. Thornburg; Mr. Thornburg was the assistant political agent. It must have been especially sweet for them to be there, for Thornburg had wired them in Dir, just before they made the attempt, saying "ice, snow and mud on Lowari" made the trip inadvisable.

Then to the palace for dinner with the *mehtar;* his brother, the prime minister; the Thornburgs; a Dr. Kekyll; several officials who were relatives of the *mehtar;* and the chief of the bodyguards. The state dining room was "fantastic, with chandeliers and artificial flowers." AZ noticed that practically no Pathan (or Chitrali) wore glasses, because they do little close reading, and are always watching out for the distance—apparently a reference to the dismal way that succession often was passed in Chitral. After dinner they saw native dances of Chitral and Hunza in the ball room. "All of the dancers were men, of course. In fact, we didn't see a woman, except on the road, the whole trip. The women are kept secreted away from curious eyes. The ones we did see would turn their heads and cover their faces." As an aside, he noted, "Most of the time they were working hard carrying wood if they were local inhabitants or doing most of the carrying, mostly on their heads, moving their goods & chattels from the high lands to the low lands for the winter. You'd pass any number of families with their worldly possessions (which didn't amount to much), livestock & all walking along the road."

After breakfast the next morning, they were off on a hawking expedition. AZ says he "drew a spirited ex-polo pony," who thought he was still on the polo field. For a city boy from the Philadelphia suburbs, it was a strange experience, and "it took all my strength to hold him down to a slow trot." He described the hunt: "Hawking consists of going to a high place where the river is narrow, getting about 200 men to beat the brush, rousing the birds to flight (chicors—like partridge), releasing the hawks (falcons) as the chicors fly by and watching the kill. Not my idea of real sport. It took all morning—the efforts of 250 men with the net result of 10 chicors killed." The *mehtar* was greeted by his subjects, who kissed his hands and offered gifts in recognition of his feudal power, which extended to confiscation of land. He was surrounded by his body guards, horsemen, and the falcon trainers, and others who served him and his guests tea every ten minutes or so. It was a rare opportunity to see the sport of kings.

After lunch they went on a jeep ride about thirteen miles up the Ludko River valley to see the antimony mines for which the area is famous. Remembering enough of what he heard, and writing it down like a good intelligence officer would, we have AZ's summary:

Mines produce about 2½ tons of ore daily, varying from 30% to 65% antimony metal. It averages around 35%. Expected production this year is about 750 tons; next year 1,000 tons. Number of workers varies. Started this year with 80 in January, labor scarce in summer, but after the harvest labor is again available. Present diggers number 200 in five workings. Dynamite and powder are used.

Pay 8 to 10 annas [former unit of currency, worth 1/16 rupee] per day, with shelter provided. Transport costs more than the mining. Cost of ore at mine head—Rs150 [rupees] per ton. Visible supplies, perhaps 50–60,000 tons. Syndicate is hoping to import Nepalese diggers. Deposits might end overnight. Deposits now being worked are on spurs, with no digging downward as yet.

As antimony is of low melting characteristics, engineer feels it
might disappear at any moment. Transport system is from mine
to depot on men; from depot to Ashret by lorry [truck]; by mule
and donkey pack to Dir; lorry from Dir to railhead at Durgai.
Refinery is at Bombay.

Also found in Chitral are galena (lead ore), orpiment, sulphur
and copper. Sulphur tested only 37%. Low grade iron pyrites also
found. Low grade mica is also found in Chitral.

After the trip to the mines, they went to an arranged shoot of *markor*
(mountain deer that come to lower altitudes in the winter). Riding in the
mehtar's car to his summer bungalow, they spotted two of them across
the river. Enders killed one but did not have time to recover it, as they
were soon leaving for the journey home. AZ found it all very interesting,
and indeed exciting, "something very few have had the opportunity to
do." He remarked to his wife that he was "the first Navy man in Chitral,
and there had been only one other American there before us." Who the
other American was remains a mystery, although I think it may have
been Milton Bramlette, an American geology graduate student who was
on an expedition with Sir Aurel Stein in the fall of 1930.[37]

AZ took a photograph of Tirich Mir in the morning, probably the first
still photo ever taken by an American. This face was the route by which
it was first ascended seven years later. AZ wrote it was the "land of the
fairies," referring to the local legend that says it is the abode of magic.
Their final good-byes included exchanges of gifts, and the *mehtar* gave
them *chagas* (native coats) similar to those that they had received from
the *nawab* of Dir.

The trip back up to Drosh was straightforward, for they knew the
route already, and they also knew that the road was clear. They left at
5:30 p.m. on 20 November, and arrived in time for a late dinner. They
called on the governor of Drosh, who was another brother (always hoping
to be the heir apparent) of the *mehtar* of Chitral. At that time, the *mehtar*
had no legitimate sons, and some believed the governor of Drosh would
be heir to the throne. It was reported that the *mehtar* was soon to marry
a princess of Dir, the widow of his predecessor as *mehtar*—and indeed

he did marry her. The succession was complicated, as always, with many wives and consorts, and many candidates.[38]

The travelers spent the night at the Drosh Fort Mess, where they had stayed on the way into Chitral Village. The trip north, visiting the rulers of the three semi-independent principalities and crossing the Lowari Pass, was the unique accomplishment of the journey. They had only to make it over the Lowari Pass going south, and they were home free. That would require careful work, but they had passed the most perilous part of their journey.

On 21 November they had breakfast and lunch at Drosh Fort Mess. The Thornburgs had come with them from Chitral, and they enjoyed a game of polo and had drinks with them before they left at 2:00 p.m. They arrived at Ashret at 2:45 p.m., and then the hard work began. They inched their way for 5.3 miles to Ziarat at 4:45 p.m. The movies show a harrowing trip in the jeep, but the time alone tells the tale: 2.2 miles per hour. They could have done it faster by walking. They left the jeep at the Scout Post, and spent the night at Ziarat. They were poised to go to the summit the next morning.

On Monday 22 November the travelers waited until late in the morning so the sun could warm the pass. Leaving at 11:00 a.m., they still had a hard time of it, with forty-five minutes on one difficult zig-zag turn, and a slow trip for the rest. It took two hours to cover the 3.5 miles to the summit, which they reached at 1:00 p.m. From there, they picked up speed, and made better time: 3.9 miles to Gujar in twenty-five minutes, and 10 miles from Gujar to Dir in one hour and forty minutes. It is still pretty slow. The total elapsed time from Ahsret to Dir, a distance of 19.2 miles, was seven hours, of which six were spent on the actual trip. They were glad to spend the night at the Dir Rest House.

The 160 miles from Dir down to Peshawar were on good gravel roads, and the trip went smoothly. They had a late lunch at Malakand with the political agent, Kenneth Packman, recounted their historic trip to him, and displayed the gifts that they had been given by the *mehtar* of Chitral and the *nawab* of Dir. They arrived in Peshawar in time to sign the guest book at Government House, and had dinner at their hotel. As AZ wrote to his wife, they were "pretty well tired out." It was Tuesday 23 November, the twelfth day since they left Karachi, and they were back to catch up

on what had happened since they had left. Most importantly, the viceroy
was there, meeting with the governor. They may have heard about the
Cairo Conference of Churchill, FDR, and Chiang Kai-shek that had begun
on the previous day.

Part 3: Peshawar Again, and on to the Khyber
Day 13 through Day 17 (24 November–28 November)

> The Viceroy had heard we'd been up the Lowari
> to Chitral in a jeep so came over to where we were
> standing and asked all about it.
> —Zimmermann, Peshawar, November 1943

The viceroy's schedule shows that he was planning to be in Peshawar on
23 or 24 November, which is why Bromhead was due to return to give
his report. There was flexibility on the departure to Chitral, but only so
much, for they needed to be back for a garden party on 27 November.
And there was flexibility on the departure after the garden party, when
they would go on to Quetta. But the garden party on 27 November was
a must.

They rested in the morning of 24 November, and had lunch at Dean's
Hotel. Dinner was at the Services Hotel with the Bromheads and the
deputy commissioner, Dr. Khan Sahib; his English wife, May; and their
daughter.[39] AZ reported that he was "a very light-skinned Mohammedan
as are his wife and daughter," apparently not realizing that the wife was
actually English. "A delicious dinner and Scotch for a change. I've been
pretty busy, and seeing many interesting things and meeting interesting people." Indeed he was. The next day, Thursday 25 November, they
were invited to dinner by Dr. Khan Sahib at his home. Most of the day,
however, he spent composing a fourteen-page handwritten letter about
the first part of the trip. The letter passed the censor on 2 December and
his wife received it on 9 December. She typed it and circulated it to her
friends.[40]

AZ believed that the next day Enders would be taking him up to the
Khyber Pass. For unknown reasons, the plans were changed, and he went
to the Khyber without Enders on Saturday. So on Friday 26 November he

was free. He walked around Peshawar, looking at the sights of this amazing ancient city, and taking movies. His camera was loaded with black and white film, and the scenes were untitled. But here, and elsewhere in the NWFP, and later in Karachi, he filmed soldiers on parade with children scampering about, weaving in and out of their lines. Whether he was intentionally or unconsciously reproducing the scenes of *Wee Willie Winkie,* the British children looked very much like Shirley Temple in Gene Markey's movie. The original story was in AZ's library of the works of Rudyard Kipling, and his children had seen the movie (probably with their parents) in 1937. It was not the first example of "life imitates art" on this trip, and vice versa—mimesis and anti-mimesis—and there would be more to come.[41]

He had dinner that evening at Dean's Hotel with five others: Colonel and Mrs. Carter, Mrs. Liepur, and the Bromheads. He had previously met Mrs. Liepur on 15 November, the night before he left Peshawar to begin the trip north. At that time, he referred to her as "one of few [Western] women who can talk Pushtu," There is no indication as to where Enders was during these days in Peshawar.

On Saturday 27 November Bromhead and AZ drove to the Khyber Pass, and proceeded on to the border with Afghanistan. As AZ described it, always measuring, they entered the Khyber tribal territory at Jamrud, nine miles from Peshawar. They encountered many blockhouses, tank traps, and winding roads. The outpost at Landi Kotal was at twenty-four miles, and Landi Khana was thirty-two miles from Peshawar. It was only a few yards from there to the border, and the famous sign that read, "FRONTIER OF INDIA. TRAVELLERS ARE NOT PERMITTED TO PASS THIS NOTICE BOARD UNLESS THEY HAVE COMPLIED WITH THE PASSPORT REGULATIONS." The railroad ran to Landi Khana, and disappeared into Afghanistan. The Afridis were on both sides of the pass, "a strong tribe, good fighters," and the Shinwari were along the pass and continued into Afghanistan. The Mullagaris, who AZ described as "bastard Mohmand," lived a short distance to the North.

The area had long been restless. Bromhead told the story of a Sikh general who was killed in battle two hundred years before. Hoping that it would show they meant business, the British "pickled his body and stuck it in one of the windows of the fort at Jamrud, where they periodically could show it to the enemy." AZ was told that in 1930 an Afridi *lushkar* [light cavalry] surrounded Peshawar, and since 1937 the Axis had caused unrest among Afridis. In 1938 parts of the Afridi tribe started a march on Jelalabad, the first major city on the Afghan side of the border, to loot it and embarrass the Afghan government. They were stopped by a blockade and effective bombing and made to pay a penalty in guns.

They got back in time to change for the garden party in the afternoon. Although it was not mentioned in Cunningham's memoirs, the visit to Peshawar appears in the viceroy's notes. AZ wrote,

> That afternoon the governor of the Northwest Provinces had a Garden Party to meet the Viceroy. Major Bromhead arranged for Enders & me to be invited. It was a grand affair in a beautiful setting on the Government House lawn. All the maliks (tribal leaders) from the surrounding country were there along with important Britishers of the community. The Viceroy had heard we'd been up the Lowari to Chitral in a jeep so came over to where we were standing and asked all about it. Enders did the talking as he has a flare for it and modesty isn't one of his virtues.

Once again, Enders is characterized negatively, as in the independent comments by Alghan Lucey (who called Enders "a bag of wind," in a letter to Donovan), and in Roderick Engert's comments (recalling that Enders was a "blowhard"). AZ did, however, at this time recommend Enders' books to his wife, suggesting especially that she read *Foreign Devil*.[42]

The day was not over until very late. "Dinner at the Services Hotel with the Bromheads, and then to the Peshawar Club for the Saturday Dinner Dance." There is a dance card for this evening at the Peshawar Club in AZ's scrapbook, but no dances were shown on the card. We do not know if he danced, or if he simply enjoyed the evening. He was, however, a sociable fellow and he was always popular with the ladies.

A trip to the Khyber and a garden party for the viceroy and a dance at the Peshawar Club, all on the same day, is almost more than one can expect. AZ's comments on the Khyber can convey only part of what he saw there. For those who have the flair for writing, let us look at comments by others—Lowell Thomas, Ernest Fox, April Swayne-Thomas, and Rudyard Kipling. They mention the forts at Jamrud, Shagai, Landi Kotal, and Landi Khana, and the fierce Afridis, but as an intelligence officer, AZ also adds that the railroad is there, too.

Comments on the Khyber Pass by Others

A gifted travel writer, Lowell Thomas described the pass in 1923 as well as anyone has ever done it:

> Few lands are more fascinating and not more wholly eastern, than remote Afghanistan, the mountain kingdom beyond Khyber Pass . . . the most famous and the most strongly fortified mountain gorge on earth, at the far end of which is the sign proclaiming that here travellers must turn back because "It is Absolutely Forbidden to Cross This Border into Afghan Territory." . . . Beyond the cliffs of Rohtas, we come to Shagai Ridge and then drop steeply down into the narrowest part of the Khyber. It was here, near the fort of Ali Masjid, that young Yakub Khan shot the sniper. The tale is nearly as old as the rugged bluffs of the pass.[43]

Ernest F. Fox saw it through the eyes of a soldier in 1937: "The fame of Khyber is not due to its physical prominence as a mountain pass. . . . But no other pass in Asia possesses such strategic importance now, or retains so many historic associations as this gateway to the plains of India."[44]

April Swayne-Thomas visited it soon after the war, but her view was similar to that of AZ: "Then with great luck *and* luxury we hired a car for a week and started to tour the Khyber. . . . The towers may belong to some tribe or they may be picketed by men of the Khyber Rifles, but they are grimly useful and no man or boy is ever seen anywhere, even in the main bazaar of Peshawar City, without a rifle on his shoulder and bristling cartridge belt at his waist. . . . They were all very vain, these ruffians, and *loved* being sketched!" [emphasis in original][45]

It is also a romantic area that stirs the hearts. Kipling's "Ballad of the King's Jest" is set near the Khyber:

> When spring-time flushes the desert grass,
> Our kafilas [caravans, Arabic] wind through the Khyber Pass.
> Lean are the camels but fat the frails,
> Light are the purses but heavy the bales,
> As the snowbound trade of the North comes down
> To the market-square of Peshawur town.[46]

Others fail to find words to describe it, leaving it for those whose have the gift. Curzon, as noted above, entered Afghanistan through the Khyber in 1887, and Rex Benson came through the Khyber in July 1914. Cornelius Engert came through to take up his position as minister early in 1942. None of them paused to comment.[47]

There was time to take some movies the next day, but AZ took no still photos. They had lunch at the Peshawar Club, and toured a gun factory in the afternoon. As AZ described it, "Shahbadin, on the road to Kohat, has a small rifle and revolver factory, making about 10 revolvers and 10 rifles per month at a cost of Rs. 160 for a rifle (Rs. 140 for a sporting model); Rs. 120 for a pistol. Guns are good considering the crude machinery that turns them out." On the way back to Peshawar, they had tea with a subhadar major named Tor Khan, a retired honorary captain; and his son, who was still in service. Both father and son had often been decorated for valor and bravery. He may have been one of the many brothers named Khan, of whom the most prominent was the man that they twice had dinner with—Dr. Khan Sahib, the deputy commissioner. AZ notes, "Water is found in good quantity at 10 to 20 foot levels below ground. Fruits, oranges, limes and tangerines may be grown here very successfully."

Part 4: The Southern Trip, to Waziristan and Baluchistan
Day 18 through Day 34 (29 November–15 December)

Most of the way we have been escorted by Kassadars.
—Zimmermann, North Waziristan, November 1943

The terrain that they would traverse is considerably different from that to the north, and they were rightly concerned about hostility from the tribes whose lands they would pass through. The land was high and irregular, and there was less vegetation than in the land north of Peshawar. The threat of war was ever present, but it was not clear who was fighting against whom, and why. They moved from their jeep to larger military vehicles and proceeded with armed guards all the way. AZ's casual mention of land mines, tank traps, bombs, artillery, and the occasional rifle shots or machine gun rounds mean this was a different type of trip.

They got an early start into North Waziristan, getting off at 7:30 a.m. for their first stop at Kohat, forty-one miles to the south, and on the other side of the Kohat Pass. The temperature shifts were dramatic—cold in the valleys and warm in the pass. They arrived at Kohat in time for a late breakfast at 9:30 with Sheikh Sahib (Khan Bahadur Sheikh Mahbub Ali Khan, OBE) and his brother, Mir Ali; they were, respectively, the district commissioner and the political agent. Both of them were stout, and both were members of the extended Khan family. The sheikh sahib was later addressed by AZ as Dear Friend.

They pushed on at 10:55 a.m. for Thal, sixty-three miles farther, and arrived there at 1:15 in time for lunch.

They were greeted at the Thal Station Mess by Brigadier Henry "Billy" Barstow, who insisted on providing an escort with armed carriers for the next ten miles.[48] AZ was not impressed with the training of the escorts, who got out of the car whenever they stopped. They arrived fifty-six miles later at Parachinar at 6:15 p.m. for tea and dinner, and spent the night at the Fort Mess. The total elapsed mileage was 160.3 for the day. Their hosts were Lieutenant Colonel Donald Francis, MBE, commandant, Kurram Militia; Major and Mrs. J. O. S. "Kenneth" Donald, political agent, Kurram; Major and Mrs. Boulter; and an unnamed Indian captain. AZ wrote, "Most of the way we have been escorted by Khassadars (local policemen). They line the road on either side (about 1/2 mile apart). Others ride in lorries ahead and behind us. . . . It makes one feel quite important having so much a fuss made of you but it's the only way to travel in this country with comparative safety. Some of the local boys just don't like strangers and might decide to take a crack at them or try a little highway robbery or kidnapping."

Baluchistan, from the Bolan Pass to Quetta, and then north through Waziristan

One of the few American tourists who preceded these travelers was Lowell Thomas, in the summer of 1923. He was arguably the first and probably the only other American to have made the trip before Enders and Zimmermann. He made the trip in the opposite direction. I know of no others except Thomas who traveled in this area before AZ and Enders, and the area was of little interest after World War II. The trip is now completely off limits to Americans. Thomas came through the Bolan Pass to Quetta, and he then headed north through some of the same places that Enders and AZ visited, ending in Peshawar. Lowell Thomas regarded the Bolan Pass as "one of the strongest strategical positions in the world," an eerily similar view to the expression that AZ voiced twenty years later regarding the Peiwar Kotal, not far north of the Bolan, that he observed was the "most potentially powerfully position in world."[49]

Lowell Thomas traveled through Quetta and the Khyber Pass about nine decades ago, just over two decades before AZ and Enders made their trip. Thomas knew the tribesmen were unpredictable and dangerous, and he was fortunate to get through his trip unscathed—and so were AZ and Enders. Thomas recalled Kipling's poetic warning to a mortally wounded soldier. Kipling said he should commit suicide, rather than risk captivity and torture: "Jest roll to your rifle and blow out your brains. An' go to your Gawd like a soldier."[50] Thomas continued,

> [W]e crossed the Sind desert by train and ascended the mountains by way of the Bolan Pass to Quetta, . . . one of the strongest strategical positions in the world. . . . From Quetta we passed through the Pink Mountains of Baluchistan . . . north to Waziristan. To reach this barren, inhospitable country after leaving the railway, you must cross the Indus River . . . near the city of Dera Ismail Khan. . . . From Tank we motor on . . . and get to our next camp before dark; men have been killed along almost every yard of this road to Jandola, and a breakdown at this hour would not be at all healthful. [We] hear, during the small hours, the occasional *plonk* of a sniper's bullet. . . . From Southern Waziristan, the land of the

intractable Mahsuds [a tribe of the NWFP], we motor north . . .
around Bannu, the Waziri metropolis, where the land is irrigated
by the Kurram River. . . . Seventy miles northeast of Bannu, we
ascend into the mountains to Kohat, one of the most notorious
cities of the Afghan frontier. . . . Not long after we passed through
the town, Afridi outlaws crept steadily into the bungalow of Major
A. J. Ellis, during that officer's absence, murdered his wife and
then carried off his beautiful eighteen-year-old daughter without
even arousing the guards who were but a few yards away.[51]

In the morning, AZ, Enders and Bromhead drove about fifteen miles
to the base of the Peiwar Kotal Pass, accompanied by fifteen rifles of the
Kurram Militia; the political agent, Kenneth Donald; Lieutenant Colonel
Francis; and—mentioned for the first time—Enders' sergeant, Tommy
Nicholson. They then hiked up to the pass on the border between Afghanistan and India. It was a rocky point, about ten thousand feet above sea
level, across which the "unfriendly" Afghans glared at the British and
Indians. They were not allowed to cross the border. AZ wrote, propheti-
cally, that this was the "most potentially powerfully position in world."
This is an eerily prescient observation, for this pass is about twenty miles
south of the Tora Bora caves, where Osama bin Laden hid successfully
while the United States tried to find and capture or kill him after 9/11. It
is a pass on one of the ancient invasion routes from Afghanistan into the
Indian subcontinent, just north of where the Kurram River crosses the
Durand Line on its way to enter the Indus River.

Photographs show the Anglo-American visitors and their escorts, the
mountains on the Afghan side, and the magnificent plain that stretch-
es down toward Parachinar on the south side of the border. They had
lunch on "One Gun Hill," which they were told was the scene of an engagement with General Roberts in the Second Afghan War in 1879, and
where a battle was fought in the Third Afghan War in 1919. From there,
they drove a few miles south to Karlachi, on the Afghan border, where
the Kurram River flows into India. They learned that Peiwar Kotal and
Karlachi are the two main routes from Afghanistan in this part of the
country. Tea, as always, was served in mid-afternoon; this time it was at

the Kurram Militia Post at Teri Mangal, at the foot of Peiwar. They then returned to Parachinar for dinner. The altitude of Parachinar was about 5,800 feet, and the tour was thirty-eight miles from start to finish. Dinner at the mess was hosted by Colonel Francis, the political agent; they were joined by Major Donald and two other officers.[52]

AZ wrote that the Kurram Valley tribesmen were Turis, who were Shias, and who had asked the British to protect them from the surrounding Sunnis. The Kurram Militia members were recruited almost entirely from Turis, and the militia had serious internal security problems. Additionally, he observed that the country around Thal was heavily filled with tank traps along roads and riverbeds. This was defense against a possible German threat during July 1942, but floods were now washing the tank traps from the riverbed.[53]

The next day they left Parachinar at 9:40 a.m., and arrived at Thal, fifty-four miles away, at 11:35. They picked up a Wazir tribal escort there, and proceeded on to Spinwam, where they were met by a Major Denning and then went on to Mir Ali. Lieutenant Colonel P. B. Jenson (or Janson) replaced Denning at Mir Ali and accompanied them to Miram Shah, which they reached at 2:55 p.m. in time for lunch. They were under constant attention by the scouts, this being very dangerous country. They planned to stay at Miram Shah for several days, where a huge airdrome was located. It is now the town that is by far the most dangerous in all of Pakistan, and it is unthinkable for Americans to visit.

The travelers learned that the Tochi Valley was occupied by Daurs, who were Sunnis and had asked for British protection. However, Daurs were considered a bad lot, having conspired with the faqir of Ipi, whose village was on the Tochi between Mir Ali and Kajourie, on the main road to Bannu. Ipi was now on the Afghan border west (and a little north) of Miram Shah. Two of his guns were reported moving on camels past Dosali. The posts at Sara Rogha and Ladha were also warned to be on the lookout for Ipi's guns, which were reported to be in the hands of twelve Mahsuds. The faqir appears here in more detail than when AZ mentioned him on 17 November, calling him a serious troublemaker. He also appears in several messages from the U.S. Embassy in Kabul. It appears that the trouble with Ipi was a major issue for the trip. He was said (or believed) to accept funding from the Axis powers, and also from the Congress Party, perhaps via the Communist Party of India. He also represented the age-old goal of this part of Afghanistan and the NWFP—to create a Pashtunistan.

They learned that Rs. 2,000 was ordinary blood money for any murder and, once accepted, settles the murder. A murder could be bought for Rs. 50–100, which is less than the cost of a rifle. A British rifle brought about Rs. 1,200, a round of ammunition Rs. 1/2/-, and a native round brought As. 6 to 8.[54] At Miram Shah they heard that Pashtun tribesmen kidnapped ten Hindu women and took them into Afghanistan, and that tribesmen had also kidnapped a Bannu Hindu shopkeeper, probably on information of his Hindu competitor. The kidnappers demanded ransom for the shopkeeper—Rs. 7,000, with negotiations under way—but none for the women, who AZ reports, "aren't considered worth ransoming."

On 2 December they stayed near Miram Shah, and passed through Razmak. This was one of the most remote areas in the realm. While in this area, they were guests of the political agent, Mr. R. H. D. Lowis, MBE. It appears that the area was often under fire, as it was when the travelers came through. Brigadier John Mervyn Hobbs, who they met, was used to being under fire.

The travelers left Miram Shah at 10:10 a.m. and reached Dosali at 11:20 a.m., having traveled a distance of 25.4 miles, escorted by Tochi Scouts. They left Dosali at 11:40 a.m., going to Iblanke Post. They saw Brigadier Hobbs on the way, who reported that he had just been shot up while out with his brigade (from Razmak) on a practice maneuver. Brigadier Hobb's brigade was made up of the 3rd Battalion of Ghurkas, a battalion of Dogras, and a battalion of Green Howards. All were camped outside the Dosali Scouts post and came under fire at 7:15 p.m. from near Iblanke Post. They received ten to fifteen rounds, apparently from a light machine gun, but no one was hurt. They did not reply, although flashes were seen about a half mile away, and a gun was trained on the spot in case of repeated shooting. AZ did not mention this in his letter to his wife, but the details are in his trip notes.

Dec. 2: Left Miram Shah at 10:10 a.m. reached Dosalli [sic] at 11:20 a.m.—25.4 miles. Left Dosalli at 11:40 a.m. going to Iblanke Post. Saw Brigadier Mervin Hobbs enroute. He had just been shot

up while out with his Brigade (from Razmak) on a practice maneuver. Arrived back at Dosalli at 1:00 p.m.—15 miles. Total miles for
day—40.4. Tochi Scouts escort went with us to Dosalli. Brigadier
Hobb's Brigade made up of 3rd Bn. Ghurkas, a Bn. of Dogras and
a Bn. of Green Howards. All camped outside Dosalli Scouts Post
and were shot at 7:15 p.m. from near Iblanke Post—10 to 15
round from a light machine gun—no reply although flashes were
seen and a gun trained on spot in case of repeated shooting. At
Dosalli was a 5.5 gun and truck which had fallen over, killing 2,
probably mortally wounding 1 and hurting 12—all natives. Had
big tikala at Dosalli with guests (besides ourselves) a Major Taylor
of the Dogras and a Captain from the Green Howards. At the
Tikala were Cumbar Kheyl, Adam Kheyl and Kukhi Kheyl Afrids'
Shiah Bangush (from near Kohat) and Khuttacks. These men
command solid platoons of their own tribesmen, but brigades of
mixed tribes are commanded by Subhadars without friction.[55]

They arrived back at Dosalli at 1:00 p.m.: fifteen miles. The total miles
for the day: just over forty miles (40.4). At Dosali, a 5.5-inch gun being
towed by a truck had fallen over, killing two and probably mortally wounding another, and hurting twelve. They had a *tikala* (ceremonial lunch) at
Dosali with guests including a Major Taylor of the Dogras, and a captain
from the Green Howards. Also at the *tikala* were three men named Kheyl,
the Afridis' Shiah Bangush (from near Kohat), and Khuttacks. AZ wrote,
"These men command solid platoons of their own tribesmen, but brigades of mixed tribes are commanded by Subhadars without friction."

Looking back on the tribes, AZ could see patterns of leadership and
success, and some areas of difficulties. All tribes above the Kabul River
were quiet and easy to handle, which he thought was because Dir, Swat,
and Chitral were ruled by autocrats. Their populations were under tribal
leaders of Mohmands and Afridis, with British supervision. Mohmands
and Afridis were democratic but were managed by *maliks* and khans, and
therefore also gave little trouble. However, in the south, the Wazirs and
Mahsuds took democracy to the point of anarchy; they would not listen
to *maliks* or khans unless it suited them, and it was also difficult for the

British to handle them. Tribes in Zhob area, on the other hand, were democratic but settled, and were willing to heed the *maliks*.

The following morning they left Dosali at 10:15 a.m. in time to travel to Miram Shah for lunch. They retraced the route that they had traveled before, arriving at 11:25 a.m., covering a total of 25.4 miles. The political agent, R. H. D. Lowis, reported that a truck had been held up near Datta Kheyl. Renegade tribesmen had captured a supervisor and wounded two men. The assistant political agent was dickering for the kidnapped man's release, for the going rate (Rs. 7,000). In another attempted hijacking of a truck, tribesmen killed three of the highwaymen, one of whom was an Afghan. In other action, the RAF dropped two 500-pound bombs on a gang of tribesmen who lived in caves near Miram Shah. Later reports said there were "no casualties, but good moral results."[56]

Sir Benjamin explained that the job of controlling the tribes was not appropriate for the Indian army (i.e., British and organized military personnel), but was best done by the scouts. The tribal behavior was based on economics, such as grazing grounds and timber. AZ wrote, "Rs. 1,000,000 worth of timber comes down the Tochi from both sides of the Durand Line just south and west of Miram Shah—mostly brought by Madda Kheyl. If this were stopped the tribe would be hard hit, it would mean war." The border had little importance here; the tribes were older than the Durand Line. He also suggested that for the scouts, in contrast to the traditional military position, a system of amnesties might be useful to entice back the deserters.

On 4 December they departed from Miram Shah at 9:30 a.m. and returned to Mir Ali, and then proceeded into South Waziristan, planning to go to Bannu and Tank. Their first stop was at Mir Ali for a "big tea" and breakfast, where they picked up Major Denning to escort them to Bannu. They arrived at Tank at 2:30 p.m., and the acting political agent "Pat" Duncan, escorted them to their final destination in Jandola by riding alongside them in the jeep. They arrived at Jandola at 3:35 p.m. Unusual for AZ, he did not make a note of the mileage. He had gradually developed a bad cold, and suffered from his ride in the open vehicles. However, the reason he did not note the mileage is probably because he was riding in the truck, and did not have access to the odometer. In Jandola, they dined with Lieutenant Colonel D. L. O. Woods, OBE, commandant of the South Waziristan Scouts.

AZ commented, "Bannu is a prosperous town compared to Tribal territories—land is rich. Passed groups of Gilzais migrating from Afghanistan for the winter. Generally speaking the whole Gilzai Tribe (including the Povindahs, or traders), and including the Suleiman Kheyl who refuse to send recruits to the Afghan Army, are friendly to the British. One small subdivision, known as the Dinar Kheyl (some 50 families), however, are sneak thieves and make trouble between Tanai and Gul Kutch."

On 5 December they left Jandola at 9:30 a.m. in Duncan's truck, in which AZ and Bromhead rode, escorted by another truck of Mahsuds. The jeep, driven by Enders and with Sergeant Nicholson on board, made a third vehicle in their little caravan. They had morning tea at Sora Rogha with Major Shahzada Khuswakht ul-Mulk, who AZ called "Kushwakht." This major was another brother—the tenth of sixteen—of the *mehtar* of Chitral. He had just returned to the South Waziristan Scouts from nearly five years at the front, having served in Malaya and Burma. They went on to Ladha for lunch, had tea at Tiarze, and arrived at their destination for the day at Wana at 7:20 p.m. It was a brigade headquarters of the Indian Army, and they were about ten miles from the Afghan border at this point.

As they passed by Ladha, a tower was hit by a 4.5-inch gun. AZ notes laconically that the "tower was shelled because its owner refused to turn over a murderer who had killed on post property. In this case the P.A. [political agent] determines what action should be taken."

AZ reported, "Khassadars are organized by section of country, in companies of 40 to 100, with hereditary subhadars, who are sometimes only boys (father to son). Companies can be moved around within tribal territory. Mahsuds have about 3,500 khassadars. They are responsible for safety on roads and can be suspended or demoted—latter is very serious because subhadar's entire family is thus demoted. They can also be fined."

He added with some irony, "Khassadar pay is Rs. 25, plus dearness allowances of Rs. 6/8 per month. Subhadars get Rs. 85 pr mo. Mahsuds steal from Wazirs and vice versa. Povindahs will fight if molested by either." He also said, "Tribal guarantees are mostly rifles (worth about Rs. 1,300 each). If fines are levied, tribal leaders are arrested and held until fines realized. Kaniguram is capital town of all three Mahsud tribes (Dre Mahsud) and has population of some 7,500. In it live Urmurs who speak no known language and are artisans (knives and guns) of Mahsuds; some now take to lorry driving." He added that Urmurs feed *jirga* members on visits to Kaniguram without charge as a "protection fee." And, "Roadworkers for M.E.S. [military engineer services] in tribal territory are locals, who have not been yet fired on for fear of blood feuds. . . . Census shows some 100,000 Mahsuds, but Duncan believes there are 150,000 with some 20,000 rifles. Janson estimates that Wazirs have more than the 30,000 rifles reputed to be held by them. Duncan reported a lorry shot up in Mahsud territory with an Afghan malik killed."[57]

AZ heard that Ipi was receiving funds from the Communist Party of India:

12 Mahsud guns, on Ipi's order were reported moving in this territory and P.A. [political agent] gave orders to fire on 10 minutes notice. Ipi was born a Daur (Tochi Valley) but has turned Turi. Stays North of Datta Kheyl, near Ghorowekht (NW of Miram Shah). His chief followers are Madda Kheyl, but only a subdivision of them. He collects money from Congressites, from the Tochi Valley and from Bannu. His followers now number less than 400 and he is hard put to feeding and supporting them. At one time he had several thousands. His followers are deserters (like Mehr Dil who was in Tirah when we went through) and he attracts men who want loot—particularly rifles. When he starts an action and is successful in an ambush or some such thing, his success often brings him support from locals who see an easy chance to loot.

They had a quiet day at brigade headquarters in Wana, and learned the story of Abdullah Jan, an Afghan brigadier, who came into Wana to get British support because the Afghan government had cut off his allowance. Nothing definite was learned about British action but Duncan said he was a troublemaker and was probably stalling for time in an effort to get his

Afghan allowances back again. Again, here was another Afghan who was making trouble south of the border.

On 7 December they were on the move again for a long day's drive, but they covered less than eighty miles. They left Wana at 9:30 a.m. and finally arrived at Fort Sandeman, just south of the border of Baluchistan, at 5:15 p.m. Only seventy-nine miles, but the map shows why. The road is full of switchbacks, and it is potentially hostile country, too. First stop at Tanai at 10:30, ten miles in an hour. They were reunited with their jeep there. They left Tanai at 10:55, crossing into Baluchistan at Gul Kutch at noon, another sixteen miles in another hour. They met Major Peter Garrett of the Zhob Militia, and had tea there. Left Gul Kutch at 12:45 and arrived Sambaza at 1:30 p.m. for lunch. They left Sambaza at 3:00, reaching the picket of Tora Gharu at 3:30, and left there at 4:30 p.m., reaching Sandeman at 5:15.

At Fort Sandeman, they stayed with the political agent for Zhob, Lieutenant Colonel C. S. Searle, MC, and his wife; and Lieutenant Colonel G. S. Keating, commandant, Zhob Militia. The senior officer present was Brigadier James Purves.[58] The travelers separated at this point: Enders stayed at the Zhob Militia mess, Bromhead stayed with Lieutenant Colonel Keating, and Sergeant Nicholson and AZ stayed with Major Garrett. They learned that in a variance from the rules of the NWFP the political agent in Zhob does not attend the *jirgas,* but hears their decisions. If the decisions require action by the Zhob Militia, the political agent, however, carries it out.

They spent the next day driving to see the sights and the problems near Fort Sandeman. They traveled in a car with the colonel of the Zhob Militia, in a convoy that included a military engineer services station wagon and two trucks of troops. Leaving at 10:00 a.m., they traveled along a new road to Shawet, which several tribes used to cross the border. At forty-five miles, they arrived at Fort Shahigu, altitude 6,695 feet. This was Suleiman Kheyl country, which this tribe controlled by chasing out the others that came across from Afghanistan. The Nasras and Gilazis, the travelers learned, had to run the gauntlet as they passed through it. Traveling on an old road across the plain for another seven miles, and on a new road for another fourteen miles, they reached the work camp of the Zhob Militia. AZ says they saw a crowd near there, which they immediately thought meant trouble, "but it turned out to be a cremation. A Hindu Army recruit had been killed and his friends had built a bonfire and were disposing of his remains. Hindus are cremated—Muslims buried as is—in shallow graves—Parsis dedicate their dead to the elements and animals—a delectable dish for the vultures." He adds, "I saw a Hindu funeral in Bombay. The body is carried on a stretcher on the shoulders of mourners without the benefit of a coffin."

They continued beyond the Zhob Militia camp for another five miles for lunch, and they returned to Sandeman for dinner at 8:00 p.m., a journey totaling 156 miles. Water is "sometimes scarce" there. That is somewhat of an understatement: what does not trickle down from the mountains requires wells drilled to a depth of eighty feet.

The next day, 9 December, was spent in Sandeman, and they prepared to go on to Quetta on 10 December. AZ had time to continue his second letter to his wife, and he reflected on the trip to date. "Tomorrow we leave for Quetta, then after a couple of days I take the train for Karachi. I'll be glad to get back . . . While it's been very interesting it's been rather hectic, none of these places have modern plumbing—I'm tired of bathing in a wash tub and washing in a basin." He said it was quite cold because of the altitude (between four thousand and ten thousand feet). "It's not so bad here—it's only 4500. My place in Enders' car is in the back seat. It's an Army car, open of course, and the breezes & dust make life far from comfortable, especially in back. I finally picked up a cold, one of the good ones. Today we rest. I hope it will do some good. . . . Most of this country is pretty God-forsaken. You marvel that anyone can scratch a living out of it. That's partly the trouble—some can't—so they take to plunder & pillaging."

On Friday 10 December they drove on to Quetta, leaving at 9:10 a.m. and arriving at the residency at 5:05 p.m. Again AZ does not make a note of the mileage, presumably because he was not riding beside the driver, and was also suffering with his bad cold. They passed by Hindubagh, where they saw and photographed a large encampment of Kariotis. They were part of the tribe of Gilzais, who have a special trade of "Karex" digging. Hindubagh was the center of chrome mines, run by a "Pop Wynn," that produced 40,000 tons annually for the United States.[59] The ore was 52 percent chromium. They heard that Wynn employs some six thousand camels and donkeys to carry ore down from the mountains. He uses a one meter (about 3.3 feet)–gauge spur track, and has some lend-lease trucks to transport his ore.

They also passed shepherds with the famous fat-tailed sheep, which, as a wool broker, AZ was especially interested in. "Their wool makes the finest carpets, and by the way, the tails are a great delicacy."

April Swayne-Thomas spent a long time in Quetta when her husband was stationed there in 1940, and she returned several times thereafter. She recorded two later visits, and she sketched several scenes in Quetta. She met Bromhead on one of these visits to Quetta, and the commissioner, Colonel Hay. She probably met both of them in Quetta before December 1941, for she mentions casually, at that time, the Japanese had captured the Quetta market for teapots. AZ met Hay in December 1943.[60] Swayne-Thomas wrote,

> A few weeks afterwards I went to Sibi which is in Baluchistan before one reaches Quetta and reputed to be the hottest place. Here they were having a Political week, a Durbar with the new A. G. G. Col. Hay. . . . Sir Benji Bromhead the Prop. Minister for Baluchistan took me about, as he is just as keen as I over the native costume. . . . Quetta is cold—beautifully *cold* (and my face cream is no longer oil). The skies are very blue and the great clouds a glistening white. . . . In spite of the cold the Hotel gardens are covered with roses and more roses, pansies, verbena, cornflower, columbine, laburnum and *more* roses. [emphasis in original][61]

Eleven December was a day of debriefing of the travelers and meetings at Baluchistan headquarters. The travelers met with Major General Robert Cotton "Robin" Money and Lieutenant Colonel John Bruce-Steer, and others who cannot be identified except by name, such as Father Wood, Major Platt, and Major Alston. They stayed at the residency with the chief commissioner of Baluchistan, who AZ refers to by the usual honorific as "governor," Lieutenant Colonel Rupert Hay.[62]

AZ wrote to his wife that the "'residency' consists of tin shacks and tents" although they were "very elaborate." Quetta had been the scene of "one of the earth's worst quakes in 1935. 30,000 people were killed out of 120,000" and they "also had a minor one in 1940. Practically the whole town was leveled." He adds, "They are building a new residence and in the meanwhile the governor & his family live in tin shacks and visitors live in tents. You'd be surprised how comfortable they've made them." In spite of the devastation, "We were royally entertained by His Excellency," and they had a grand dinner party for them that evening.

The movies and still photos amplify the events of the last day in Quetta, which appear briefly in AZ's letter and trip report. On Sunday 12 December AZ says "His Excellency" took them for a "chickor shoot"— hunting for the partridge of the NWFP. The group included Bromhead, Enders and his sergeant, and the Hay family with their little children. The political agent for Quetta, Major (later Lieutenant Colonel) Basil Woods-Ballard, MBE, CIE, and his wife and children also joined them. There were also beaters, bearers, and cooks. The Europeans were dressed for the picnic in shorts and long stockings, and Enders was in his usual fur-lined leather jacket with an aviator's hat.

They then went their separate ways: Enders and Sergeant Nicholson went by jeep over the mountains to Kandahar and Kabul, on the route that he had taken on a previous trip. Bromhead drove back to join his wife and their newborn baby in Peshawar, and AZ took the train to Karachi.

It is not clear whether AZ left on the late afternoon of 12 December, or early on 13 December. The photo at the station shows Enders and his sergeant. Since none of them mentioned that they spent an additional night in Quetta, and all were eager to return home, I presume that they left on 12 December.

AZ's trip report says only that he arrived in Karachi at 11:30 a.m. on 15 December, and resumed his duties on that date. He wrote that he was "Back 'home' again and am I glad, . . . 'be it ever so humble.' Karachi isn't a bad place at all after one has seen other parts of India. . . . I'd have enjoyed my stay more if it weren't for this damn cold which wasn't helped any by the dusty train ride home." He passed through the famed Bolan Pass without mentioning it—perhaps he was asleep by then—and much of Baluchistan, but he could hardly wait to get to Karachi.

The travelers learned that while they were on the road the conference in Cairo of FDR, Churchill, and Chiang Kai-shek had taken place (began on 22 November had concluded on 27 November). The Cairo Declaration of the United States, Britain, and China was broadcast on 1 December, reaffirming the requirement that Japan must surrender unconditionally. They also learned that a conference of FDR, Churchill, and Stalin had been held in Tehran from 28 November–1 December, but the results of this conference were yet unknown.

Four

Aftermath

The Outcome, 1944 and Beyond

Only two Americans have ever taken such a comprehensive trip of the Tribal Territory

—Zimmermann to his wife, 5 September 1944,
recalling his trip with Enders

When the travelers returned to their home bases, they found more than a month's work had piled up, needing their immediate attention. There was little time to talk about the trip, and they also did not know what they could say about it. They had not discovered anything on the trip that was unexpected, and although there had been some close calls, no one got hurt. The first trip over the Lowari Pass in a motor vehicle was a rare experience, but it did not seem like much to those who had never been there. And it must have seemed rather tame, compared to the war that was raging in Europe and the Pacific. The photos and movies had not been developed yet. And furthermore, Enders was fatigued by his trip, Zimmermann had a very bad cold, and Bromhead was concerned about his wife's premature delivery and their newborn baby, who had a cleft palate.

The needs of the service were also upon them, as Enders and Thayer unexpectedly received orders to move to new assignments before the end of the month—Enders was to go to Delhi and Thayer to London. Zimmermann was still sorting through his notes and composing his trip report, while taking his turn on duty every two or three days at the NLO in Karachi. But his letters and papers for the next fifteen months have survived, and they serve as a timeline for the immediate aftermath of the trip.

Before the end of the war, most of the Americans who were involved in the trip had moved to other places, while the British largely stayed in place until after the war was over and India had become independent. Thayer went to Europe and never returned to Southeast Asia, while Enders disappeared into a new intelligence job at CBI rear echelon headquarters. Smith was soon reassigned to work for a new command in Calcutta, and Zimmermann was left in charge in Karachi. AZ's record of the unending stream of official visitors and the seemingly unofficial but necessary social duties at the NLO over the next year are a window into the strange nature of the "war" that was being played in Karachi.

Winter of 1943–44: Return, Recovery, and Reassignments

On 19 December 1943 AZ wrote to his wife that as a result of recent personnel changes, he would soon be the senior officer present—except for the CO, "and there are rumors that he's to be changed." AZ learned that Curt Winsor, his desk officer in Washington, came through Karachi when he was on the trip to the NWFP, and expected to return on 7 January, on his way back to the United States.

On 22 December Enders wrote to AZ from Kabul, sending a length of Chitrali putthu fabric, which he said that Thayer would bring with him, on his way to London. Thayer's transfer came as a surprise. Enders was also surprised to find that he had orders to leave immediately for New Delhi, to stay for a week or two. Enders said that he and Sergeant Nicholson got out of Quetta and made the trip back without a hitch. They made the run from Kandahar to Kabul in one day, without encountering snow or rain, or "anything else disagreeable." He asked to be remembered to Commander Smith and "the boys"—indicating that he had previously met Smith. AZ spent Christmas Eve at the Harris's—"he mostly in government work"—not mentioning that Harris was the intelligence officer in Karachi who arranged for him to go on the trip. He sent his wife a *chaga* (robe of honor) given to him by the *nawab* of Dir, keeping the one from the *mehtar* of Chitral for a bath robe, and four distinctive Chitrali caps for their four children.

On 26 December Charles Thayer arrived; he was the brother of AZ's friend George Thayer, and a cousin of AZ's friend Jack Thayer, so they undoubtedly talked of their families. Thayer departed from Karachi on the 28th, on a "Number One Air Priority from Karachi to London." He rode in Ender's jeep to Peshawar—covering the distance in a "record" time of six hours. In Peshawar, Thayer, Yang (his cook), and his four dogs were "piled into a couple of compartments on the Karachi express and after two miserable dusty days, one of them being Christmas," they pulled into Karachi. He was met by Ed Macy, the American consul. When Thayer got to London, he received a letter telling him that the shotgun shells he had requested to be sent to the Afghan king had been located.[1]

Rex Benson also arrived in England during the "little Blitz" of January 1944, having spent some time in December with William Stephenson in New York City. After he returned home, the Army sent Benson a curt letter discharging him from the service. The Army allowed him to use the title of lieutenant colonel, but said he could not wear the uniform of this rank. His activities during the rest of the war, whether involving intelligence or not, were not recorded, except that he had his collection of old silver buried to protect it. In public, he resumed his duties as head of Benson Bank.[2]

On 24 December Engert notified the American Embassy in London by wire that Thayer had left Kabul that morning and expected to arrive in London via Karachi by air in about two weeks. He also notified the Department of State that the Afghan minister in Washington had telegraphed Kabul, saying that an American captain has been appointed military attaché. The legation in Washington added that the officer in question was a geologist and had been in Afghanistan before. The minister of foreign affairs wanted to know whether he was connected with an American oil company. Engert thought that, if so, he did not believe the appointment would be suitable, because the Afghans would be likely to regard him as a "concession hunter" rather than as a bona fide military attaché.[3]

Engert wrote to Enders in New Delhi on 29 December, saying the Afghan Foreign Office had sent him a note in which they alleged that Enders borrowed 1,050 afghanis (about $80.00 at that time) from an official on his journey to the North. They said they had previously sent reminders to Enders about this in August, on 10 November, and on 29 November. Engert said that he remembered seeing these notes, but he now understood that Enders had the entire file. With barely disguised hostility, Engert wrote to Enders, "I should appreciate it if you could return the file to us, together with an indication as to the reply you wish me to make."[4]

On 30 December Engert wrote a "confidential" letter to Lieutenant Colonel Edward O. Hunter in Delhi. He thanked Hunter for his letter of 16 December, and for another letter on the same subject of 15 December, regarding a mysterious plan that was proposed by Hunter, and that could not be put into writing. Hunter was an OSS officer, which complicated the situation, because Enders was in G-2. Engert said that he agreed that Hunter's suggestion (whatever it was) was worth trying, and to let General Ferris or "the British" try something else, through other channels. He hoped to be able to come to Delhi to confer with Hunter. Three days later, Enders wired Engert from New Delhi, saying that Captain Fox, the new military attaché, was the author of *Travels in Afghanistan,* and that he and Fox would soon return to Kabul.[5]

Two weeks after returning to Karachi, AZ was sent to Colombo on another courier mission. He left on an RAF plane on 1 January, departing at 6:30 a.m. (a hard time to depart, after his party on New Year's Eve), passing through Bombay, overnighting at Bangalore, spending twenty-four hours in Ceylon where he met with Lieutenant Commander George McManus, and returning to Karahi, all in four days.[6] He saw Winsor when their paths crossed for twenty minutes in Bombay. Not a word about what he actually did on this trip, but we can be certain that this was for debriefing after his trip to the NWFP. A few days later he had dinner with a man named Wilder. Looking ahead to the postwar era, AZ wrote that Wilder was with the Bombay Company, and "might some day be of some use in getting us a better wool connection in India."

Secretary of State Hull sent a wire to Engert on 7 January, saying that Captain Fox was well known to the Afghans, making it clear that the new military attaché had been properly vetted by the Army and the State Department. Fox had traveled to Afghanistan in 1937 when he was employed by an American company to search for oil and minerals, and had been recalled from service in Alaska specifically for this duty.[7]

As a special representative of FDR, Major General Patrick Hurley left Iran at the end of December 1943 for what was to be a quick trip to Afghanistan. In the event, he spent seven days there. He flew first to Karachi, and then on to New Delhi. On 28 December he wired Engert, proposing to land at the Kabul airport as soon as he could. Afghan officials asked him to delay his arrival until after 5 January. Hurley then flew from New Delhi to Peshawar, arriving on 3 January, where he was the guest of Sir George Cunningham. Hurley's plane, a military version of the twin-engine Lockheed Lodestar 18, flew to Kabul on 5 January to assess the airport; it flew back the next day with Hurley on board. Hurley's plane was unable to go beyond Jelalabad because of bad weather, and its generators burned out on the return flight to Peshawar. The general then requested a C-47 from New Delhi. In the meantime, he drove to Kabul on 8 January, traveling in a two-car convoy provided by the British. On 8 January 1944 Engert wired the State Department: "The Afghan authorities had also very courteously waived the rule that foreign military personnel in Afghanistan must wear civilian clothes."[8]

Hurley and the nine officers and enlisted personnel in his party spent the next six nights at the luxurious government guest house at Dar-ul-Aman. The Afghan government provided him with two Buick limousines and a Dodge station wagon. They traveled the streets and the marketplace of Kabul, the first foreigners to have permission to do this in uniform. Their movements, in uniform, apparently were intended to display the power of the Americans and the friendship of the Afghans, and it made the desired impression.

Hurley had dinner with the foreign minister, the deputy prime minister, the minister of education, the minister of war, and the court minister—a veritable "Who's Who" of Afghanistan. The prime minister was incapacitated by an attack of angina pectoris, but Hurley was visited at the guest house by the foreign minister and the deputy prime minister. He saw King Zahir Shah on the morning of 13 January, and they exchanged many gifts. He received a carved piece of lapis lazuli on which a gold plaque bore the date of his meeting with the king. An American crew flew Lord

Mountbatten's C-47 to Afghanistan for Hurley's use, arriving at Peshawar on 11 January, and at Kwajah Awash airport near Kabul the next day. Hurley and his party departed Kabul at 9:45 a.m. on 14 January to return via Peshawar to New Delhi.

No record was kept of Hurley's visit with Enders, so it is unknown how much time he and Enders spent together, but Enders probably was with Hurley for much of the time from 8 to 14 January, when he left. Enders had wired Engert from the American mission, New Delhi, on 7 January to say that he was returning the next day to Kabul: "Please inform General Hurley." It is likely that Enders arrived back in Kabul on 8 January, as he said he would, in time to type the report (or to have it typed), and that he presented the five-page report to Hurley in person on 13 January, the day Hurley met the king. The report is a summary entitled "Afghanistan in General" and does not mention any of Enders' extensive travels in Afghanistan, or his trips across the border into India.[9]

Lohbeck says Hurley reported that Afghanistan "was now on the verge of becoming an important factor in the war planning of the United States for two reasons": (1) the hope of discovering oil, and (2) the possibility of building a road through Afghanistan to China.[10] Buhite says Hurley did little while there except converse briefly with government officials, but "the mission was a success . . . better U.S.-Afghan relations resulted."[11]

Enders' account of Hurley's visit was far more upbeat than Buhite's or Lohbeck's. Enders pointed out that this was the first time a general had visited Kabul, in uniform, and as an official guest of the government. "A common remark heard by the M.A. [military attaché] was: 'It's easy to see why the General was chosen as a personal representative of the President.'"[12] Enders cited his military bearing, crisp speech, and confident opinions. Before Hurley arrived, the speculation was that FDR would send an American plane to take the prime minister to Egypt for a conference or to a good doctor, and that the United States was about to invade Afghanistan. After Hurley departed, the rumors were that he had come to map out a road, to be constructed by American engineers, or to develop the oil resources of Afghanistan, or to build a railway linking India and Russia, or to construct a road through Afghanistan to China, or to discuss "commercial aviation concessions from Afghanistan for the post-war period."[13] We will never know what Hurley actually discussed or promised, for he wrote nothing about this visit.[14]

Engert sent a secret wire to Colonel Hunter at rear echelon head-quarters on 15 January, saying that he had given further thought to his letter of 30 December (which was not preserved), and had talked it over with Enders. It is apparently on the same subject that he mentioned in his letters of October 1943. He says that both of them agreed that the suggestion needed to be "handled with the utmost caution and the few people connected with the Legation are involved, the better."[15] He adds that Enders' successor would *not* be used or even informed of the plan, so he could say ("if necessary") that no member of his staff had been involved with it. In other words, this was for the OSS; G-2 would be kept out of the loop, in violation of the usual protocol. He added that the question he had discussed with General Cawthorn was a different issue.[16]

On 13 January AZ wrote that Winsor had recently been with him for four days. Winsor had again lost the letters that he brought from AZ's family at home. AZ continued to receive a stream of visitors, some of whom were important, and others who thought they were. Smith departed Karachi on 18 January, leaving AZ in charge, and officially designated as executive officer. A "commodore and a general" visited them during the night of 31 January–1 February 1944; the general could have been almost anyone, but as far as I know, there was only one American who was called "commodore" in that region, at about that time, and he was Commodore-select Milton "Mary" Miles.[17] He would remember AZ, as we will later see, and he had already picked Lieutenant Commander Smith to work for him in Calcutta. AZ also mentioned that he ran into his friend "Buzz" Sloan at the American consulate.

Thayer began his new job in London at the European Advisory Commission in mid-January, where he worked with the ambassador, who he called, familiarly, "Gil Winant." In London, he met Brigadier Fitzroy Maclean, "who was then heading an Anglo-American Mission to Tito." Maclean invited him to join it. His move to the OSS was approved by Donovan, the ambassador, and Secretary of State Edward Stettinius. He was commissioned as a major and went to parachuting school. His focus was on his new job, and Gordon Enders' trip to the NWFP had become ancient history.[18]

Also in mid-January, AZ received a long handwritten letter from
"Benjie" Bromhead on the letterhead of Services Hotel, Peshawar. Bromhead's son had been born on 21 December. There were complications
that kept his wife in the hospital for three weeks. In addition, the boy had
a cleft palate and cleft lip that would require surgery in another country.
He said that he "saw HH the Mehtar of Chitral here the other day and
he told me that your H.Q. out here had promised him a jeep—he was
delighted, and is going to start improving the Lowari." Bromhead regret-
ted that he had no plans in sight to visit Karachi (and indeed, they never
met again), adding, "Nancy joins me in sending our best wishes and good
luck for 1944."[19] A week later another handwritten letter from "Benjy"
enclosed the mess bill from the South Waziristan Scouts. He sent greetings from several men, including "Doc" Hasset at Miranshah, "Father"
Wood from Quetta, and the district officer frontier constabulary at Hanger,
the "rather small place we passed through between Kohat and Thale."[20]

At the end of January Hull wired Engert that Captain Fox could be the
assistant military attaché and they wanted Enders to remain as military
attaché. Two days later Engert replied that Najibullah Khan had approved
Fox as military attaché, and the reason that they wanted an assistant was
because the Soviets had recently appointed one and this would "avoid the
impression that they had yielded solely to Soviet demands."[21] Fox, who
had been promoted to major, arrived in New Delhi on 7 February 1944. He
was met by Enders, who learned that he was to return with Fox and finish
up his affairs in Kabul. They left New Delhi on 11 February, expecting to
reach Peshawar on 13 and Kabul on 17 February. They actually arrived on
19 February, and they spent more than a month in the turnover.[22]

On 14 February Engert sent a "strictly confidential" wire to the
Department of State, reiterating his 22 June and 22 November 1943 comments about Afghanistan and the Soviet Union. He added that Afghan
officials doubted the sincerity of any pledges made by the Soviets at the
Moscow and Tehran Conferences. They believed the pledges were only "a
cynical attempt to disguise territorial ambitions," and the Soviets actually intended to become "the dominant voice in Europe and Asia."[23]

Engert was concerned throughout 1944 about Afghanistan's imports
and exports, and for what America should be doing in regard to Afghan-

istan's foreign trade. The issue was complicated by the desire of Britain to maintain control of shipping across its territory (mainly from Karachi to the Afghan border), and to be the primary source of goods needed by Afghanistan. The issue got into details about tonnage of wool and pistachio nuts and almonds, as well as strategic issues of petroleum and trucks. Engert argued on behalf of Afghanistan, saying the "importance of providing Afghanistan's minimum essential import requirement is inherent in its geographic position as a Middle Eastern country." He noted that cessation of imports "might rouse the turbulent Afghans to widespread disturbances" in the tribal areas "abutting on India," and could be a "focus of Moslem disaffection in the post-war period." By the end of the year, he was pleased to say that the governments of the United States, the United Kingdom, and India had met the needs of Afghanistan, and had prevented the outbreak of "tribal uprisings along the Northwest Frontier of India."[24]

AZ recovered his health in February and began to function as the acting CO of the NLO; he began to submit monthly reports to the ONI, via JICA/FE in New Delhi. He could not transmit copies to his family, and unfortunately only a few have been preserved. More "friends of Freeman" (meaning OSS officers in transit) passed through Karachi, and the *New Yorker* cartoonist, Saul Steinberg, stopped for a brief visit on his way to China. Though AZ did not say so, Steinberg was also working for the OSS.[25] He wrote, "Watch for his cartoons in *New Yorker* of 15 January." And for the first time, AZ also showed interest in writing about the trip: "I'm trying to write a story about the trip illustrated by the pictures I took, but it's taking a long time to do. I seem to have so little time for it and I labor so over writing." He would return to this subject several times, but it eventually faded from view.[26]

Winsor told AZ in February that his chief, Lieutenant Commander Sadler, had recommended AZ to become the CO at Karachi when Lieutenant Commander Smith was "recalled" (using the Navy term for being relieved of command under less than favorable conditions). Smith's personal vouchers had been "carefully checked," and Smith had been directed by telegram to (1) submit a certified inventory property account, (2) eliminate counterintelligence activities and discharge Sheikh and Madame Dubash, and (3) cut down the style of operation of the mess. It might take some time to get Smith his new orders, so Winsor said AZ should be prepared to be patient. Winsor also tantalized AZ with the notion that he might get a promotion when he became CO. However, in a second letter on the very same day, Winsor confirmed that his superiors said that Smith will leave, but unfortunately, AZ will probably not get a promotion as CO. He added that the ONI had decided that the way to handle the accounts at Karachi was to assume that "all of you junior officers probably boarded at the mess under oral or written orders."[27]

Lady Nancy Bromhead wrote to AZ in February from the Services Hotel, Peshawar, thanking him for the gift of a shawl. It was the last letter he received from her. She said that Ben had been away for more than three weeks and was expected back the next day. He had been to Delhi and was now in Dera Ismail Khan. All of their plans had been uncertain until they decided what to do for their newborn son and heir, John Desmond Bromhead, who had recently undergone plastic surgery in Buenos Aires.

In March 1944 AZ settled into a routine that he would follow for the rest of his time in Karachi. He and two other officers staffed the NLO, and there were three enlisted personnel, so if all three officers were well, each was on duty every third day. All three worked during the days on classified business, which AZ rarely, and only indirectly, mentioned in his letters to his wife. Most of his off-duty hours were spent with British officers and their wives, and he increasingly used British slang in his letters. He had some interactions with American officers and the American consulate, and with expatriate American business persons. The interactions with Americans increased over the next few months after he was designated as the CO at the NLO in Karachi.

After dinner with the revenue commissioner, AZ wrote to BSZ: "They had three other men from various parts of the Province. I can feel pretty much at home now in such a group having travelled about this country a bit." That led him to muse, "Do you think I should write up the trip thru the NWFP? I don't think the Navy wants it & I don't think it will be good enough to be published and I hate to put in the time. If you *really* think there's a hope I'll go ahead with it." This was the second time that he mentioned writing up the trip for a civilian publication. AZ had learned that evening that the viceroy would pay a visit to Karachi at a garden party on 13 March at the governor's house. He took color movies at the party and mentions those who were in the movies: "Mr. Macy (the consul) by himself—the Harris's (he in uniform)—the Coughlans (civilian), also General Hind—the Viceroy & the governor & wife of Sind." A photo taken at the garden party was enclosed with this letter. The photo shows the Viceroy shaking hands with Sardar Bahadur Mir Allahdad Khan Talpur. AZ could have reminded the viceroy of his trip to the NWFP when he met him in the receiving line, but if he had recalled previously meeting the viceroy in Peshawar, he surely would have mentioned it in his letter.[28]

By coincidence, on that same day Engert wrote to the Department of State, referring to his dispatch of 17 January 1944, in a strictly confidential wire expressing the Afghan minister's expression to the British minister that his government was anxious to secure a firmer control over its tribes in the Eastern and Southern Provinces, and "that in order to carry out such a policy Afghanistan would require certain assistance from Great Britain in the equipping and training of its regular army. He expressed the hope that the United States and Great Britain would be able to supply some military equipment to Afghanistan immediately."[29]

AZ learned early in March that his friend Joseph Freeman Lincoln, now in the OSS, would be coming out to India, but would not be coming through Karachi. He spoke of Peachy Durand, also in the OSS, daughter of "Bitz" Durand, who was a mutual friend of theirs and the Lincolns. He said he would meet her if she came to Karachi, or would have someone else meet her if she came to Bombay or Delhi. He would try to have his nephew Dick Kelley meet Peachy if she came through Delhi, and said that Dick had, by coincidence, recently bumped into Enders there—confirming that Enders was in Delhi in March 1944. He also congratulated his wife for the article that she had written that had been published in *Vogue*.[30]

More "friends of Freeman" continued to pass through Karachi; three groups came in March 1944. Back in good health again, AZ began to repay his debts by inviting the British to the NLO. Weekends were often spent at the Sandspit beach, and he went to the races with a mysterious fellow named Tommy Weston, "an RAF bloke," who owned several horses. AZ played golf occasionally, although the course was unusual—there were cow tracks in the fairways, and just dirt—not even sand—in the "greens." AZ also took several reels of movies while walking through Karachi. The descriptions are tantalizing, although none of the reels has been found. He concludes by mentioning that he took movies at the garden party in honor of the viceroy at the governor's house, he met Wavell for a second time.

> The next roll shows a building operation—how women work along with the men (women & children are street cleaners here—they have plenty to do)—the children of our servants who live in our compound & finishing with the garden party to meet the Viceroy. . . . That happened this afternoon and was quite an affair. I'm sorry I didn't have more film but it will give you some idea—I tried to take some of the people I've been talking about but can't very well identify them—Mr. Macy (the consul) by himself—the Harriss's (he in uniform)—the Coughlans (civilian) also General Hind—the Viceroy & the governor & wife of Sind.[31]

He was also taking care of a large group of visiting American officers in March. By then, Smith had left for Bombay, "quite unnecessarily," AZ wrote, although it appears that he was glad to be out from under him.[32]

By the end of March, Ernest Fox had been in Kabul for six weeks. By this time, there was plenty of time for his book, *Travels in Afghanistan,* published in May 1943, to make the rounds in Kabul. There could be no doubt that he was knowledgeable about the geography of Afghanistan, more than most of the people in Kabul, and for that matter, more than most people in all of Afghanistan. He was a fearless explorer, who wrote of the Afghans that their "honor is their bond; their hospitality is full and generous."[33] But most of the book told, undiplomatically, of nine months of travail among the people of the country, worrying that they had lied to him, misdirected him, cheated him again and again, and would desert him. In spite of his expertise, Fox was probably marginalized; he does not appear after 22 September 1944 in the correspondence from the American legation in Kabul.[34]

Spring of 1944: False Hopes for an Early End to the War

On 5 April AZ rode on a small warship, and he was thrilled to dine on board with the captain in his cabin. It was probably a PT boat, on the way to the invasion of France, Operation Overlord, the invasion that would take place on 6 June. At about this time, AZ received another letter from Bromhead to thank him for his letter and check. This was the last letter AZ received from Sir Benjamin, although he received a final telegram from Benjy on 22 September 1944.[35]

Winsor wrote to AZ in April and complimented the NLO in Karachi, saying, "A revised summary on Karachi is in the works and with the good reports you and Howard [Voorhees] sent in should be one of our best."[36] He said that once a month an officer in the India area would come back as a courier. AZ could look forward to this sometime in the next year, and it would be up to Markey to decide who would go. "The colonel has hinted that I might go out again in the fall on another junket." But by the time AZ's turn came up, Markey had been relieved and had returned to the United States. A handwritten letter from Winsor was carried out by Sid Sweet, a "close associate in the Far Eastern Division," saying that the recall of Smith had been delayed for unknown reasons.[37]

Peachy Durand and Anne Carter Greene were due in Bombay on 10 April, but he heard nothing from either of them. Peachy went on to the regional OSS headquarters at Kandy, and Greene, who was with the American Red Cross, went to Calcutta.[38] AZ vowed to his wife, "I will continue to write up my NWFP trip but I'm afraid it's going to take a long time for me to finish it. There just isn't the spare time and letter writing consumes most of what there is." As every writer knows, it is not just time that you need to do the writing—it is something else that is intangible, the itch, and he never finished the job.

In April, Elizabeth Enders wrote to Hurley, offering him some thirteen uncanceled Afghan postal stamps to show to FDR ("and he can keep them if he so desires"). She added that Enders had been sent to New Delhi as a military observer, but "he is already homesick for Kabul," and that he "enjoyed your visit to Kabul." Like Engert's wife, Sara, Elizabeth Enders was pushing her way up to FDR. Sara Engert, who became a friend of Eleanor Roosevelt, made the leap to the White House, but there is no answer from Hurley to Elizabeth Enders' letter in the file.[39]

Sometime in mid-April, AZ finally became CO of the NLO in Karachi. He had been acting in this capacity for about six weeks, but now it looked like Smith was gone for good, and he was in charge. Winsor wrote on 23 May to say, "Thank God you're rid of him at last. I hope now you get the responsibility and opportunities that you desire."[40] Winsor said that Commander "Off" at ONI would put in a strong letter for AZ's promotion, but he was, in the end, not promoted. In one of the few instances in which AZ's actual intelligence work in Karachi is mentioned, Winsor said, "We would like you as a long range project to send us material on 604, 100 to 600 of the Index Guide for your area. You may have to be careful about getting this dope for fear of misunderstandings, but it might prove useful if the area were some day to fall into enemy hands." But Smith was not quite gone yet; he would not be officially detached until May.[41]

A lecture on "The Constitutional Issue in India" was given to British Army officers in Delhi in May 1944. At some point thereafter, AZ received a copy of the lecture from his friend, John Harris, the British intelligence officer in Karachi. AZ forwarded this report to his chain of command on 5 July. The lecture was so sensitive that the lecturer (who was probably Harris himself) could not be identified in the transmittal message by AZ. The report remained classified until 18 November 2011, when it was declassified for me under the FOIA. AZ said nothing about it to his wife, but he was also busy preparing a secret forty-page bound report on "Port Facilities in Karachi," which he submitted to his superiors in JICA/CBI on 15 May. This report also went to G-2 in Washington.[42]

Engert wrote to the consul at Karachi, Clarence Macy, in May, noting that "cashmere from Afghanistan" was on a shipping priorities list of 29 March. He thought this was the first time that cashmere had been mentioned as an exportable product of Afghanistan. By this time, AZ and Macy were close friends, and Engert's report would be something that would have interested AZ, as a wool broker in civilian life.[43]

Reading AZ's letters, it was hard to believe there was a war going on. Milton Miles was hardly a friend, but it appeared that way to him, too. Miles called it *A Different Kind of War* in his memoir about the CBI theatre. AZ continued to go out to weekly dinners with a bridge game, which included British civilians and officers, and Greek traders with Ralli Brothers, and their wives. He was usually the only American in the group. Eric Layman was there; he was ADC to the fortress commander, General Hind. Another frequent partner was Lady Vere Birdwood (later Baroness Birdwood), whose husband was stationed in the NWFP.[44]

AZ and his executive officer, Lieutenant Howard Voorhees, went to the British Officers Club on 7 June 1944 for a farewell party for the naval officer in charge. It was on that day he learned that Operation Overlord had begun—the invasion of France. (Karachi was five hours earlier than Greenwich Mean Time, where D-Day was on 6 June.) He immediately wrote to his wife, before the world knew that it was the real invasion, "What do you think of the war news? I hope it means this damn war will be over soon. I've had enough and I know you have." Two weeks later he wrote, "Well here it is one whole year away from home. . . . There's only one way it can end but still German and her stupid satellite nations still go on." But he was wrong; Germany had many tricks yet to play, including the V-1 and V-2 rockets, the Battle of the Bulge, and the possibility of making an atom bomb before the United States did; and Japan would fight from island to island, retreating but not surrendering, for another fourteen months. Other visitors in the first week of June included Captain Gene Markey, USNR, who had been the senior ALUSLO in the CBI and liaison to SEAC. He was being promoted and reassigned, and was on his way home from Ceylon. Two weeks later the new liaison officer for Colombo came through on his way to replace him.

This was apparently the last time that AZ saw Gene Markey, but since he already knew that Markey had been famous before the war, he must surely have enjoyed reading about Markey's later exploits. Markey is largely forgotten now, but his life after the war continued to be fabulous. In October 1944 Markey resumed his friendship with Myrna Loy at the restaurant "21" in New York, and they became constant companions. In 1945 Loy was offered the female lead role in *The Best Years of Our Lives,* which became the most successful movie of the decade. In 1946 Markey married Loy at the San Pedro Naval Base, with Fleet Admiral William Halsey as his best man. Markey by then was wearing the broad gold stripe of a commodore. The marriage lasted four and a half years, and fell apart as Markey continued his philandering ways: "nothing less for Gene than a duchess or a countess."[45]

After Markey was promoted to rear admiral he insisted on being called "Admiral Markey," even by his grandchildren. He was a special assistant to Secretary of the Navy James Forrestal, and retired from the

Navy in 1956. He was the model for "Egan Powell," played by Burgess Meredith in the movie about war in the Pacific, *In Harm's Way* (1965), starring John Wayne. Markey was the godfather for a child of his friend and neighbor, Douglas Fairbanks, Jr., the movie actor who was awarded the Silver Star as a naval officer in the war. Lord Mountbatten was one of the child's honorary godfathers.

In 1952 Markey married his fourth wife, Lucille Voorhees Parker Wright, the very wealthy widow of the man who had owned the Calumet Farm racing stable.[46] Under the management of Gene and Lucille Wright Markey, Calumet Farm dominated the scene in Bluegrass Country. Their horses entered the Kentucky Derby eight times between 1951 and Lucille's death in 1982, and won it four times. It seems very likely that the Zimmermanns would have recognized Markey's name when they read about this, although they never mentioned him to their children. Markey died of colon cancer in 1980. Lucille created the Markey Trust for medical research, endowing it with her entire estate. The Markey Center for research on cancer and cancer-related diseases at the University of Virginia was a major beneficiary of the trust, and it continues to this day.

Summer of 1944: Trips to Kandy and Baluchistan

The monsoons arrived in June, the first rains since January. At Sandspit AZ watched but did not swim in the rough, warm seas, where, he said, "Only fools go in over their depth." Parties brought the diplomatic community together to spy and be spied upon. On 3 July the American vice consuls gave a party at which the Afghanis, Iranians, Iraqis, and others were present, and on 4 July the two U.S Army generals and the Macys gave a party for "everybody important in town including the governor aur billi (Hindustani)." At another affair, "A Mr. Tennyson was there, great-grandson of the poet," and AZ was an official guest at the Royal Navy base, Badahur, in Karachi.[47]

AZ forwarded an intelligence report to his chain of command (JICA/CBI and DNI) on 5 July, marked confidential. The report had come to him from John Harris, the British central intelligence officer in Karachi. It was a nine-page typewritten "transcript of a lecture delivered to British Army officers at Delhi" on about 1 May entitled, "The Constitutional Issue in

India." The lecturer "could not be identified," but it was probably Harris, who chose to remain anonymous. AZ said that it gave the "background of the Indian political situation and defends the British for the actions they have taken" prior to Gandhi's release from prison, and that it "probably presents the best British opinion on the Indian political situation as it stands today." Copies of the document went to Army G-2, OSS, the State Department, and to his desk officer at ONI. All of the other reports and files that were preserved from the NLO in Karachi in the National Archives had been declassified previously—probably in the 1980s—except this one. I requested it through the FOIA, and it was released to me, with only the original classification (confidential) redacted. The typewriter, spelling, and punctuation suggest that it had been typed in a British office. The lecturer said that, in his opinion, Indians "do not realize that there has been a very big change in public opinion about India"; that "freedom has already been granted and the people of England wish them to enjoy it, if they could only combine for a constructive purpose." The problem is that many Indians, especially the sectarian leaders, wish to take "a short cut to the sort of power they want for themselves." The sense of frustration voiced by the lecturer with the leaders of India, especially Gandhi, was echoed by AZ in a letter to his daughter at about this time.[48]

On 12 July AZ planned to leave at 6:30 a.m. on an overnight flight on a flying boat to Colombo for a meeting of area ALUSLOs, to return via Agra and Delhi. Delays due to weather and engine trouble pushed the departure back to the evening of 14 July. He thus missed a party in Karachi that was being held for John Godfrey, admiral commanding, Royal Indian Navy, and formerly the British DNI. While in Ceylon, AZ planned to visit Kandy, which was "of course quite important right now."

He shared a room in Colombo at the Officers Club with a friend from Philadelphia, Lieutenant Commander Hampy Barnes, who had seen "a lot of action in the Pacific."[49] He was joined by Lieutenant Commanders Curren and Dawson, ALUSLOs from Bombay and Calcutta. There were about fifteen officers in the mess, one of them "a survivor who had some hair-raising stories of Jap atrocities that you probably will hear about later. Machine-gunning life boats would be considered humane compared to the further things they did." Of Ceylon, AZ said, "You go through beautiful groves of cocoanut trees skirting the picturesque coast line, rock bound with waves breaking high. The people are very interesting, a lot cleaner and more intelligent looking than Indians." On 17 July, he drove to Kandy, where he had "a good look at headquarters, personally conducted by Commander Linaweaver, our senior naval officer there. . . . We had lunch with Linaweaver and then stopped at OSS headquarters and saw *Peachy* [emphasis in original].[50] I hadn't known she was in that part of the world till the night before when Hampy happened to mention 12 beautiful American girls were in Kandy connected with OSS and sure enough one was Peachy. She looks very well and healthy although she's had a touch of dengue." His air trip back to Karachi, from 8:00 a.m. to 9:30 p.m., went through Delhi, with a stop for lunch at Bangalore and three hours for dinner at Agra. "I saw the Taj Mahal from the air but no closer."[51]

This letter is the only time he mentioned the acronym "OSS" in his correspondence to his wife. He also mentions, by allusion, the failed assassination attempt on Hitler that had occurred only two days earlier, and the NWFP, where "some people" were stationed, probably in the Navy. This is the only time that any other Navy activity in the NWFP appears in his letters. There is not a word about what he did, officially, in Delhi and New Delhi. This was probably the time that he saw Auchinleck (whose photo is in his loose snapshot file), although he does not mention it. He also heard about Enders while he was in Delhi. He wrote,

> Gordon Enders has evidently written an article on Afghanistan for the Sat Evening Post. I haven't seen it yet. I imagine it is one of the May issues or perhaps early June. When I see it I'll give you the exact issue. Perhaps he'll write one about our trip thru the NWFP—maybe use my pictures. I kind of suspected he would, that is why I've never been too enthusiastic about doing it myself. I thought by the time I got around to it he would have an article already published. Besides that's what he normally lives on anyway. He is now back in the states, having contracted a bad dose of malaria.[52]

In this letter AZ also mentions three VIPs who "landed on us today but are leaving very early in the morning—two are Captains and one a

Commander. A marine corps Colonel who was naval attaché at Chungking for about two years left today." By this time, AZ had become increasingly an anglophile: He told his daughter that "I'm afraid I'm inclined to agree with the person who thinks India should not have her freedom now. I think there would be chaos. The average Indian thinks only of himself, is dishonest and ruthless." On the last day of July, AZ's nephew Dick Kelley dropped in on his way home. "I'll try to send some pictures with him—of the NWFP and of my last trip." Kelley developed a fever of 102 while he was at the NLO, and was hospitalized for eight days, with malaria complicated by "ptomaine poisoning."[53]

Also in July, trouble continued on the Afghan-Indian border. Engert reported that the rebel leader Abdurrahman, known as "Pak," was next in importance to the faqir of Ipi. And Winsor wrote to AZ, introducing Lieutenant (jg) Marshall Green, who was in Op-16-FE with Winsor, suggesting that AZ could discuss anything in confidence with him. He said that Captain Markey would not be returning to India, and his successor had not been named. He also encouraged AZ, as his own CO, to institute a request for promotion, which would be an odd and unlikely way to go about it.[54]

August passed, and with it, finally, the monsoon rains. In the meantime AZ's day job continued and he could say nothing about it, other than the "usual ships came through." He was alone because his executive officer was hospitalized with a skin infection, and the Coast Guard lieutenant "wasn't allowed to do some things." AZ, too, was in bed with a fever for three days, but he roused to play bridge with General Hind, the fortress commander, who he called "a genial old bird." Two days after the Allies invaded southern France, AZ was hopeful again: "What do you think of the news? I don't see how the Germans can go on. They must be dizzy trying to figure out where the next blow is going to fall." He continued to have visitors from Philadelphia, whose missions are unknown but apparently secret. He used nicknames and none can be identified except Hampy Barnes, who was a friend of Mac Aldrich.

I found an unsigned and unaddressed handwritten copy of a letter of 22 August as a loose document in the AZ-WP. It was copied in AZ's handwriting. By the context of the letter, I have no doubt that the original letter was written on 22 August 1944 by Commodore Milton Miles, USN, to the DNI, Rear Admiral Roscoe Schuirmann, USN. It was obtained by Curt Winsor and shown to AZ at the time he visited the NLO in Karachi on 25 February 1945. Winsor referred to this letter in his letter to Colonel W. L. Bales on 9 March 1945. He allowed AZ to make a copy of it. I note the letter at this point in chronological order, because it shows the relationship of Commodore Miles at this time to Winsor and Zimmermann. Winsor will be covering his tracks from this point on, and AZ was the odd man out. August 22 was, by coincidence, the same day that Thayer's brother-in-law, Charles Bohlen, approved Thayer's recommendation to deny a requested Afghan-American military exchange.[55]

In this letter, Miles wrote to Schuirmann, "I think you may have to fire somebody." He enclosed a photocopy of a personal letter that Winsor wrote to AZ, showing what Miles calls Winsor's abuse of trust, and Winsor's favoritism toward Zimmermann and Voorhees, who he said were Winsor's "particular good friends and buddies." Miles says, "I don't know Winsor. I have met Z & V [Zimmermann & Voorhees]. My personal opinion of Z is that he is a very nice fellow personally but he does not have much on the ball either from an administrative or naval standpoint. However I don't know much about him and withhold judgement on him because I might do him an injustice." Miles wrote very harsh words about Winsor, who "must have distorted the facts of the Karachi situation to suit his own ends," adding, "Smith has had an injustice done to him. That is why I have spread myself at considerable length in my forwarding endorsement to his unsatisfactory fitness report and in this note to you."[56]

On 2 September AZ was off on a strange intelligence mission, traveling on a camel into Baluchistan. He and a British intelligence officer traveled about fifty miles to investigate a "thing" that washed ashore. The message about it came by carrier pigeon. The "thing" turned out to be a life raft from a Liberty ship, which apparently had gotten loose in the monsoons. He wrote for permission from Bromhead and Winsor to write an article about the NWFP trip, and his wife planned to edit his story and send the pictures to *Life* magazine. He decided that it was necessary to say something about the reasons for making the trip to the NWFP:

As to why I was there: it was a very nice gesture on British Intelligence's part (with whom we have the finest cooperation) to invite

one of our officers to make the trip that had been already instigated by the Military Attaché to Kabul (Maj. Enders) to give him
an opportunity to see what was on the other side of the fence.
Then again I think the British are anxious to let her ally have a
look at some of her problems in India to counteract the crack
pots who came over here and after six weeks write a book about
the oppression of the Indian people and how they should unques-
tionably have their independence.[57]

Anyway I took the trip and took the pictures and there are
very few people and I might say only two Americans [AZ and
Gordon Bandy Enders] that have ever taken such a comprehensive trip of the Tribal Territory.

As far as peddling them to a magazine is concerned I'm sure
I should have Sir Benjamin's permission and also the Navy Dept.
I've written them both today—just in case. As far as story goes—I
started one some time ago—a bit more in detail than anything
I've written in letters to you—but with the changes that have
taken place here I gave it up more or less because I thought it a
forlorn hope. Anyway pictures and story would have to be cleared
before publication but, if what they have in hand, Life or Town &
Country want to go ahead, I'm game. Hampy Barnes, when I saw
him in Colombo and mentioned the subject, told me I was crazy
not to go ahead as he had had several things accepted by maga-
zines and they were hungry for material and paid well. He also
said the Navy Dept. approved of this sort of thing when routed
through the proper channels.[58]

The trip in Baluchistan was very interesting. I took lots of
pictures. I saw the negatives today and selected about 40 to be
enlarged. I'll weave a story around them in the spritely manner
of *Life* and send them to the Navy Dept (care of Curt Winsor). If
they approve, I'll ask them to send the story and pictures to you
so you can peddle them as you like.[59]

The story was never submitted to *Life* magazine, and the pictures
were never published.

AZ received a prompt reply from Winsor, who wrote, "I see no objection to your sending in your photos + an article to Life. I'll be glad to clear it with the Public Relations Office here. Col. Bales concurs." He also mentioned some changes in the ALUSLOs in the CBI theater and named Markey's replacement as a Captain Collins, who, in fact, never did arrive.[60]

Bromhead wired AZ, giving approval for submission of a story about the NWFP trip:

Indian Posts and Telegraphs Department
O PE—PESHAWAR—25 STE 31 LT ALBERT
ZIMMERMANN 254 INGLE ROAD KARACHI =
MANY THANKS YOUR LETTER THAT ALL RIGHT GO AHEAD
HOPE VISIT KARACHI SELF NEXT MONTH WRITING FROM
KASHMIR BEST WISHES = MAJOR BROMHEAD[61]

This was AZ's last communication with Bromhead, who was appointed political agent for North Waziristan in February 1945. He served in that position until the independence and partition of India in April 1947. Bromhead retired from the service as a lieutenant colonel. "Benjy" Bromhead died in 1981, and his wife, Lady Nancy, died in 2005. They were survived by their three children: Diana (b. 1940), Anne (b. 1942), and John Desmond Gonville Bromhead (b. 21 December 1943), who inherited the title of sixth baronet, but who has declined to use it. In 2003 he was living at the family estate, Thurlby Hall, Auborn, Lincolnshire.

FDR sent Patrick Hurley and Donald Nelson, head of the War Production Board, to China at about this time. Hurley carried a letter from FDR to Chiang stating his assignment: Hurley was "to coordinate the whole military picture under you [Chiang] as Military Commander-in-Chief—you being, of course, the Commander-in-Chief of the whole area." Hurley was "to help iron out any problems between you and General Stilwell who, of course, has problems of his own regarding the Burma campaign and is necessarily in close touch with Admiral Mountbatten."[62] Hurley traveled via the Pacific, Siberia, Moscow, and Tehran, arriving in Chungking on 30 August 1944.

For much of the month of September AZ was in bed with fever, which he thought was probably due to dengue. He was nonetheless able to get his reports in on time to the ONI. He may have not thought carefully about his request for a promotion, which he mailed on 5 September without an endorsement by a senior officer, but he got up to welcome an admiral and a commander who came to Karachi on 8–9 September, "the first admiral that ever visited." Others were ill, too: Macy was in the hospital with dysentery and tapeworm, and another friend had pneumonia. The transients continued to pass through: a "friend of Freeman and Clarence" named Fischer, who was doubtless in the OSS, and others who were unnamed.[63]

AZ wrote to his wife, "Benjie Bromhead replied to my letter by telegram saying everything was in order for me to use the NWFP pictures and story. How is the situation? Is anybody really interested or should it just be dropped. Curt Winsor also replied that he would get a release from the Navy Dept." And more trouble was reported on the border of the NWFP, as Engert reported that in addition to the faqir of Ipi and "Pak," another "brigand" was operating in the southern part of Afghanistan, a man named Mazrak Khan known as "Mazrak."[64]

Fall of 1944: Trying to Sell the Story and the Pictures

Sickness continued to be a problem at the NLO in Karachi. AZ's executive officer was back in the hospital with a fever of unknown origin, originally thought to be dengue but that was bacillary dysentery. One of the enlisted men had amoebic dysentery, and AZ himself had a troublesome fungal infection of his foot. He was depressed and his wife was angry because she thought he was not trying hard enough to come home.

AZ asked his wife if she had seen the "article on the Khyber Pass in the Sept 30th *New Yorker?* He makes it sound like a very fearsome place. I thought it quite tame, I was rather disappointed. It didn't hold a candle to the many other places we visited in the NWFP but it shows what a guy with imagination can do." AZ was becoming increasingly discouraged. After dinner at the Harrises—Harris was the British intelligence officer in Karachi—he wrote to his wife that "these special engagements are all very empty to me." Winsor saw BSZ briefly and talked with her on the phone, and then wrote to AZ, saying, "I wouldn't count on your return till mid winter, however." He added flippantly, "I'd write Bowen off, if I were you."[65]

After an "at home" at the consul from Iran, AZ brightened up a bit: "It was quite interesting and the first of this sort of thing I've done. It was in the late afternoon and they served tea and cakes. The governor and his wife were there as well as the rest of the burrah sahibs [important men] and memsahibs [important women] about town." And the Navy Day party on 27 October was a great success, in spite of his overall gloomy spirit: "We had H.E. the Governor of Sind and his wife Lady Dow, the two American generals Warden & Haddon, our Consul etc etc in fact about all the pucca [important] people in town, altogether about ninety."[66]

Early in November AZ was "pretty browned" when he learned that his request for home leave would not be granted. He would not be going home for Christmas and would not get a courier position, for reasons that were in a letter that was not saved. He may have crumpled it up in disgust. But on 5 November he sent home a slightly redacted version of the five single-spaced pages of his NWFP report, which passed the censor and was ready for his wife to edit for publication. Information about the period 24–26 November 1943 in Peshawar (including the governor's garden party and meeting the viceroy) is missing from this report, but it is in AZ's letters to BSZ. In this report AZ mentions a number of items that suggest additional reasons for the trip, and for his being invited to be on it. In the report he mentions "Bolshies" in the Chitral portion; attempts by the Axis to foment trouble with Hindus in India and to help the faqir of Ipi; Ipi as a major troublemaker along the Border; mines and tank traps that were laid in anticipation of German Nazi invasion in 1942; and unrest characterized by shelling and bombing by the RAF in the Waziristans. He also comments on the characteristics of the various tribes as he observed them, or on reports that he received about them. The five pages are well typed, with only a few typos and mistakes in spelling, and few signs of erasures. I therefore suppose that they were typed by one of the yeomen in Karachi, for I do not think AZ would have the skills to do this.

In mid-November, Clarence Gauss arrived in Karachi on his way home after serving as Ambassador to China. "Mr. Macy asked me to put him up.

The Ambassador had an interview with H.E. the Governor of Sind, and a party at General Warden's, the commanding general in Karachi and the head of S.O.S. [Services of Supply]." After many false starts, Macy and AZ finally put him and his party on General Stratemeyer's personal plane.[67]

Patrick Hurley had been in China since the end of August. He had initially refused the offer to become ambassador, but by 18 October, when the irascible Stilwell was replaced by Wedemeyer, it looked as if harmony might be achieved. Hurley accepted the position on 17 November after receiving a personal plea from FDR. It may have been impossible for anyone to negotiate the thicket of intrigue in politics in China at that time, with the Communists and Kuomintang fighting each other, the OSS and naval intelligence and G-2 spying on each other, and Britain ready to pounce on its former colonies when Japan surrendered. And as Hurley expected, it was a disaster for him, and he lasted only a year; he resigned on 26 November 1945.[68]

AZ learned that he could only be replaced by a lieutenant commander, and the ONI did not have anyone available. On 20 November Captain Harold Bowen, deputy DNI, sent a letter to AZ:

Dear Al:

I have your letter of 12 October and we have likewise received your request for change of duty. As soon as I have an officer at hand whom I can recommend to take over in that area, we will start him on his way. I hope that it can be arranged that you may be back in this country by Christmas but frankly I cannot hold out much hope along those lines. Captain Baltazzi feels that the officer at Karachi as at the other posts should be the rank of lieutenant commander and at the present moment we have no one at hand. . . .

As you probably know, a regular Navy captain has been appointed Senior Naval Officer, India-Burma-Ceylon and has reported in today in preparation for assuming his duties. He will have full authority over all naval groups in India. . . .

It was unfortunate that you did not get your courier trip in but I believe things will work out better in this way as we would have relieved you at the end of eighteen months anyway. There is nobody that feels you have been moping around or bemoaning your fate. . . . This courier trip business will be straightened when Captain Davis reaches there inasmuch as he will have authority to shift officers from Jica and between the posts in order to better the situation in any way he believes to be in the best interests of the naval service.

. . . my very best to Howard and warmest personal regards to yourself.

Sincerely,
[s] Bowen[69]

This is a warm and personal letter from Bowen, who was a highly dec-orated officer, and it shows serious concern for Zimmermann. However, AZ commented to his wife, "I'm pretty bitter about it. The last I heard there were 35 Lt Cdr's sitting around Wash. doing nothing." AZ was con-ditioned to think ill of Bowen because Winsor had previously said, "I'd write Bowen off, if I were you." It is hardly a surprise that AZ had learned to distrust Winsor, but on the other hand he did not know who he could trust. And Winsor was also having problems, some of which were self-induced, in the ONI.

One of the lieutenant commanders who were "doing nothing" in Washington was Henry Groman, who at about this time was picked to go to Karachi. Winsor wrote to AZ that he can "expect to be relieved on or about 1 March by Lt Cdr. Henry Groman." Winsor said that Groman's orders called for "25 days leave upon his return and then to go on duty at Port Director's School in N.Y. City. . . . Course lasts about 9 weeks." AZ got his hopes up too soon; Groman never arrived. AZ did not mention it in his letters home, but the audit and financial responsibilities at the NLO in Karachi continued to be a problem, in which AZ sparred at long dis-tance with Lieutenant Commander Smith. Each of them made his points in letters to the ONI, with copies sent to the senior ALUSLO in New Delhi. Smith had gone to work for Commodore Miles, who became his cover, while AZ, who was probably correct about Smith's devious deal-ings, depended on the uncertain support of Curt Winsor at the ONI.[70]

"Last night an Indian by the name of Thakirdas Gokalda gave a dinner for me at the 'Karachi Club Annexe'—the pukka Indian boat club. He's in the wool businesses and is represented by Stuart Lamsbury, who had given me a letter of introduction to him. There were about 4 or 5 other men—Europeans—who also are interested in wool." AZ returned to Karachi in 1950 to continue the wool trade that he developed during the war.

December was another month filled with hollow pleasures and disappointments. AZ received a call from Delhi offering him a courier position to go home, but it was promptly canceled. He then reset his goal to be home by March 1, a date that would also elude him. At Christmas time, "three naval officers on an anti-typhus mission dropped in who had just arrived from the States. One (a Commander Steel[e]) was with the Rockefeller Foundation before the war . . . a friend of Harry Schroeder's." Another was C. Rollins Hanlon, who later became famous as a cardiac surgeon. Schroeder and Steele were already well respected and both had successful careers in medical research after the war.[71]

AZ believed his plans to return home were being finalized, although he did not yet realize that he would not be relieved by his neighbor, Groman. Another OSS man came through Karachi:

Yesterday Cy Polley called up from the Airport and I invited him in for dinner. He's on his way to China. I got pretty well up to date on some of our mutual friends. He told me a rather amusing story—not so amusing to the one who told it to him though. Knowing he was headed this way Browning Clement told him to call a man he knew that had been here. He wasn't home but he talked to his wife. She had just been to a cocktail party where several people had heard of my coming home and expressed their pleasure (I have no idea who they might be). It didn't please her very much as her husband was coming out to relieve me. He tells me Bryce Blynn is in Italy and is just about to be made a full colonel.[72]

In contrast to Engert's contemporaneous reports of troubles caused by "Pak" and Ipi, Governor Cunningham, in Peshawar, later recalled that peace was maintained on the frontier in 1944. He made trips to Thal, walked to Tochi, and attended an Afridi *jirga* in April which demonstrated "their extreme friendliness."[73] The faqir of Ipi was still in North Waziristan, but Cunningham said he was unable to stir up trouble. A boundary dispute between the Mahsuds and Wazirs near Rasmak threatened, but it, too, subsided. In November Cunningham flew to the Middle East to visit troops of the Indian Army from the NWFP. The political world was not as comfortable, however, as pressure built for Indian independence and, increasingly, for partition into the countries of India and Pakistan.

Winter of 1944–45: The War Winds Down

On New Year's Day 1945, AZ wrote to his wife: "Still nothing new on when I set off. We are expecting Capt. Davis any day now. He is coming out to head all our offices in India & Ceylon. He probably will know when Groman is due to arrive." But Davis did not stay to talk, and a lieutenant with him brought the bad news that Groman would not get to Karachi before 1 March, at the earliest.

On 19 January Winsor tantalized AZ with additional possibilities, none of which would come to pass. AZ spent a couple of days in bed with a cold, and then went to a party for General Hind, who was about to be relieved as fortress commander. "He's a great guy and everybody is sorry to see him go." More farewell parties, as the war was winding down: "Everybody seems to be changing jobs. Saturday afternoon Eric Layman, Gen Hind's A.D.C. was married. Howard and I were the only Americans invited which was quite a compliment." He took Kodachrome movies of the event, which have not been found, though his still pictures are in the album.

"We've had a Capt [Frederick Shrom] Habecker staying with us the last few days awaiting a plane to Colombo to be on Mountbatten's staff. Peachie [sic] is gathering quite a name for herself."[74] Habecker wrote to AZ in January from HQ, SACSEA (Headquarters, Supreme Allied Command, South East Asia), grateful for all the help he had received in Karachi. Habecker had met Peachy Durand and gave AZ's message to her: "She is one of many attractive girls in this immediate theatre. Captain Paul Linaweaver will probably arrive Karachi via R.A.F. plane, either Tues (30th) or Wed. (31st). Huntingdon will confirm by wire."[75]

AZ sent home some drawings of himself and others that were made by a Coast Guard combat artist named Joseph Paul Di Gemma, who, apparently unknown to AZ, had been a well-known artist before the war. His sketch of AZ is shown in this book; several others are in AZ-WP, Scrapbook. At the end of January AZ's wife visited the National Geographic Society, where she left his photos of India and Ceylon. She received a response from Kip Ross of the Society, expressing "great interest" in them. She immediately responded with a letter saying that her husband would be able to tell more about them after the war, when the "reasons for the trip can be told." The following week, Ross returned AZ's four-page letter and 193 prints, saying that four articles about this area were now "under consideration," and, at best, AZ's article would be in line for publication. BSZ said that AZ would stop in to see Ross after he returned from India in March, and Ross said that the Society might buy some of the photos. The matter then rested until AZ returned and continued the discussion in October 1945.[76]

Captain Tom Thornton visited Karachi for several days again early in February, waiting for transportation back to Cairo.[77] AZ commented, "By the looks of things maybe I'll be home just in time to celebrate VE day. Germany looks about done though she's looked that way before." He began again (correctly) to suspect that his relief would not arrive, and that he would be informed of that at the last minute. His next-door neighbor in Pennsylvania, Clarence Lewis, who was a first lieutenant in the Marines and in the OSS, came through Karachi at about this time, and stayed with him. Winsor arrived on 25 February and in a very brief visit told him that he would soon be relieved. He said that AZ's relief was due in Cairo that very day. But in fact, he did not arrive; he had developed amoebic dysentery and had not even departed from the United States. "I had a hunch about this latest bomb shell . . . I can't help thinking there has been some skullduggery afoot." His new boss, Captain Davis, arrived again for a long visit on 26 February, and interrogated AZ at length about the NLO in Karachi and its past problems. After Davis left on 1 March, AZ wrote, "We had various people in to meet him—Gen. Warden (U.S. Army) and Colonel Shirley for lunch on Tuesday and a dinner party Wed. night. . . . It was a bit of an ordeal having someone pry into your affairs using a fine tooth comb."[78]

On 9 March Winsor wrote to AZ:

I enclose a copy of a letter I wrote to Col. Bales on the advice
of Capt. Davis. The Captain said he had talked to you at length
about the mess etc. but that he could only get you to answer
direct questions. While I can well understand your reticence, I
do think that the Captain is the person to whom one should tell
the whole story since it is his specific duty and he has orders
from CNO [chief of naval operations] to get to the bottom of
it. Perhaps you feel that you have told him everything but he
seemed to think you had not.

I'm very sorry on your account to hear that Groman isn't
coming. . . . I hope to drop in at Karachi about the 5th or 7th of
April for a day or so but will advise you later. . . . I had an interesting week in Calcutta and got down to Akyab. I didn't see Smith.
He's laid up in the Hospital with a bad case of Dengue and pneumonia.[79]

The letter of 9 March that Winsor wrote to Colonel W. L. Bales was
an attempt to rebut the charges of favoritism and unprofessional conduct
that were levied against him by Commodore Miles in his letter to Rear
Admiral Roscoe E. Schuirmann in August 1944. The letter addressed the
unfavorable fitness report that Lieutenant Commander F. Howard Smith
received for his service as CO and president of the mess in Karachi—a
matter that apparently came to the attention of the chief of naval operations, Fleet Admiral Ernest King. Winsor wrote to Bales from Delhi, where
he was on courier duty:

Dear Colonel:

I have been to Karachi, Delhi, Calcutta, and Akyab so far and
believe I've been able to help clarify the picture of what we do and
do not want in the way of reports. I've also been of some value,
I think, to Captain Davis who certainly has taken hold of all the
loose strings and is pulling them together into a coordinated, unified outfit. Both he and [Lieutenant] Castle are now well. I saw
quite a bit of Eddie O'Connor at Calcutta and hope he gets the

Karachi job, but pursuant to your instructions I have steered my course away from all matters of administration and personnel.[80]

There is one matter which I believe I should call to your attention pertaining to the Smith affair at Karachi. When I made my trip last year, Colonel Boone wrote for me a letter of authority in which he designated me as his "personal representative," in just those words, to take up all matters affecting FE with the several posts out there. Colonel Boone . . . and Captain Green (ALUSLO Eastern Fleet at the time), directed me to inquire into the mess situation at Karachi concerning which reports had been coming in from officers returning from duty in the theaters and couriers. You saw my report in which Lt. Comdr. Sadler "heartily concurred" and for which Captain Schrader praised me in writing.

The junior officers in Karachi were in a dither about the mess for which they expected to be checked on the pay and they weren't getting along with their C.O. . . . I wrote them a letter explaining . . . that Zimmermann would probably take over and that their pay would be checked unless they could show that they had been ordered by Comdr. Smith to live and eat at the mess. . . . *This letter was never received by either of these officers* [emphasis in original]. It was intercepted and opened by Comdr. Smith, photostated by him and given to Commodore Miles who wrote a letter about it to DNI saying that the Director might want to fire me, and that Smith was being persecuted whereas he should be promoted, etc. The Commodore added that the letter had been obtained legitimately. I don't see how this could be. I knew nothing about this until Captain Davis showed me the photostat of my own letter and told me about Commodore Miles who may now be in Washington, and for all I know, "gunning for" me.[81]

One thing, Colonel, I wish to make clear: Neither Zimmermann nor Voorhees are particular friends of mine. I knew neither of them before I entered the Service. . . .

Captain Davis, who approved of my writing this letter, sends warm regards . . . Looking forward to getting back and working under you again, I am,

Very sincerely,

[s] Curtin Winsor[82]

AZ told his wife, "After waiting ten days, after receipt of the news about Groman, I called Capt. Davis in Delhi to ask if there was anything new in my situation. I got promptly sat on for calling on such a 'trivial' matter." But the squeaky wheel gets the oil. Two days later, "Delhi called this morning to say my relief's orders were there. He is being sent over from Calcutta and should arrive here in about a week, which will allow me to leave April 1st. I'll be going home on top priority, reporting directly to Washington." On 31 March AZ wrote again about another delay: "My relief came last night and brought the news I was not to be the courier. . . . That means of course all my plans in the last letter go the way the previous ones have. It's all so damn discouraging."

On 3 March Roderick Engert wrote from Kandy, Ceylon, to his father, Cornelius Engert, a few lines in pencil beginning "Dear Pops," to show that he was well. Roderick was then in the OSS, translating Hindustani documents.[83]

Spring of 1945: Victory in Europe

Zimmermann's orders to depart Karachi were endorsed on 8–9 April by the new CO, Lieutenant Commander Edward F. O'Connor. AZ departed Karachi on Air Transport System on 10 April and arrived in Miami on 17 April 1945. After he returned to the United States he had thirty days of leave, which he spent at home. On 19 May he reported to headquarters, Third Naval District, New York City, for an eight-week course of instruction at Port Director School. While there, he developed recurrence of a peptic ulcer and was evaluated at St. Albans Naval Hospital from 23 July until September. A medical board recommended on 11 September that he be released from active duty, and he was sent home on terminal leave. Both AZ and his wife developed peptic ulcers and required treatment before the war was over.

Charles Thayer spent the rest of the war with Tito's forces, having some hair-raising escapades that he tells of with some humor. The chief of the American mission was Colonel Ellery Huntington, a former Yale football player who was brave but rather elderly; he was soon recalled and Thayer replaced him. One of his amusing experiences involved John R. "Tex" McCrary, who Thayer first met when McCrary flew in to Belgrade in a camera plane, not paying any attention to clearances: Tex was a "grimy unshaven Air Force colonel" looking tired and bleary eyed. He set up a movie unit to film the activities of the U.S. mission, complete with a sturgeon in a bathtub. McCrary had been at Yale, where he was in Skull and Bones; he later married the beautiful actress Jinx Falkenberg and died in 2003 at the age of ninety-two.[84]

Thayer felt the brunt of Tito's anger when Anglo-Americans occupied Trieste and stood firm. In May 1945, when Tito expelled the OSS and SOE missions, Thayer already had already left for Washington to be briefed on his next position—chief of OSS in occupied Austria. Thayer was in Washington for about three days and then caught the first plane he could for Austria. The Germans were surrendering piecemeal, in large units, all across Europe. VE Day was celebrated in Britain on 8 May and in the USSR on 9 May.[85]

Summer of 1945: Victory in the Pacific

The Potsdam Conference concluded on 2 August, and the war in the Pacific drew to an end in the same month. The United States dropped the first atomic bomb on Hiroshima on 6 August. On 8 August the USSR declared war on Japan, and on 9 August, the United States dropped the second atomic bomb on Nagasaki. Emperor Hirohito issued a radio broadcast on 15 August announcing "unconditional surrender" of Japan, and VJ Day was declared. On 2 September representatives of all parties signed the instrument of surrender on the deck of the USS *Missouri* in Tokyo Bay. Japanese forces surrendered over the following six weeks in various locations across Asia.

While AZ was resting and recovering from his ulcer at home, he continued to correspond with Kip Ross of the National Geographic Society. On 4 October he sent a selection of his NWFP and Baluchistan trip photos to Ross. On 14 December Ross offered $175 for the lot. AZ's active duty in the Navy concluded at midnight on 30 December 1945.

In July 1945 Lord Wavell called a conference between the Congress Party and the Muslim League at Simla; Cunningham regarded the conference as a failure. The war ended without a comment in Cunningham's memoirs. The transborder area was relatively quiet, and in February 1946 he resigned the governor's position and returned to his home in Scotland. He was succeeded by Sir Olaf Caroe, who had been for the past six years foreign secretary to the government of India. Caroe was not successful in this position, and left the NWFP on a "leave of absence," from which he did not return.

Wavell spent the rest of the war and served into the postwar era in India as viceroy. At the end of October 1945 he had Auchinleck in to tell him to prepare for trouble and a struggle with Congress, as Wavell and Auchinleck previously had in August 1942. Cunningham arrived to talk with Wavell, and Wavell discussed the problem of disarming the tribes on the frontier with Cunningham, Auchinleck, Caroe, and other members of the council. "The majority had held, quite rightly I think, that disarmament could only come by economic penetration and improved social conditions." Auchinleck and the other generals insisted on immediate disarmament as the key. Cunningham and Caroe supported the majority opinion: "So the old see-saw of frontier policy goes on, much as it has for the last 100 years, without getting any nearer to a permanent solution."[86]

Cunningham was invited to return to the NWFP to serve as its governor when India became independent and was partitioned. He was sworn into office in Peshawar on the day of independence, 15 August 1947, taking the oath under the constitution of Pakistan. He resumed his tours of familiar places: Miram Shaw, Nowshera, Bannu, Kohat, and Tank. There were riots, Muslims and Sikhs were displaced, and there was the imminent threat of war with India over the fate of Kashmir. After Gandhi was assassinated in January 1948, the situation became especially tense, but war was averted in the NWFP. Finally, suffering from high blood pressure, Cunningham resigned as governor in March 1948; his resignation was effective in April. He was rector of St. Andrews' University in Fife, Scotland, from 1946 to 1949. He declined other appointments, and died suddenly on 8 December 1963.[87]

In August 1945, having failed in his quest to become ambassador to India or to be offered any other suitable post in the foreign service, Engert retired and left Kabul. He then traveled to Moscow overland, visiting Nepal, Bokhara, and Samarkand. His health was still excellent, and he was looking for another job. From 1946 to 1947 Engert was assistant and acting diplomatic advisor to the United Nations Relief and Rehabilitation Administration (UNRRA). He was a representative of the International Bank for Reconstruction and Development (IBRD) for the Middle East, India, and Pakistan from 1948 to 1951. Engert then became a founder and member of the board of directors of the American Friends of the Middle East, Inc. In 1954 he was made honorary commander of the Order of the British Empire (CBE). Engert was also a fellow of the American Geographical Society and the Royal Geographical Society. He was an active member of the English Speaking Union, of which he was head of the Washington bureau from 1951 to 1958. (Rex Benson was honorary treasurer of the English Speaking Union when he was knighted in 1958.) Engert's wife, Sara, died in July 1972. Their son, Roderick, attended Yale after serving in the OSS, and had a career in government service. Cornelius Engert died at his son's home in Washington, DC, in May 1985.

1946: The War Is Over, but Peace Is Elusive

In January 1946 AZ replied to Ross at the National Geographic with explanations of the photos of Gadani, Saidu, Thal, Dos Ali, Kaniguran, Gulzai, and Quetta. AZ insisted that one of the photos was Gadani, in Baluchistan, and explained to Ross why this could not be the NWFP, which was an entirely different province. On 11 February he sent Ross twenty additional photos of Tatta on the Indus and Karachi. In January or early February AZ was promoted to lieutenant commander, and on 15 November he was asked if wanted to stay in the USNR. He was highly recommended by the Fourth Naval District intelligence officer, and he replied that he wished to remain in the USNR.[88]

After Hurley resigned as ambassador to China, his career in public service came to an end; he ran unsuccessfully for the Senate in 1946 and 1948. His postwar personality increasingly verged on "fear, suspicion, insecurity, and rage" and "his efforts in the Middle East were largely those of the gadfly." It was said that he was "superficially spectacular but actually rather average, neither an outstanding statesman nor a great man. He was not the first American to go far on modest talent, nor the last." Dean Acheson dismissed him "as a cowboy who struck it rich."[89]

Thayer continued as OSS chief in Austria until 1946, when he was named political commissioner on the U.S.-USSR Commission for Korea. He served for six months in Seoul negotiating for the unification of Korea, and was awarded the Legion of Merit. He was head of the Voice of America from 1947 to 1949. In 1949 he was appointed U.S. political liaison officer to the newly formed West German government at Bonn. In 1952 he transferred to Munich as consul general and land commissioner for Bavaria. In March 1953 attacks on his loyalty by Senator Joseph R. McCarthy inspired a State Department investigation into his diplomatic career, and he resigned from the Foreign Service. He then lived in Munich, where he wrote *The Unquiet Germans, Bears in the Caviar, Hands across the Caviar,* other books, and many articles. He was the brother of Avis Howard Thayer, wife of Ambassador Charles Eustis "Chip" Bohlen. He died during heart surgery in Salzburg, Austria, in 1969, and was interred at the cemetery of the Church of the Redeemer Cemetery in Bryn Mawr, Pennsylvania. His cousin John Thayer Jr., brother of the George Thayer who was mentioned in Zimmermann's letter from the NWFP in November 1943, is buried there; so, too, are Albert and Barbara Zimmermann.[90]

In November 1946 Wavell took what would be his final trip to the NWFP. In Peshawar he had an hour of interviews, and then a garden party, a meeting with the Khan Sahib, and a dinner party. It was sad for him to see that the Khan Sahib and Caroe were at odds, and very much on edge. The next day he drove to Landi Kotal for a dignified and impressive *jirga* of the Afridis, who said that for the usual bribe they would forgo taking back the Khyber Pass. After lunch, a less dignified *jirga* of the Ahmadzai Wazirs was followed by drinks and dinner in the Wana Brigade mess. On 17 November he traveled some of the same route that Enders, Bromhead, and Zimmermann had taken. It was still peaceful at that time. Wavell went by car to the Malakand Pass and Chakdarra, at the junction of the Dir and Swat Valleys. He lunched with the *nawab* of Dir, and on to Saidu, the capital of Swat, where he met with the *wali,* "a nice friendly old man." After a chickor shoot, he drove back to Peshawar, about a three-hour drive. "It is always pleasant to visit the N.W.F.P." But Wavell's son-in-law and aide-de-camp, Simon Astley, was killed in a road accident in Quetta in 1946, leaving his daughter Joan with an infant child, a reminder of how dangerous it could be on the border.[91]

Wavell was peremptorily dismissed by Prime Minister Clement Atlee on 31 January 1947 and given a month to depart. Churchill and the Conservatives did not believe that he tried hard enough to keep India in the empire, and that he was too cozy with Gandhi, Nehru, and Jinnah. Atlee agreed, and Wavell's career as a public official thus came to an end. He was granted an earldom at the end of his viceroyalty, took his seat in the House of Lords, and did various ceremonial duties for the next three years. He developed liver cancer and died in 1950 at age sixty-seven. He was survived by his wife and three daughters, who Enders met on his way to Kabul, and by his son, Archie John, second earl Wavell, who was fatally wounded in an attack by the Mau-Mau in Kenya in 1953.[92]

The pressure of civilian activities and the letdown after the war was over led AZ to reconsider his plan to stay in the USNR; in fact, he stayed only two years after he was promoted to lieutenant commander. He submitted his letter of resignation on 28 April 1947. It was promptly accepted, although it was not until 11 September before he finally turned in his ID card and was done with the Navy.

Others Who Learned of the Trip, after It Was Over

Zimmermann had a very fine relationship with British naval personnel in Karachi. They undoubtedly learned of his trip after he returned, and of many details about it. The British naval officer in charge and his staff, and their intelligence officers, provided intimate details about the Port of Karachi that AZ summarized for the ONI. He would have offered his observations about the NWFP in conversation with them. This is the way intelligence is shared: "You tell me something, and I will tell you something in return." His frequent bridge partner, Brigadier (later Major General) N. Godfray Hind, was the commander of British forces in Karachi, and he certainly would have heard of the trip. He would have enjoyed hearing what Zimmermann thought of the various British generals he met in his trip south of Peshawar, and in Quetta. How much Zimmermann told his British and American civilian friends about the trip is unknown, but he remarked at one point that they were impressed by the range of his travels throughout India.

Zimmermann also played host to many important visitors, including the U.S. ambassador to China (Gauss) and a U.S. senator (Richard Russell), and many unnamed others. None was entitled to know about the trip, if it was still a secret. But by the time they came through Karachi, Zimmermann knew that his day-by-day trip notes had passed the censor and had gone to his wife, and by the fall of 1944 he had been cleared by the ONI and the British (Bromhead) to send it to civilian publishers. The cat was then out of the bag, so to speak.

Who would have learned of the trip from Gordon Enders? He surely wrote to his wife, Elizabeth, about it. They had a lively correspondence, but whatever he wrote to her about the trip has been lost. After the death of his first wife, Enders married a widow named Elizabeth Gallagher, and his books, papers, and photographs have since disappeared. He would have talked about it to anyone else who would listen. He loved to talk, and as Zimmermann wrote, "Modesty isn't one of his virtues."[93]

Enders was ordered to transfer to New Delhi as a military observer in December 1943, shortly after he returned to Kabul. In New Delhi, his mentor was Lieutenant General Raymond Albert "Spec" Wheeler, with whom he had flown out to India in November 1941. Wheeler's office had moved to Ceylon in the fall of 1943, but his presence was still felt in New Delhi. When he arrived in India in 1941, Wheeler was a brigadier general, the senior U.S. Army officer in India. Promoted to lieutenant general in the fall of 1943, he was appointed to the staff of Admiral Lord Louis Mountbatten. He served as principal administrative officer of SEAC and, from February 1944, as deputy supreme commander. Enders would have told General Wheeler about the NWFP trip if he had had the chance to do so.

The Army general staff, which included Enders' department—G-2— was wary of the OSS. But the OSS officers in New Delhi would likely have heard of Enders' trip, if only because he would not have been able to keep quiet about it. We recall that Alghan Lucey, who probably knew Enders from their time together in Shanghai before the war, called Enders "a bag of wind" in a letter to William Donovan, head of the OSS. In addition, Enders' brother Robert was in the OSS, which would have made it a bit easier for him to communicate with that agency. And his former boss's son, Roderick Engert, would soon join the OSS in Delhi as translator. Roderick Engert would later recall Enders as a "blowhard."[94]

The story of the trip to the NWFP by Enders and Zimmermann in 1943 began to recede into distant memory after the war was over, and it was eventually all but forgotten. If either of them had published anything about the story, it might have become at least a footnote in history, but for various reasons they did not. Zimmermann tried for a while to get the *National Geographic* to accept his story, and he also had hopes for *Life* magazine. The *Geographic* was interested, and bought his pictures for possible use in the future. As noted above, the *National Geographic Magazine* had published four articles about India in 1946, but AZ's photos were not included. The NWFP then gradually receded from view, and the *Geographic* never asked for anything more from him. Enders was a fine writer, and could tell a good story, but he had no photos of his own, and Zimmermann had been the recorder of the trip. Zimmermann did not trust Enders, and Enders was a proud man. He remained in the Army after the war, and what he did was so secret that he did not want to call attention to his work. He only published one article after the war, and all of his papers have been lost.

Intelligence officers are wary of discussing their work. If they publish something about what they do, it is possible to have the work reviewed in advance, to avoid disclosing anything that should be kept in confidence. But in conversation they learn to turn the question, and to obscure the details. So Zimmermann did not discuss the trip (or anything about his wartime service) with his children, nor did Enders with the young people in his family. Enders mentioned once that he took an interesting trip with another American, but said no more about it.

Gordon Enders completed his career as an intelligence officer in the U.S. Army, with the rank of colonel. He served in China, and then in Korea, where he was assistant chief of staff for intelligence. He was probably serving there at the same time that Charles Thayer was there, although there is nothing in Thayer's books that mentions Enders. He was a lecturer on the same circuit that Eleanor Roosevelt was on, and he was an avid photographer, with some sixteen cameras. He published at least one article in the postwar period. Enders later worked at Fort Meade, Maryland, where the National Security Agency is located.[95]

Enders retired in 1962 and relocated to the Albuquerque, New Mexico, area, which he had first visited as tourist in the early 1930s. In retirement he continued his interest in photography, and was best known for his photographs of the Sandia bighorn sheep. His wife says that he was on the summit of Sandia Mountain on the day before he died, on 2 September 1978. He was survived by his brother Robert, who had been in the OSS; and his second wife, step-daughter, and several nieces and nephews. Enders was recalled by Robert's son and daughter as a kind man who loved to tell stories (as did Robert), but they never knew exactly what to make of them. Robert Enders wrote a biographical note for Wooster College, saying that Gordon had received the Legion of Merit and several foreign decorations. His last address of record was in Bernalillo, New Mexico. He was buried at the Santa Fe National Cemetery.

Albert Zimmermann returned to his family and to his partnership as a successful wool broker, with little outward indication that he had been affected by his four years in service. After a few months of desultory work on the story of the NWFP trip, he set it aside and finally gave up trying to publish it. His wife completed filing his letters and papers. She put his photos in an album, and the most interesting papers in a scrapbook, but these were soon forgotten. He played golf, traveled, and sang in the Orpheus Club, just as he had before the war. He made a trip to Karachi with his wife and daughter in 1950, renewing his friendships there, and doing a bit of business, too. His children were successful in school and college. One was a CIA officer in Jordan before she was married. Three received advanced degrees. One of them became a physician, and one became a biologist. His older son, Warren, became a Foreign Service officer, and was the last ambassador to serve in Yugoslavia before it disintegrated. By coincidence, one of Warren Zimmermann's daughters married the grandson of Maj. Edward "Fruity" Metcalfe and Lady Alexandra Curzon, who appear above as cameos in the history of the Great Game. And the epitaph on the tombstone of Percy Chubb, Warren's father-in-law, appears to be a nod to *Kim*. The epitaph, "He hath chosen the sea," is an answer to the rhetorical question, "Who hath desired the Sea" that Kipling asked in his poem, "The Sea and the Hills," which appears in *Kim*. Albert Zimmermann died unexpectedly at age fifty-nine of a cerebral hemorrhage on 24 July 1961, and was buried in the cemetery of the Church of the Redeemer in Bryn Mawr, Pennsylvania.

Outcome of the Trip

We can now look back on the trip and answer the following questions: What was the purpose of the trip? That is to say, what were the travelers looking for, and what did they hope to accomplish? What did they find, and what, in fact, did they achieve?

I will focus principally on the Americans—Enders and Zimmermann—because they had an ambitious agenda. The trip was Enders' idea, he "instigated it," wrote Zimmermann, and Zimmermann was sent along to keep an eye on him. The goals for the British were different. They wished to introduce the Americans to the people and the geography of the NWFP and northern Baluchistan, and to keep the Americans as safe as possible on their way.

The main purpose of the trip was to show the Americans the problems that the British had with the tribes of the NWFP and Baluchistan, and how they dealt with them. Why the British would want to show these problems and their responses to the Americans is another question. The issue was never addressed in the letter from IB Quetta, in the orders that Zimmermann received, in the letters he wrote home, or in his trip reports. I believe it was mainly to give "cover" for the trip—a statement of purpose that could be used as a legitimate excuse to introduce the American officers to the VIPs along the way, both the local rulers and the British and Indian officers. There was no perceived important national intelligence issue here, and the border between India and Afghanistan was not a significant U.S. national concern at that time. That this line, known as the Durand Line, might become an area of vital interest to the United States and the world was not mentioned as a future possibility by any of the travelers. The search for Osama bin Laden was not anticipated. Any serious student of the Great Game, however, could see that this area had been contested for at least two millennia and this contest (whether or not called the Great Game) was likely to continue. It would be the same game, but with new players.

Some expected that the United States would replace Britain in the Game, and that it would not be a surrogate for Britain—it would have its own goals. Engert believed this, and he wrote about it; his warnings and cajoling letters were looked at with some amusement, a form of diplomatic localitis. Thayer, on the other hand, warned that Afghanistan would attempt to draw the United States into its age-old conflict with Russia. And he thought the United States should resist this. Enders saw the United States as the successor to Britain in the Great Game with Russia, and he foresaw the present outcome of Tibet's struggle with China. He would, therefore, have predicted (correctly) that China, once it had expelled Japan, would turn its attention to the west; it would gobble up Tibet, and then focus on India.

What Else Did the American Travelers Find?

The Americans saw that the British dealt with the three hereditary rulers (the *wali*, the *nawab*, and the *mehtar*) with tributes—gifts, bribes, medals, and titles—and were allowed to keep their thrones as fiefdoms for their families. The *maliks* of the various tribes, each of which was somewhat different, were dealt with by tributes and gifts, and sometimes by a show of force. Honorifics were important in dealing with such men. Local customs were strictly observed at greetings, meals, and departures. It was important to appreciate the five pillars of Islam. Enders and Zimmermann saw respect for such customs as the use of the right hand for eating, and how women were excluded or sequestered from society. A formal education system for migratory tribal children was nonexistent ("they wouldn't know what a school is," wrote Zimmermann). Alcohol was officially prohibited, although the custom of abstinence was sometimes observed in the breach. The *mehtars* received rifles, and opportunities for employment of their young men in the *khadassars*.

Peace was kept by negotiations and decisions made at *jirgas* and *loya jirgas* of the village and tribal elders. Armed force was used only as a last resort. Force might be used to retaliate for an attack on the British (Indian) armed forces, or to pursue a bandit raid, a hijacking, or a kidnapping. Force was not employed against random shots fired from rifles, but a mortar attack would provoke a serious reaction, even bombing by the RAF. Everyone on the frontier carried a gun (British, Indians, tribesmen, and Americans, too). Random shots were expected, but if the shooting appeared to be purposeful, or if an officer was harmed, the British had to retaliate. If several native troops were injured, the British retaliated, too. *Badis* were allowed to be settled by the ancient code known as *pashtun-*

wali (the ethical code of the Pashtun), grim as it was. "Blood feuds" were mentioned in AZ's notes, but not the Pashtun word for this. Boundary disputes between families or tribes were settled by the British, and both parties usually accepted the settlements. Groups of outlaws, or bandits (often called brigands) were pursued with armed force, but nonviolent smuggling had to be tolerated, even when it was opium. The *maliks* appreciated this as one of the benefits of British rule.

It was not easy for the British to deal with the *mullahs.* They were teachers of Islam, and as such they had a special place in society. The *mullahs* often incited rebellion against the British, and they had the force of Allah and the Koran behind them. The *mullahs* could award the title of *ghazi* (warrior) to one who killed a *kafir* (infidel). If such a warrior died, he would have a special place in heaven. At the time of the trip by Enders and Zimmermann, an insurrection against British rule was being led by the faqir of Ipi, based in North Waziristan. The faqir was never found or defeated by the British, and his insurrection was believed to be supported by both the Axis and the Communists. The best that the British could do with the faqir of Ipi was a policy of containment, and it was not very successful.

The "Indian problem" was a preoccupation of the British and the Americans, which Enders and Zimmermann saw at first hand. It was a catch-all phrase that meant many things to many people. It referred to the desire of many Indians (Hindus, Muslims, and others) for independence from Britain, without specifying what would happen after independence was gained. Some, including most Hindus and some Muslims, favored a single country for the subcontinent. Some, who were mostly Muslims, wanted a separate state, and some of them wanted a division into two Muslim states. This division finally occurred: three states (Pakistan, India, and Bangladesh). But in 1943 no one knew that would be the outcome.

Pashtun irredentism was yet another problem that Enders and Zimmermann encountered, although little could be done about it by the British. This was referred to as the problem of "Pashtunistan," the desire of the Pashtuns to disregard the Durand Line and to be united. For some, Pashtunistan could then control all of western India (Pakistan) *and* Afghanistan. Some Pashtun leaders in the tribal areas and other Pashtuns in the NWFP hoped for such an outcome, and some still do.

Another issue was the possibility of encountering surrogates of the Axis. It was believed that the Nazis supported the faqir of Ipi in some way, and the Italians had been, until recently, even more effective in their undercover operations. The American legation in Kabul believed the Germans were inept and the Italians were now on the side of the Allies, so no trouble was expected from those countries, and none was encountered. The Axis sympathizers were of course always a possible concern, but a small one, especially in Turkey, the Balkans, and Iran. And the legation knew that the Japanese had many sympathizers in Afghanistan, but they were not known to have any operatives along the southern border. We saw previously that the U.S. Navy was concerned that the neutrality of Afghanistan might allow whatever was in a diplomatic pouch to travel between Berlin and Tokyo via Kabul. The Germans had planned to make a run for India in 1942, and AZ mentioned remnants of the tank traps to block Rommel, should he get to the NWFP, in his notes and letters. AZ and Enders did not encounter any Axis or Axis-supported activity, in the event.

The Russians were another issue. The Great Game, after all, was all about Russia and Britain, and the Americans were looking at this from the British perspective. AZ mentioned the work of "Bolshies" on two occasions, but it was Russia operating at a distance. The American legation believed that of the two opponents in the Great Game, Afghanistan feared Russia, and mistrusted Britain. Now that Germany was in retreat, the Russians were expected to renew their efforts in Afghanistan. The Afghans even considered the possibility of a Russian invasion, at least down to the Hindu Kush range, and considered that Russia might deploy ethnic Uzbeks and Tajiks to do its bidding, even without directly invading Afghanistan. The American legation believed that the British had learned their lesson in the three wars they fought with Afghanistan, and Afghanistan knew that the Americans knew this, too. The British would not seek a military solution to any problems they had with the government in Kabul, or with tribes on the Afghan side of the border. The Great Game was quiet at this time. Enders and Zimmermann did not expect to see Russian activity along the border, and, as expected, they did not encounter any.

As intelligence officers, Enders and Zimmermann were looking at other aspects of the economy and resources of the NWFP, and they found much to record—albeit briefly in the original notes, and largely redacted from the final trip report. They mentioned the details of mining for antimony and chromium, and they were interested in water resources, lumber, mutton and wool, fine cashmere cloth, and fruit and grains. Enders would have known that this area has gold mines and other precious metals and ores, especially lapis lazuli. There is enough coal and iron to smelt steel for weapons—a major product of the local workers. Lumber is now said to pass illegally in huge trucks, operated by the Chinese, from Chitral directly into Afghanistan. The lumber passes by a route or routes that were not constructed at the time of Enders' and Zimmermann's visit, and no such activity was expected or encountered. Having trained in electrical engineering, Zimmermann duly recorded his observations about hydroelectric power, but this was just good basic intelligence; no surprises here.

Oil was always the prize that was most often sought in Afghanistan. The search by an American oil conglomerate was behind the exploration of Afghanistan that Fox and his partners conducted in 1935, to no avail. Alexander the Great had found oil north of the Oxus when he invaded this country, and Patrick Hurley was an oil man, too. His fortune derived from his work as a lawyer in the oil business. But Enders and Zimmermann did not expect to find traces of oil in their trip, and they found none.

The Americans were also tasked to look for ways to reach China by alternative ways, to support the Allied war efforts. This was not in their written orders, but abundant sources show that many efforts were made by others, before and after their trip. They were looking for opportunities to reach China by road, by air, and by railroad. And because Zimmermann was in the Navy, which was responsible for worldwide U.S. government communications, he was surely looking for opportunities to improve radio transmissions. The Tolstoy expedition to Tibet had been recalled because of the belief that China would object to a high powered radio there. The U.S. 10th Air Force had a weather station in Peshawar, and it needed to have better radio facilities. Naval Group China said it had a depot near the Khyber Pass, and the NLO in Karachi had applied to send a lieutenant to Kabul on a special mission in December 1942. Some of these goals were expressed in the report from Enders to Hurley in January 1944, and the rest appear in various places in other documents that I reviewed for this book. All of these operations were undoubtedly intended to support the role of the United States in China, not to play in the Great Game with Russia on the Afghan border.

Finally, as with any explorers, Enders and Zimmermann must have wanted to have a grand adventure, one that would set a record if possible, and would push the limits of safety. They accomplished this by being the first to cross the Lowari Pass in a motor vehicle. And Zimmermann overcame his modesty to mention that he was the first Navy person ever to travel to those places.

Five

Afterword and Closure, after September 11, 2001

The new Great Game does not stop at the Khyber Pass
—Lutz Klevemann, *The New Great Game*, 234

The trip taken by Major Gordon Enders and Lieutenant Albert W. Zimmermann in November–December 1943 was a seminal event, though long since forgotten, in American diplomatic history, and in the history of Central Asia. Although a few other Americans had visited this region as tourists and explorers, this was the first time that American officials had been invited to visit this part of the world. With an invitation from senior British officials in the area, including the governors of the NWFP and Baluchistan, Enders and Zimmermann traveled along the south side of most of the border between Afghanistan and what was then India, and is now Pakistan. The British established the border, known as the Durand Line, in 1893 to divide the territory they ruled from that of Afghanistan, and it continues to be the de facto border between Afghanistan and Pakistan. The Americans were military intelligence officers, traveling in the open and in uniform, with their personal side arms discretely hidden. They were welcomed by the hereditary local rulers of three semi-independent states in the NWFP, by leaders of the Pashtun tribes and local members of the government, and by British civilian and military officers, including several generals.

175

The trip was also important in the annals of exploration. In spite of many adverse warnings, Enders forced his jeep in a successful ascent of the Lowari Pass, coaxing it upward and even having it pulled up on occasion. He thus became the first person to drive a motor vehicle over this pass. His passengers, Zimmermann and their British guide, Sir Benjamin Bromhead, and a local militia officer, photographed the ascent and descent with still and moving photography. This pass, which is the border between the states of Dir and Chitral, is even now usually closed for the winter, which is when they crossed it. It is the southern route to Tirich Mir in Chitral, the highest peak in the Hindu Kush range. Others have previously tumbled from horseback on this pass, and a later ruler of Chitral died there in a plane crash. Alexander is said to have crossed the pass, and the intrepid Francis Younghusband crossed it several times. When Churchill, as a young subaltern, visited this area, he reached only the base of the pass. Curzon, too, was unable to cross it. When he was a young soldier, the viceroy of India, Lord Wavell, had a hair-raising horseback trip over the Lowari Pass, and he was therefore interested in hearing all about the trip from the Americans after they returned to Peshawar.

The stated mission of Enders and Zimmermann was to see what problems the British were having with the tribes along the border, and how they dealt with these problems. Their eyes and ears were open, however, to all other issues that would be of interest to intelligence officers at that point in World War II, and that might be of interest to the United States in the postwar era. They were greeted enthusiastically by the *wali* of Swat, the *nawab* of Dir, and the *mehtar* of Chitral, whose titles and perquisites were later abolished. They saw hydroelectric power generated in the Swat valley, the terraced hillside agriculture of Dir state, and the antimony mines of Chitral. They feasted with the rulers, known as *maliks,* of each of the federally administered tribal areas. They were shown the principal crossing points across the border, including (from north to south) the Kunar, Khyber, and Kurram Passes, and the valleys of rivers that zigzagged along the border, such as the Kabul and Kurram. They went to the border at Peiwar Kotal, a few miles south of the infamous Tora Bora caves, which Zimmermann presciently referred to as the "most potentially powerful position in [the] world."[1] After concluding their trip on the NWFP, Zimmermann returned to Karachi through the Bolan Pass, which is the southern approach to Quetta, while Enders returned to Kabul through the Khojak Pass, the northern route into Quetta.

Zimmermann's notes and photographs provide a fascinating look at an area that seemed to most people to be remote and of little interest to the United States, and that rapidly faded from view in the early years of the Cold War. The Soviet invasion of Afghanistan in 1979 led to a reawakening of interest in the border between Afghanistan and Pakistan; the mujahedeen, who finally pushed the Soviets out of Afghanistan in 1989, welcomed American support, and Americans again visited this area during the period from 1979 to 1989. Whether any Americans have made the same trip that Enders and Zimmermann did is unknown, but if they did, the circumstances were very different from the relatively peaceful trip of 1943. It is unlikely that any would have made the trip in the open, and in uniform, as Enders and Zimmermann did.

After 1989 and the subsequent collapse of the Soviet Union, this area again fell from strategic view. Afghanistan eventually came under the control of religious conservatives, the Taliban, who provided a safe haven for Osama bin Laden and al Qaeda, when no place else in the world would have them. After the attacks of September 11, 2001, America returned to the area in an attempt to find and kill bin Laden and to defeat al Qaeda. The mujahedeen who defeated the USSR and became the Taliban thus became the enemies of the United States and its allies, the North Atlantic Treaty Organization (NATO). The war of the United States and NATO against the Taliban of Afghanistan drove them into Pakistan, in safe havens on the south side of the Durand Line, in the very same areas that Enders and Zimmermann traveled in 1943. The Afghan Taliban were given refuge by the Pakistani Taliban. And following the ancient tradition of "the enemy of my enemy is my friend," Arabs and other members of al Qaeda also found it possible to hide in Pakistan. The United States' search for bin Laden and other leaders of al Qaeda, and the attempts to destroy the border-crossing Taliban—especially with the recent use of unmanned drones—has led to profound difficulties with the government of Pakistan, and anger by the people who live in the NWFP (now the Khyber Pakhtunkhwa Province) and Baluchistan.

Americans in uniform have visited on a few occasions, however, in recent years. Americans were allowed to offer humanitarian aid in the aftermath of the earthquake in northern Pakistan on 8 October 2005, when some 78,000 were killed in the provinces of Khyber Pakhtunkhwa and Punjab. More than thirty U.S. helicopters eventually reached the scene. Americans were also invited to offer humanitarian aid after devastating floods in the Swat Valley in August 2010. The United States sent 250 American troops immediately, plus a three-ship force with three thousand Marines and nineteen helicopters. They are said to have supplied 500,000 halal meals, twelve prefabricated bridges, and many rescue boats and water purification systems. The American military personnel restored a bridge in lower Dir, providing access to Dir and Chitral. But when American soldiers from Afghanistan were invited to attend a conference near the border in North Waziristan in 2007, after a meal and what appeared to them to be a successful meeting, their hosts ambushed them and killed a U.S. Army major; the rest of the Americans had to fight their way out. This event occurred at a place called Teri Mangal, near the border crossing at the apex of the parrot's beak just south of Tora Bora. This was the same place, or very near, that in Zimmermann's report was called Peiwar Kotal, in North Waziristan. And on 1 May 2011 the hunt for Osama bin Laden was conducted without notifying Pakistan, for fear that the information would be leaked. Members of the Navy's Seal Team Six flew across the border to Abbotabad, near a major Pakistan army base. They found and killed bin Laden. They were extracted by air, bringing his body with them. Pakistan reacted angrily to this event. A few other episodes mentioning U.S. Special Forces acting as advisers or conducting operations in Pakistan have been mentioned in the media. There are surely others that have not been mentioned, or that are so highly classified that their existence has not been disclosed.[2]

Plus Ça Change, Plus C'Est la Même Chose

Two quotations about South Waziristan, one from 1943 and one from 2011, show the changeless nature of the area.

> Most of the way we have been escorted by Kassadars (local policemen). They line the road on either side (about 1/2 mile apart). Others ride in lorries ahead & behind us. . . . Since we've been here, this is what has happened—a road engineer's lorry held up—the supervisor kidnapped being held for ransom. At Dasali,

where we spent a night, about twenty shots were fired from a hill into the Army camp fortunately not hurting anyone—we were in the Scout post 1/2 mile away. . . . Another lorry was held up and three of the highwaymen were killed, one an Afghan. The RAF bombed some outlaws who were living in caves. Such is life on the Northwest Frontier. (Zimmermann to his wife, from Wana, South Waziristan, 6 December 1943)

One of Pakistan's most wanted militant commanders, Ilyas Kasmiri, was killed in an American drone strike in the tribal territory of South Waziristan . . . in a strike on a compound in Laman, near Wana. . . . He is reported to lead a unit called the 313 brigade, and is suspected of a number of high-profile attacks, including . . . the navy base in Karachi. (*New York Times,* 2011)[3]

As with many previous invaders of Afghanistan, the coalition of U.S. and NATO forces has found it easier to come into the country than to find a way to get out. Although some things have changed since the 1940s, much remains the same—or is worse, from the point of view of the United States. As the saying goes, the more things change, the more they stay the same.

Closure

The United States has accused Pakistan's Inter-Services Intelligence Directorate of sponsoring the Haqqani network, which has attacked coalition forces, Afghan government leaders, and the Indian embassy in Kabul. Many leaders in Pakistan, at this writing, appear to desire to have an unstable and weak Afghanistan, instead of a strong, stable, united Afghanistan. They especially wish to prevent Afghanistan from developing an alliance with India. The United States has a difficult role to play in this regional struggle, which involves vital interests of Iran, Russia, and China, as well as Pakistan and India. Americans are seen as intruders in this game, especially when they play it with a heavy hand.[4]

When everyone is dead the Great Game is finished.
Not before.
—Rudyard Kipling, Kim

Notes

Acknowledgments

1. Until about 2005 all that was known of this trip was a pair of letters that Albert Zimmermann (AZ) wrote to his wife in November and December 1943 in pen and ink. She copied the letters in typescript, and shared them with her children and friends. AZ wrote the first letter in Peshawar, about mid-way on the journey, on 25 November 1943. It mentions his trip by train to Peshawar, where he met the other two travelers. The letter tells of their visits to meet *maliks* (kings or tribal chieftains) of the tribal territories, the *wali* (ruler, Arabic) of Swat, the *nawab* (ruler, Urdu) of Dir, and the *mehtar* (ruler, Persian) of Chitral. It tells of their unique journey by jeep over the Lowari Pass, of Zimmermann's trip to the Khyber Pass, and of the garden party in Peshawar where the viceroy, Lord Wavell, came to hear of their trip. Zimmermann's daughter, Helene, preserved a typed copy of this letter. The second letter was remembered, but its location was forgotten until many years later.

   On 25 February 2007 my wife and I discovered the other letter about this trip, along with many other documents and photographs related to the trip and to the rest of Zimmermann's career in the Navy, a box of letters written from India to his wife, maps, orders, movies taken by AZ in India, a scrapbook of AZ's Navy records assembled after the war by his wife, and other items related to AZ's family. These items were in the attic of AZ's daughter, Barbara. When the items were gathered together, they were inventoried and placed into two footlockers, which they filled completely. The two letters about the trip had been passed by military censors without any deletions, and only a half-dozen or so words (principally names of places on commercial postcards) were deleted from all of this correspondence. This book is principally derived from these papers, which I refer to as the AZ–Wartime Papers (AZ-WP).

Key Documents and Players

1. The two documents are in the AZ-WP Scrapbook, p. 16(R).
2. The author of the letter of 28 October 1943, known only as "Intelligence Bureau, Quetta," remains unknown, although the travelers probably met with him in Quetta at the end of their trip.

Chapter 1. Background

1. Montaigne (1580): *Le jeu n'en vaut pas la chandelle,* which means "the game is not worth the candle." William Moorcroft (1825), in Bokhara: *Le jeu vaut bien la chandelle* which means "the game *is* worth the candle." Jablonsky, *Churchill: The Great Game.*
2. Lieven, *Pakistan,* 342.
3. L. Thomas, *Beyond Khyber Pass,* 3.
4. The chronology of the Great Game is from Rasanayagam, *Afghanistan;* Hopkirk, *Great Game;* Goodson, *Afghanistan's Endless War;* and Kleveman, *New Great Game.*
5. Hopkirk, *Quest for Kim,* 6–7 ("noble one"); Hopkirk, *Great Game,* 350 ("domains of the Emir" and "sphere of influence").
6. Hopkirk, *Quest for Kim,* 6–7; Meyer and Brysac, *Tournament of Shadows,* xxxvii; Hopkirk, *Great Game,* 350–1, 353, 362; Curzon, *Persia and the Persian Question.*
7. Hopkirk, *Great Game,* 481 ("fought for the throne" and "five successive rulers"), and 482–4; Curzon, *The Pamirs and the Source of the Oxus;* and Curzon, *Russia in Central Asia in 1889.*
8. Hopkirk, *Great Game,* 498 ("good place").
9. Ibid., 482–4, 494–500; Curzon, *The Pamirs and the Source of the Oxus;* Curzon, *Russia in Central Asia in 1889;* Churchill, *Malakand Field Force.*
10. Hopkirk, *Great Game,* 504. Curzon died in London on 20 March 1925. See Goradia, *Lord Curzon;* Rolandshay, *The Life of Lord Curzon;* and Courcy, *Viceroy's Daughters.*
11. Kipling, *Verses, 1889–1896;* Kipling, *Kipling Stories;* Amis, *Rudyard Kipling;* Gilmour, *Long Recessional;* Ricketts, *Kipling.*
12. Hopkirk, *Quest for Kim,* 6–7.
13. Hopkirk, *Trespassers on the Roof of the World;* Goodson, *Afghanistan's Endless War,* 36.
14. Hopkirk, *Setting the East Ablaze,* 174 ("the Soviets agreed").
15. Smith, *OSS,* 234 ("possible military supply"), and 234–5; *Foreign Relations of the United States* (hereafter *FRUS*) 1943, "China," 624–5; Tolstoy, "Across Tibet from India to China"; Tung, *Lost Tibet;* Meyer and Brysac, *Tournament of Shadows,* 540–50; and Yu, *OSS in China,* 76, 83, 87, 159–63, 297n, 308n.
16. Hopkirk, *Setting the East Ablaze,* 242 ("well and truly over"), and 120–3, 174–5, 240–2; Brobst, *Future of the Great Game.*

Chapter 2. The Travelers, and Others Who Were Involved in the Trip

1. G. Enders, *Foreign Devil.*
2. Ibid., 208 ("Before Chanti left Almora"); see also G. Enders and Anthony, *Nowhere Else in the World,* 64; and G. Enders, *Foreign Devil,* 81, 121.
3. G. Enders and Anthony, *Nowhere Else in the World,* 119 ("Armenian massacres"), and 146. William A. "Bill" Eddy (1896–1962), was born in Sidon, then in Syria, the son of Presbyterian missionaries. He was a U.S. Marine Corps officer in World War I, was wounded and awarded the Navy Cross, the Distinguished Service Cross, and two Silver Stars. In 1941 he was naval attaché in Cairo and with the OSS; he was envoy to Saudi Arabia; and he was interpreter for FDR and King Ibn Saud.
4. G. Enders and Anthony, *Nowhere Else in the World,* 150.
5. G. Enders, "Prohibition in Old India," 1003–4. Andrews was ONI civilian Secret Agent #241 from 10 June 1918 until March 1919 (Harris and Sadler, *The Archaeologist Was a Spy,* 305–9, 370).
6. Anthony was also coauthor with Franks Buck of *Bring 'Em Back Alive* and *Wild Cargo.*
7. [Enders] Anon., "Flying Gold Out of Tibet."
8. Fatehpur-Haswa is in the state of Uttar Pradesh, in north central India, about sixty miles northwest of Allahabad.
9. Etawah, in Uttar Pradesh, is about 110 miles northwest of Fatehpur. It is about fifty miles east of Agra and the Taj Mahal, and approximately due south of the great mountain Nanda Devi.
10. Wavell was then commander in chief, India. Brigadier General (later Lieutenant General) Raymond Albert Wheeler and his staff were en route from Washington via Karachi to Tehran, where he was to establish an Iranian mission for the United States. He traveled with his chief of staff, Lieutenant Colonel (later Brigadier General) Don Shingler, and Brigadier General (later Major General) Russell L. Maxwell, who became commanding general, U.S. Army Forces in the Middle East (USAFIME) on 15 June 1942. Wheeler's group went through Honolulu to India.
11. Written at Dean's Hotel, Peshawar. See more about the hotel and its history in Zareef, "Dean's Hotel."
12. Sir George Cunningham, governor of the NWFP; and Lieutenant Colonel Sir Reginald Lindsay "Rex" Benson, military attaché of Great Britain in Washington from 1941 to 1944 (see below).
13. Rai Bahadur Tirah Singh joined the United Province Police Force during the British Raj and later became deputy inspector general of police of the NWFP.
14. State Department Archives / Microfilm Publication #1219, Afghanistan / Boxes 4–7, Afghanistan 1940–45 / Box 4.
15. G. Enders, "Afghanistan's Strategic Geography."
16. NARA II, RG 165 (Records of the War Department General and Special Staffs), Entry 7 Afghanistan 5000–6400 Box 4 NND 745008, Geography (5900), 5930 [hereafter abbreviated to RG 165]; 128 Kabul 8 November 1943, addendum to 22 October and 4 November, ref M. A., #103 of 1 September.

17. From Enders to the minister in Afghanistan (Engert), 4 November 1943, in NARA II, RG 165 Entry 7 Afghanistan 5000–6400 Box 4, NND 745008, Geography (5900), 5930-Afghanistan's Strategic Geography.

18. Dreyfus' official title was envoy extraordinary and minister plenipotentiary in Tehran from 7 July 1939 to 12 December 1943. He had the same title in Kabul, where he presented his credentials on 19 May 1941. Dreyfus was ambassador extraordinary and plenipotentiary to Kabul from 21 April 1949 to 19 January 1951.

19. His nickname has no consistency in its spelling. He and others spelled it Benjy, Benjie, and Benji. Sometimes a "Sir" was added. The Bromhead baronetcy is a title in the baronetage of the United Kingdom.

20. Letter from IB Quetta to J. R. Harris, 26 October 1943 (above, in Key Documents and Players).

21. Dorwart, *Conflict of Duty,* 207–9: At the height of the war, early in 1943, "the ONI directed twenty-nine attaché posts manned by 156 officers (mostly reservists), twenty-two observer posts with seventy-nine officers, forty-three liaison offices with eighty-four officers. . . . No matter what the title, each officer received from ONI a little kit including a Hoey Position Plotter, various stationery and supplies, a .38 revolver, belt and holster, a *World Almanac,* fifty rounds of ammunition, and sometimes a gas mask and steel helmet. . . . The designation 'naval liaison officer' arose from war experience, probably at the behest of the British as part of a ship routing agreement." Dorwart says three of the offices were in India: Bombay, Calcutta, and Karachi.

22. One of the mutual friends of AZ and Curtin Winsor, his desk officer in the Far Eastern Division of ONI, was Henry Rawle Pemberton. He is one of those named by Baltzell, *Philadelphia Gentlemen,* 298: "The quantitative backbone of the book is based on the 770 Philadelphians of various class and ethnic backgrounds listed in *Who's Who in America in 1940,* an index of the elite leadership structure."

23. The photos were later returned to AZ with a letter dated 21 June 1949 from L. V. Boardman, special agent, FBI. The two photos returned to (and taken by) AZ were of a wedding at St. Paul's Church, Philadelphia, before 1937, showing German Bund members in uniform.

24. On 13 June 1942 FDR "suddenly dissolved the COI and established in its place the Office of Strategic Services (OSS), transferring control of it from the White House to the JCS," and although Donovan "lost control of the Foreign Information Service," which became the Office of War Information (OWI), he was named director of the OSS (Brown, *The Last Hero,* 237, "suddenly dissolved" and "lost control"). Joseph Freeman Lincoln, a prolific author, was a major, later a lieutenant colonel, in the OSS. Lincoln also was a neighbor of "Bitz" Durand, whose daughter Peachy Durand went to Kandy as a civilian OSS secretary. Clarence Lewis was an OSS officer and first lieutenant in the U.S. Marine Corps. His daughter Susan was the best friend of Zimmermann's daughter Helene.

25. Dorwart, *Conflict of Duty,* chap. 15 (162–71). For background on the Room, see Andrew, *For the President's Eyes Only;* Hyde, *Room 3603;*

Persico, *Roosevelt's Secret War;* Smith, *OSS;* Stevenson, *A Man Called Intrepid;* and Dorwart, "The Roosevelt-Astor Espionage Ring." Malcolm (Mac) Aldrich, president of the Commonwealth Fund, died at eighty-six in 1986. He graduated from Yale, where he was a member of Skull and Bones and captain of the football team. He was a friend of the Zimmermanns before the war, and their friendship continued in East Hampton after the war. His cousin Winthrop Aldrich was a member of the Room. The Room was chaired by Vincent Astor. FDR directed the director of naval intelligence (DNI) to provide orders to Astor to vet civilian recruits for the ONI on the East Coast.

26. Dorwart, *Conflict of Duty,* 194–206 (chap. 18). The chapter title (p. 194) refers to Zacharias and his career goal, which was never achieved.

27. The Navy career of Rear Admiral Harold Cecil Train (1887–1968) included command of USS *Arizona* (BB-39) until 5 February 1941, when he was relieved by Captain Van Valkenberg, who was killed by a direct hit on the bridge on 7 December 1941. Train was promoted to rear admiral and served as DNI from July 1942 until September 1943, when he was relieved by Rear Admiral Roscoe E. Schuirmann (September 1943–October 1944), who in turn was relieved by Rear Admiral Leo H. Thebaud (October 1944–September 1945). For Zacharias, see Dorwart, *Conflict of Duty,* 194–206; Zacharias, *Secret Missions;* Zacharias, *Behind Closed Doors;* Wilhelm, *The Man Who Watched the Rising Sun;* and Pfeiffer, "Sage Prophet or Loose Cannon?" Zacharias was awarded the Legion of Merit near the end of the war and retired as a rear admiral.

28. Edgar P. Snow, correspondent of the *Saturday Evening Post,* became famous for his close relationship to the leaders of Communist China. He encouraged the visit of President Nixon but died of cancer just before Nixon arrived. His ashes were divided between America and China. Tom Treanor, a reporter for NBC and the *Los Angeles Times,* was killed in France on 21 August 1944. Quotation is from Treanor, *One Damn Thing after Another,* 140 ("despite protestations"). AZ's comments are from his intelligence report to JICA/CBI and DNI, 5 July 1944 (obtained by FOIA request).

29. Thomas A. Thornton was commander and later captain, USNR. He was deputy chief, JICA-ME in RG 38, Serials JICA 1943–44, Box 19; and in Box 20, he was officer in charge, naval section. He later became chair, JICA/ME; under that title a folder of his papers are filed in the FDR Library. For Eugene "Gene" Markey, see Markey (below) for his profile up to November 1943. He was at this time a commander, USNR, and was en route to become the senior ALUSLO in CBI, based in New Delhi. General Strong was probably Major General George Veazey Strong, chief of U.S. Army Intelligence (G-2). Henry Hotchkiss appears in the list of Foreign Service appointments for 1943 as assistant naval attaché and assistant naval aviation attaché in Cairo.

30. Madame Dubash's invitation to AZ for this dinner on 20 July 1943 is in the AZ-WP, Scrapbook, p. 12(V). She appears in several subsequent let-

ters from AZ. Her given name, Nadia, first appears on 24 October 1943 when AZ refers to her as the "girlfriend" of his CO, Lieutenant Commander F. Howard Smith.

31. Harris and Sadler, *The Archaeologist Was a Spy,* App. 5 "General Instructions," 381–2, e.g.: "In employing natives or residents to obtain information the greatest care must be used." Dorwart, *Conflict of Duty,* 211: In December 1944 "the department ordered that funds for the collection and classification of information could not be used for dinners, luncheons, and entertainment."

32. Brigadier (later Major General) N. Godfray Hind, CSI, MC was the commander of British forces in the area. His wife was Marguerite "Poppie" Hind. AZ first mentions going to dinner at the residence of Brigadier Hind on Saturday 31 July 1942. Major Smyth was the military secretary to the governor of Sind Province.

33. "Richard B. Russell (Dem.-Ga.) was a Senator from 1932 to 1970. He chaired the Armed Services Committee from 1951 to 1953 and 1955 to 1959" (http://www.senate.gov/artandhistory/history/common/generic/Featured_Bio_Russell.htm). "Ambassador Clarence Edward Gauss was a career Foreign Service officer. He was ambassador to the Republic of China from 1941 to 1944. He resigned the post in November 1944, and was replaced by Patrick Hurley" (http://history.state.gov/departmenthistory/people/gauss-clarence-edward). On 20 August 1943 HQ, China-Burma-India Training Unit (Prov) was activated at Karachi, India, with Brigadier General Julian B. Haddon as commander.

34. IB Quetta to J. R. Harris, 26 Oct 1943 ("clear to the American Legation").

35. AZ to BSZ, Letter 86, 6 September 1944 ("already instigated").

36. Mitchell, *Cunningham.*

37. Ibid.

38. Cunningham's diary quoted in ibid., 34–7.

39. Ibid., 41–43.

40. Ibid., 60 ("just appeared on the scene"); see also 60–61.The faqir of Ipi (1897–1960) is a controversial figure to this day. He appears in the trip report of AZ, and in *FRUS.* His birth name was Mirza Ali Khan. He was the son of a religious teacher, who was considered to be a holy man himself. The faqir came from the village of Ipi, between Bannu and Razmak. His rebellion died out after Pakistan achieved independence.

41. Mitchell, *Cunningham,* 87 ("was not expected"), 87–9.

42. Afridis were the tribe of Pashtuns who lived (and still live) on the road to the Khyber.

43. Remark on 9 January 1944. Mitchell, *Cunningham,* 108 ("more peaceful"), 102 ("shadow of the war").

44. Mitchell, *Cunningham,* 108 ("bad affair" and "ordinary exercise").

45. Ibid., 177 (Kipling, quoted by Cunningham in his Rectorial Address to St. Andrews University, 9 April 1947).

46. AZ wrote that it was a party for Smith's fiftieth birthday, but it must have been his fifty-first.

47. AZ to BSZ, 25 August 1943.
48. Miles, *A Different Kind of War,* 271 ("most of his work had been for SACO"). On p. 268, Miles offers another possible connection to the mission of AZ and the others in November–December 1943, which does not appear in any other place that I have seen: "Naval liaison officers . . . had supplies stashed all over the Indian subcontinent, including the Khyber Pass up on the border of Afghanistan."
49. IB Quetta to J. R. Harris, 26 October 1943 ("up to Smith"). Full text in Key Documents and Players.
50. J. Engert, *Tales from the Embassy.*
51. Ibid., 23 ("the more times").
52. Ibid., 31 ("sniff around"), 33 ("unofficial" and "gather much").
53. Ibid., 91 ("never been taught"); and 67–83. C. Engert, *A Report on Afghanistan,* given in a letter to Wilbur J. Carr, assistant secretary of State, 29 April 1928, referenced in a footnote on J. Engert, *Tales from the Embassy,* 50; Cornelius Van Engert Papers, Special Collections, Georgetown University (hereafter CVHE Papers).
54. J. Engert, *Tales from the Embassy,* 25.
55. Sara Engert also was helpful to her husband. She corresponded with First Lady Eleanor Roosevelt, and her obituary is in FDR papers for Engert, Sara—in Vertical Files—copy of her obit in *New York Times* (28 July 1972).
56. *FRUS* 1941, vol. 3 (Near East and Africa, Afghanistan), 255–9; vol. 3, 259 ("American diplomatic mission"). Dreyfus was directed to read C. Engert, *A Report on Afghanistan,* 48, 211–2.
57. *FRUS* 1942, vol. 4, 48 ("name the regular Minister"), 51.
58. *FRUS* 1942, vol. 1, 604.
59. CVHE Papers, Box 8, Folder 10.
60. Ibid.
61. State Department Archives / Microfilm Publication #1219, Afghanistan / Boxes 4–7, Afghanistan 1940–45 / Box 5.
62. CVHE Papers, Box 8, Folder 2.
63. *FRUS* 1943, vol. 4, 20 ("weakening of the present regime"), 21 ("traditional menace").
64. Buhite, *Hurley,* 110 ("officer" and "enter Afghanistan"); see also Lohbeck, *Hurley,* 188, 194–6, 202; *FRUS* 1943, vol. 4, 22 (Hull to Engert); *FRUS* 1943, vol. 4, 24 ("nothing less than a brigadier').
65. *FRUS* 1943, vol. 4, 23 ("Afghans are convinced").
66. *FRUS* 1943, vol. 4, 24 ("very much interested"); the name of the director of IB Quetta was not given.
67. CVHE Papers, Box 8, Folder 2.
68. *FRUS* 1943, vol. 4, 26 ("little room for doubt").
69. *FRUS* 1943, vol. 4, 48, 50, 51 ("very much hampered").
70. CVHE Papers, Box 8, Folder 19.
71. Ibid.
72. CVHE Papers, Box 7, Folder 75.
73. Ibid.

74. CVHE Papers, Box 8, Folder 2.
75. Ibid.
76. *FRUS* 1943, vol. 4, 36.
77. *FRUS* 1943, vol. 4, 30 ("relates to")
78. State Department Archives / Microfilm Publication #1219, Afghanistan / Boxes 4–7, Afghanistan 1940–45 / Box 5.
79. CVHE Papers, Box 8, Folder 20.
80. Ibid.
81. Roderick Engert, telephone conversation with the author, 13 August 2009.
82. Other officers at the NLO in Karachi: Hebford 3 December 1943 to 2 April 1944; Baker 26 December 1943 to 15 March 1944 (AZ-WP, Box 1, File 1–6, "India-Northwest Frontier"). Halla's arrival date was not given; he is first mentioned in AZ's letter to his wife on 4 May 1944.
83. Jeffery, *Secret History of MI6.*
84. The principal sources for Benson's family and his public life are Wake, "Benson, Sir Reginald Lindsay (1889–1968)," 194–6; and Wake, *Kleinwort Benson.* See also, "Sir Rex Benson, Banker, 79, Dies: Was Military Attache Here from 1941 to 1944," *New York Times* (28 September 1968) [d. 26 Sept 1968]; [Benson] Knighthood awarded. *The London Gazette* (18 July 1958), 4514; and [Benson] Benson, Lt.-Col. Sir Reginald, in "Philip Morris's predecessor, Benson & Hedges" (http://www.smokershi story.com/Benson.html). For his military history, and work in military intelligence, see Brown, *Secret Servant,* and Hyde, *Room 3603.* Dorril, *MI6,* says Benson was in MI6. The index shows one reference to Benson in the text, in which Colonel Rex Benson is referred to as one of the "senior MI6 officers" who were "in the highest circles of the intelligence 'old-boy network' at the beginning of the Second World War" (p. 456); the other man mentioned here was Kock de Gooreynd. Benson also appears at least twice in Dorril's notes: "Rex Benson was an MI6 officer and Menzies's cousin" (p. 810, n1); and "the British-American-Canadian Corp. chaired by [Sir Charles] Hambro with former MI6 officer Sir Rex Benson and former US Secretary of State Edward Stettinius" (814, n27).
85. The background of Rex Benson, his family, his childhood, and his career in banking is summarized from Wake, *Kleinwort Benson.*
86. Benson's career as a soldier is in his papers at the King's College London / Liddell Hart Centre for Military Archives / Lieutenant Colonel Sir Ronald Lindsay Benson, AIM25, in King's College London. I did not review these papers.
87. Wake, *Kleinwort Benson, 194* ("working as a stoker").
88. The career of Stewart Menzies is described in Brown, *Secret Servant.* Dorril, *MI6,* Notes (p. 810, n1, and p. 814, n27) say Sir Rex Benson was in MI6. The index in Dorril shows one reference to Sir Rex Benson, on page 456. On that page Colonel Rex Benson is referred to as one of the "senior MI6 officers" who were "in the highest circles of the intelligence 'old-boy network,' at the beginning of the Second World War."

89. The marquess of Willingdon had been governor of Bombay and Madras, governor general of Canada, and then the viceroy of India. His wife was a sister of Countess De La Warr and the aunt of Lady Avice, Menzie's first wife.
90. Ruth Donovan's diary quoted in Brown, *Secret Servant*, 355–6; the date is on p. 324. Sir William Stephenson was not a member, but he was involved with the Room. See Persico, *Roosevelt's Secret War;* Hyde, *Room 3603* (foreword by Ian Fleming); and Dorwart, "The Roosevelt-Astor Espionage Ring"; Stevenson, *Intrepid's Last Case;* Stevenson, *A Man Called Intrepid.*
91. Brown, *Secret Servant*, 256 ("should not deal").
92. Ibid., 386.
93. AZ to BSZ, 21 August 1943.
94. Hill, *Intimate Relationships*, 109–43. Macy left Karachi sometime after 1944, was consul general at Istanbul 1947–48, and retired in 1948, according to Denslow, *10,000 Famous Freemasons.* He died in 1984, and was buried Ft. Logan National Cemetery, site T1, 1433.
95. Fort, *Archibald Wavell;* Wavell, *Other Men's Flowers;* Wavell and Moon, *Wavell;* Connell, *Wavell;* and Lewin, *The Chief.*
96. Connell, *Wavell*, 48 ("sharp crisp winter" and "sense of humour").
97. Ibid., 54.
98. Ibid., 54–7.
99. Ibid., 39 ("thirteen years of my life"), 46 ("conflict seemed"), 57 ("trouble on," "stiff little," "from the Khyber"); Fort, *Archibald Wavell*, 38 ("1890 poem").
100. Fort, *Archibald Wavell*, 86 ("taciturnity"), 87 ("poker face"), 246 ("oyster").
101. Ibid., 250.
102. Wavell and Moon, *Wavell*, 39 ("more tired and depressed").
103. Wavell, *Other Men's Flowers.*
104. Hay, *Two Years in Kurdistan.*
105. Thayer, *Bears in the Caviar;* and Thayer, *Diplomat.*
106. Thayer, *Bears in the Caviar*, 243–52; 247 ("a jeep rolled").
107. Thayer, *Diplomat*, 57 ("written in his autobiography").
108. Thayer, *Bears in the Caviar*, 257–8, 258 ("advice for the British").
109. State Department Archives / Microfilm Publication #1219, Afghanistan / Boxes 4–7 / Box 5.
110. Thayer to Department of State, August 1943 ("constrained"), ibid., Box 5 ("scrupulously living"); Thayer, *Bears in the Caviar*, 258–9 ("tribes never actually rose").
111. Thayer, *Bears in the Caviar*, 265 ("Northwest tribe").
112. Thayer, *Diplomat*, 75, 88.
113. Ibid., 185 ("Italy switched sides").
114. Thayer to Department of State, 30 November 1943, enclosed with Dispatch No. 348 of 8 December 1943 ("The Axis aim"). The document was initially classified as Confidential, but it was declassified on 28 January 1980. Microfilm 1219, Box 5.

115. Thayer, *Diplomat,* 158 ("Contrary to myth"), 159 ("A typewriter we borrowed").
116. Thayer, *Bears in the Caviar,* 284 ("got himself confused").
117. Ibid., 292–3 ("to go to London").The highest peak in Afghanistan is Noshaq, 24,850 feet.
118. Thayer, *Guerrilla,* xi ("West Point training"), Foreword, by Sir Fitzroy Maclean. Maclean knew Thayer from his first trip to Moscow, prior to coming to Afghanistan. He and Thayer agreed in London in 1944 to a new mission for Thayer in Yugoslavia.
119. The ONI was in the office of the chief of naval operations (OPNAV). ONI was OP-16. The Far Eastern Division (aka Far Eastern desk) was referred to as "FE," so Winsor's division or desk was in OP-16-FE, although he was not the head of the division. Winsor to AZ, ALS written in Delhi, 9 December 1943, in AZ-WP, Winsor File.
120. Morris Duane was born 20 March 1901. He and his wife resided at Bryn Mawr, Pennsylvania, and, as did the Zimmermanns, attended the Church of the Redeemer there. He was a commander in the U.S. Navy in 1944. Henry Rawle Pemberton was born in Philadelphia on 27 April 1898. He graduated from the Episcopal Academy of Philadelphia in 1915, where he was said to be the "most musical" member of the class.
121. JICA, or Jica, was abolished after World War II. So-called "joint intelligence" organizations (intelligence sections and divisions of the Joint Chiefs of Staff) are now usually referred to as "Defense" or "Armed Forces" rather than "Joint"; examples are the Defense Intelligence Agency (DIA) and the Armed Forces Medical Intelligence Center (AFMIC). Winsor to AZ, 15 September 1943, 2 ("ONI staggers along").
122. Winsor to AZ, 9 December 1943, in AZ Wartime Papers.
123. Gene Markey was a well-known Hollywood producer before and after World War II. He married four women: Joan Bennett; Hedy Lamarr; Myrna Loy; and Lucille Wright). This brief background on Markey is based on biographies of his wives, especially Rhodes, *Hedy's Folly,* esp. 127–9, 134, 154, and 204; and Leider, *Myrna Loy.* Also see Gene Markey's own books, including *His Majesty's Pyjamas* and *Women, Women, Everywhere;* films produced by him, such as *Wee Willie Winkie* (DVD, B&W, 100 min, 1937); and films inspired by him, such as *In Harm's Way* (DVD, B&W, 167 min, 1965). See also Prescott, *PT Skipper,* 107.
124. USNLO to AZ, 8 November 1943, Temporary Additional Duty orders (see Key Documents and Players).
125. Dorwart, *Conflict of Duty,* 209. ALUSLOs in Bombay and Calcutta appear in AZ's letters from Karachi, which also mention New Delhi and Colombo. It appears from Dorwart that the stations at Bombay, Calcutta, and Karachi are the only ones with ALUSLOs. New Delhi and Colombo were headquarters locations.
126. Leider, *Myrna Loy,* 157 ("gift of gab").
127. The movie *Wee Willie Winkie* was filmed on the Iverson Movie Ranch. The location of the British camp in Kipling's story cannot be identified,

because it is imaginary. However, Kipling sets many of his stories in the area of the Khyber Pass and to the north, along the Afghan border (Mills, "John Ford, USN"). Ford was wounded filming the Battle of Midway, and he was recalled for service in Korea; his photo as a rear admiral shows fifteen service ribbons. Ford, who had "a yen" for Myrna Loy and called her the "only nice girl in Hollywood," was in New Delhi with Markey, according to Leider (*Myrna Loy,* 256), and was in the wedding party when Loy and Markey were married in 1944. Ford's work with ONI has never been fully revealed.

128. In 1941 Lamarr and composer George Antheil invented an electronic technique that they patented in 1942 that was used to scramble communications and guide torpedoes; it has since been used in Wi-Fi communications. See Rhodes, *Hedy's Folly,* 242; and Natalie Angier, "From the Lab to the Red Carpet," *New York Times* (1 March 2011).

129. Lohbeck, *Hurley;* and Buhite, *Hurley.*

130. Lohbeck, *Hurley,* 97.

131. Ibid., 179 ("the only non-Russian"), 171 ("port near Colombo"); Buhite, *Hurley,* 109 ("that Stalin was" and "believed Hurley").

132. Buhite, *Hurley,* 116 (all quotations this paragraph).

133. Lohbeck, *Hurley,* 202 ("meeting regularly"); Buhite, Hurley, 122 ("a variety of reasons" and "Chiang's concurrence").

134. Lohbeck, *Hurley,* 209 ("neither Britain nor the Soviet Union").

135. Ibid., 217 ("just a few minutes before").

136. Buhite, *Hurley,* 124–9, 130–1; Lohbeck, *Hurley,* 217. Lohbeck says on 21 December he sent a report to the president. FDR forwarded Hurley's report to the State Department with an accompanying message on 12 January (p. 225), which FDR described in a letter to Hurley on 25 March. Stettinius acknowledged the report of 21 December in a letter to Hurley of 2 March.

137. Roderick Engert, telephone conversation with the author, 13 August 2009.

138. Fox, *Travels in Afghanistan;* and Fox, *By Compass Alone.*

139. Fox, *By Compass Alone,* dust jacket comment. Quotations from dust jacket are available online. He is referred to as Colonel Fox.

140. Fox, *Travels in Afghanistan.*

141. Ibid., 112 ("the foreign engineer").

142. Ibid., xviii ("great hope").

143. Fox, *By Compass Alone.* His death date is from the Social Security Death Index. Her obituary is from *TC Palm* (6 December 2009).

144. "Francis Verner Wylie Video Interviews," http://www.ovguide.com/francis -verner-wylie-9202a8c04000641f80000000153713d3

145. Andrew, *Defend the Realm,* 4, 108, 137, 442 ("For almost a quarter"). "During the 1920s the Service's most active imperial liaison had been with the Delhi Intelligence Bureau (DIB or IB), whose diminutive London office, Indian Political Intelligence (IPI), was situated in MI5's London headquarters," 236. See also 442–7. The names and the acronyms in

British intelligence evolved over time, and since they were kept secret at the time, it is difficult now to be accurate in usage. For example, ibid., 3: "The Security Service (MI5) and the Secret Intelligence Service (SIS or MI6) began operations in October 1909 as a single organization, the Secret Service Bureau, . . . The Bureau was staffed initially by only two officers, . . . Commander Mansfield Cumming RN and an army captain . . . Vernon Kell. . . . Cumming and Kell parted company to become the first heads of, respectively, SIS and MI5."

146. King's Police Medal awarded in 1933: "SUPPLEMENT TO THE LONDON GAZETTE, 2 JANUARY, 1933. 15: King's Police Medal awarded to Denys Pilditch, Assistant to the Deputy Inspector General of Police, Criminal Investigation Department, United Provinces."

147. M. V. Kamath, "A Selective Memory," *The Hindustan Times* (21 November 1998). After Pilditch retired, quotes from an unnamed newspaper in Melbourne, Australia, 26 October 1948 and 14 March 1950. Holt, *The Deceivers;* Wolpert, *Shameful Flight;* Liddell and West, *The Guy Liddell Diaries;* and Aldrich, *American Intelligence and the British Raj.*

148. Cutting, *The Fire Ox and Other Years;* Dorwart, "The Roosevelt-Astor Espionage Ring"; Meyer and Brysac, *Tournament of Shadows,* 541; "Cutting, C. Suydam"—a thin file of letters in President's Personal File, box 4556–4612, PPF 4596, FDR Library; Nicholas F. Brady, letter to George J. Hill, 14 October 2009. Brady was formerly secretary of the Treasury; he was the step-grandson of Suydam Cutting.

149. Cutting, "Cheetah Hunting," in Plimpton, *As Told at the Explorers Club,* 167–72.

150. Major General Sir Stewart Graham Menzies, KCB, KCMG, DSO, MC. The MI6 was formed as a branch of military intelligence (hence the term MI6, in which MI stands for military intelligence), but it gradually grew apart from the MID (military intelligence department), and it now stands on its own. For more on Menzies and MI6 and MI5, and the failure to identify officers within MI6 who were traitors, which occurred on Menzies' watch, see Brown, *Secret Servant;* Jeffery, *Secret History of MI6;* Dorril, *MI6;* Andrew, *Defend the Realm* [MI5]; Philby, *My Silent War;* and Page, Leitch, and Knightley, *Philby.* I can find no record to show that Menzies ever visited India.

151. For MI5's activities in India, see Andrew, *Defend the Realm.* Pilditch does not appear by name in the Index in the official histories of MI5 (by Andrew) and MI6 (by Jeffery).

152. Jeffery, *Secret History of MI6,* 584 ("extremely hostile").

153. Ibid., 584, 587–8.

154. Brown, *The Last Hero;* Smith, *OSS;* Hersh, *The Old Boys;* E. Thomas, *The Very Best Men;* Casey, *Secret War;* Dulles, *Secret Surrender;* Dulles, *The Craft of Intelligence;* Grose, *Gentleman Spy;* Hyde, *Room 3603;* McIntosh, *Sisterhood of Spies;* Miles, *A Different Kind of War;* Smith, *OSS;* Yu, *OSS in China;* Yu, *The Dragon's War;* and Donovan, William J.—President's Secretary's File—Box 153; FDR Library.

155. Brown, *The Last Hero,* 160, 164 ("Make Donovan"), 165 ("supplementary activities" and "espionage, sabotage"). Zimmermann later received an invitation to meet Admiral Godfrey when he was commander of the Indian Fleet, but he apparently missed the opportunity because he left that day for SEAT and Regional OSS Headquarters in Kandy, Ceylon. Whether he met Godfrey later is unknown.
156. Donovan's itinerary from September 1943 to February 1944 from Brown, *The Last Hero,* 359–508; and Yu, *OSS in China,* 128–34.
157. Mountbatten was properly styled as The Right Honourable The Earl Mountbatten of Burma, and by the end of his life his honorifics included KG, GCB, OM, GCSI, GCIE, GCVO, DSO, PC, FRS—the latter in recognition of his work as an inventor, which included a patent for naval use.
158. AZ to BSZ, 6 December 1943: "Enders did the talking as he has a flare for it and modesty isn't one of his virtues."

Chapter 3. The Trip

1. AZ to BSZ, 30 October–3 November 1943.
2. AZ to BSZ, 10 November 1943.
3. Fagin may have been a false name; there is no one who graduated from West Point with that name who could have been this person. His dress is quite unusual—it is reminiscent of *Kim's* dress when he was in disguise on the train: recall the story of Agent E24 and the two amulets. General John H. "Nonnie" Hunter II died in 1992.
4. L. Thomas, *Beyond Khyber Pass,* 29.
5. AZ to BSZ, 25 November 1943.
6. Swayne-Thomas, *Indian Summer,* 60 ("The Vale of Peshawar"). See also 45, 60.
7. Connell, *Wavell,* 45–46 ("conflict seemed imminent").
8. Wavell and Moon, *Wavell,* 38–9 ("enjoyed visit to the N.W.F.P.").
9. Churchill, *Malakand Field Force,* 25 ("it was impossible"), 15, 23–26, 95 ("Nothing in life"), 136 ("history repeats"); Green, *Alexander of Macedon,* 379.
10. Rolandshay, *The Life of Lord Curzon,* 129, Courcy, *Viceroy's Daughters,* 81 ("Be careful"), 91, and dust jacket. Many years later, a grandson of Curzon's daughter Alexandra (Curzon) Metcalfe married a granddaughter of AZ.
11. J. Engert, *Tales from the Embassy,* 34–5; L. Thomas, *Beyond Khyber Pass,* 34–5, 45, 96 ("most of their wives"), 255 ("back into British India").
12. Fox, *Travels in Afghanistan,* 3 ("once the residence").
13. Ibid., 2–3; Hopkirk, *Great Game,* 493–4; Jeffers, *In the Rough Rider's Shadow,* 153.
14. Quotations from Reeve, "Peshawar Remembered," http://www.khyber lodge.co.uk/about-khyber-mainmenu-26/peshawar-remembered-main menu-43.html
15. Kleveman, *New Great Game,* 237–8, 234 ("Only by obtaining"), 238 ("Great Pashtunistan").

16. AZ's trip report is the basis for all that follows, unless I indicate otherwise.

17. Charles Thayer and his brother-in-law Charles "Chip" Bohlen, George Kennan, and Llewellyn Thompson were regarded as the four most knowledgeable Russian experts in the State Department. Charles and his brother George Thayer were first cousins of AZ's good friend and fellow Orpheus Club member, John W. "Jack" Thayer Jr.

18. Kipling's poem about Gunga Din was in AZ's library in Haverford, in Kipling, *Verses*.

19. W. G. Dildine, "Model Monarch Rules Model State of Swat," *Cleveland Plain-Dealer* (18 February 1951).

20. AZ to BSZ, 25 November 1943, p. 8.

21. AZ, "Notes on Chitral Trip / Nov. 15–23," five-page typescript, marked up by AZ in pencil, the penultimate draft of a typescript entitled "Notes on Chitral Trip / Nov. 15–23, 1943," 16 November, p. 1 ("there is no evidence"), AZ-Wartime Papers, in NIP Special Collections.

22. Churchill, *Malakand Field Force*.

23. AZ, "Notes on Chitral Trip," p. 2, 16 November 1943, quoting Bromhead.

24. Churchill, *Malakand Field Force*, 10–22, with ellipses ("After crossing the Malakand Pass"); also see 55–7, 65–7.

25. Swayne-Thomas, *Indian Summer*, 62–4 ("Malakand and Swat").

26. AZ, "Notes on Chitral Trip," p. 1 (17 November 1943).

27. Ibid., paraphrasing what Bromhead said: "Mollah is tribal priest and Malik is Tribal leader. Propaganda against Ipi was that he tried to combine both offices in himself which was against the Koran."

28. Green, *Alexander of Macedon*, 382–4 ("Alexander moved on north").

29. The odd, tortuous course of the Kunar River is described by Mitchell, *Cunningham*, 118fn. Kipling's fictive story of "The Man Who Would Be King" is set in the kingdom of Kafirstan, immediately north of Chitral and Swat (Kipling, *Kipling Stories*, 307–57).

30. Khan, "A Short History of Chitral and Kafirstan"; Shirazi, "Chitral."

31. AZ-WP, Movies. AZ took movies on many occasions during his twenty-two months or so overseas. A VHS tape of the two reels of film was made August 2007 and converted to DVD on 3 June 2011; it is in the Special Collections of the Naval Institute.

32. AZ, "Notes on Chitral Trip," 1–2 (18 November 1943).

33. Ibid., 2 (18 November 1943).

34. This is not Ziarat, Baluchistan, an entirely different city. This Ziarat does not appear on a Google map of Pakistan.

35. I spoke by phone on 20 January 2010 to Colonel Harry Reginald Anthony "Tony" Streather (Ret.), OBE, who as a captain was the official government representative when a Norwegian party made the successful first ascent of Tirich Mir in 1950. He was one of those who ascended the mountain at that time. He later was famous for climbs elsewhere in the Himalayas, most notably on K-2, where he survived the famous fall with Charles Houston, Robert Bates, and several others on the American expedition in 1953 (Houston and Bates, *K2*). Streather said he was aide-

de-camp to Sir Ambrose D. F. Dundas, KCIE, CSI (1899–1973), the last British governor of the NWFP. Streather never met Bromhead, but he had "heard about him many times—he was somewhat of a character." He had not heard about Bromhead's trip in 1943 but said that "it was all part of the Great Game. . . . The Russians got interested in this area again a bit later, somewhat after 1943." I asked if he had ever been to Peiwar Kotal and the Kurram Valley, where the travelers went in 1943, and he replied, "Yes, I have been in one of the Tora Bora caves" near there.

36. Muzaffar-ul-Mulk was the third of sixteen sons of H. H. Mehtar Sir Muhammad Shuja ul-Mulk, *mehtar* of Chitral, KCIE (1895–1936). He succeeded to the throne on 29 June 1943. He died in 1948, and his son Saif-ur-Rehman (b. 1926) was *mehtar* of Chitral until he was killed in an airplane crash at Lowari Pass in 1954. The title passed to Saif's son, Saif-ul-Mulk Nasir, who held the title until 1972. Pakistan abolished the titles of the rulers of the former states of Pakistan, including Chitral, in April 1972.

37. Milton Bramlette (born circa 1896), a graduate student at Yale, accompanied Sir Aurel Stein on his fourth trip to the northern Pamirs (Meyer and Brysac, *Tournament of Shadows,* 390).

38. This man was the fourth of the sixteen sons of Shuja ul-Mulk, *mehtar* of Chitral, and the next in line of succession after the present *mehtar.*

39. Khan Sahib later became premier of the NWFP. After Pakistan became independent in 1947, he was a prominent legislator in the new country. He was chief minister of West Pakistan until he resigned in 1956. From *New Encyclopaedia Britannica,* vol. 25, *Pakistan,* 290.

40. AZ to BSZ, 25 November1943, handwritten, from Peshawar.

41. AZ mentions the word "Sikenada" at this point, by which I believe he means Sikandar, a reference to Sir Sikandar Hyat Khan, chief minister of the Punjab. Kipling, "Wee Willie Winkie," in *Prose and Verse,* vol. 6, frontispiece and 287–304.

42. Mitchell, *Cunningham,* 107–8; Wavell and Moon, *Wavell,* 39; Lucey, letter to Donovan, in Yu, *OSS in China,* fn33, p. 295 ("bag of wind"); and Roderick Engert, telephone conversation with the author, 13 August 2009: "Yes, I saw Enders several times, and he certainly was flamboyant, a blowhard in fact."

43. L. Thomas, *Beyond Khyber Pass,* ix ("few lands"), 3, 45, 68, 73 ("the most famous"), 78 ("Beyond the cliffs"), 81, 96–7.

44. Fox, *Travels in Afghanistan,* 5 ("The fame of Khyber").

45. Swayne-Thomas, *Indian Summer,* 60 ("great luck"), 61 ("towers may belong" and "all very vain"), 62.

46. Rudyard Kipling, "The Ballad of the King's Jest," in *Verses 1889–1896,* 79–83 (quote from p. 79). From the set of Kipling's writings in AZ's library.

47. Rolandshay, *The Life of Lord Curzon,* 129; Brown, *Secret Servant,* 59; Cornelius Engert in *Time,* 10 August 1942.

48. Barstow (1894–1961) was assistant adjutant and quartermaster general of India from 1940 to 1942.

49. L. Thomas, *Beyond Khyber Pass,* 7 ("strongest strategical"); AZ, Notes on Chitral trip, p. 7 (in AZ-Wartime Papers, NIP Special Collections): "most

potentially powerful." The full quotation, on Tuesday, 30 November 1943, is "Climbed to Paiwar Kotal (pass to Afghan) Afghan unfriendly wouldn't let us look over top alt abt 10,000—rocky path—scene of engagement 1919 with Afghans Gen. Roberts most potentially powerful position in world."

50. Kipling, quoted by L. Thomas, *Beyond Khyber Pass,* 16 ("go to your Gawd").

51. L. Thomas, *Beyond Khyber Pass,* 7 ("crossed the Sind" and "strongest strategical"), 8 ("From Quetta" and "north to Waziristan"), 9 ("leaving the railway"), 10 ("Indus River"), 13, 16, 19, 24, 25 ("From Tank we motor on"), 28 ("Southern Waziristan"), 29 ("Kurram River" and "Seventy miles"), 39 ("Not long after"). At Tavistock, Devon, a stone is inscribed: "Ellen Mary Ellis (1923) wife of Mjr A J Ellis DSO."

52. General Roberts actually fought the Battle of Peiwar Kotal on 2 December 1878, not 1879.

53. Young, *Rommel.* The Germans had planned to be in Cairo by Christmas 1940. But the plan failed, and on 3 November 1942 the Afrika Corps began its long retreat across North Africa.

54. According to Boulger, "Unity of Coinage for the Empire," the system was based on the notion that "a penny in England" is equivalent to an "anna in India." This equivalence continued until after World War II. There were 240 pence to the English pound sterling (12d = 1s, & 20s = 1 pound). There were 16 As. to 1 Rupee (Rs.). And the U.S. dollar was pegged to the pound, too: $5.00 to 1 pound. If you work this out, you will find that 1 As. = 1 pence (d) = about 2 U.S. cents. And 16 As = 1 Rs. = about 32 U.S. cents. The anna is no longer used as a unit of currency in India or Pakistan. The value of "blood money for a murder" in the NWFP in 1943 was estimated at Rs. 2000. The value of INR 2,000 is now approximately US$35.70.

55. AZ, "Notes on Chitral Trip," 5.

56. Ibid., 4 ("no casualties"), 3 December 1943.

57. Ibid., 5, 5 December 1943.

58. Brigadier James Jarvie Purves (1898–1974), was CO, 21st Indian Brigade, 1942–1943; http://www.generals.dk/general/Purves/James_Jarvie/Great_Britain.html

59. I could not identify "Pop Wynn" or "Karex."

60. Swayne-Thomas, *Indian Summer,* 21, 105–7.

61. Ibid., 21 ("A few weeks . . . native costume"), 107 ("Quetta is cold").

62. On 11 December, AZ met with Major General Money, who was in India for the first time as commander 6th Indian Brigade, and Colonel Bruce-Steer, formerly of the 15th Punjab Regiment, who was now at Baluchistan headquarters. He also saw "Father Wood, Major Platt and Alston." Platt was perhaps John Rowley Innes Platt (later Brigadier J. R. I. Platt, DSO, OBE), who could only have been in Quetta for a short time. Alston was probably Lieutenant Colonel (later Brigadier) William Lowry Alston, commander of 8th Battalion, the Rajputana Rifles, stationed at Kakul, and would also have been a transient in Quetta. AZ's notes for 12

December say that he went for a chickor shoot and picnic lunch with the governor/commissioner, Lieutenant Colonel Rupert Hay, and his family, and Major Woods-Ballard, the Political Assistant. If "Father Wood" and Major Woods-Ballard were actually different people, "Father Wood" was perhaps a euphemism for IB Quetta—counterpart to J. R. Harris (who was IB Karachi).

Chapter 4: Aftermath

1. Thayer, *Bears in the Caviar,* 296, 297 ("piled into a couple of compartments"), 299–302. Letter from the State Department to Thayer at American Embassy, London, 23 December 1943. State Department archives/Microfilm File #1219, Afghanistan / Boxes 4–7, Afghanistan 1940–45 / Box 4.

2. Rex Benson returned to his home in Chichester, Sussex, for the rest of the war. He continued as chair of Benson Bank, which merged with the Lonsdale Investment Trust in 1947. He retired from the chairmanship of Robert Benson Lonsdale in 1959 but remained on the board and oversaw the merger of RBL with Kleinwort Sons & Co. in 1961. In 1958 he was knighted "for his contribution to the work of the English Speaking Union," which he had served as honorary treasurer for many years. He was elected vice president of the English Speaking Union in the year before he died. On 6 June 1968, the day after the funeral of his cousin Sir Stewart Menzies, Benson published a long letter in *The Times* in which he said that Menzies, like *Kim,* had a "habit of 'acquiring knowledge' which he put to good use in his later professional life." Benson died three months later in Naples, Italy, at age seventy-nine. His widow, the former Leslie Foster, died in 1981. His son David married the daughter of the twelfth earl of Wemyss, and his son Robert's daughter Lucinda was a godchild of Princess Margaret. References for Benson's postwar life: Brown, *Secret Servant,* 124, says Benson was "chairman of the English Speaking Union." Wake, "Benson," writes, "in 1958 he was knighted for his contributions to the work of the English Speaking Union." *New York Times* (27 September 1968): "Sir Rex, who was knighted in 1958, was an active member of the English Speaking Union . . . of which he became vice president last year." *The London Gazette* (18 July 1958), 4514: "The honor of knighthood was conferred on . . . Lieutenant-Colonel Reginald Lindsay Benson, D.S.O., M.V.O., M.C. . . ." (approved by the queen, 12 June 1958). "Lieutenant-Colonel Reginald Lindsay BENSON . . . Honorary Treasurer, English Speaking Union of the Commonwealth."

3. CVHE Papers, Box 8, Folder 20.

4. CVHE Papers, Box 7, Folder 69.

5. Brigadier General Benjamin Greeley Ferris (1892–1982) was deputy chief of staff, U.S. Army Forces, CBI theater of operations, 1943–44; CVHE Papers, Box 7, Folder 69; Box 8, Folder 21.

6. McManus was a lieutenant commander in 1942 and 1943, when he was on the Foreign Service roster as a naval attaché and assistant attaché for air. In 1946 he was with the Central Intelligence Bureau. He later gave

testimony to Congress on Operation Mongoose, the failed attempt by the CIA to assassinate Castro.

7. CVHE Papers, Box 8, Folder 21.

8. Ibid.

9. Ibid.

10. Lohbeck, *Hurley,* 226 ("now on the verge of becoming").

11. Buhite, *Hurley,* 133 ("the mission was a success").

12. G. Enders, in Hurley Papers, Oklahoma University Special Collections: "Report of Military Attaché, Kabul, Afghanistan, on General Hurley's Visit to Afghanistan," 1/18/44 (five pages, typed), in Hurley Collection, Box 493C, Folder 4, also in Box 83, Folder 7. Index in University of Oklahoma Libraries Western History Collections / Patrick J. Hurley Collection, 4 ("A common remark").

13. Ibid., 4 ("commercial aviation concessions").

14. Another issue—Navy supplies for China—may have played a role in the decision to send a naval intelligence officer to the NWFP, although nothing more about this has ever come to light. Milton Miles wrote that supplies of SACO (Sino-American Cooperation Organization) were "stashed all over the Indian subcontinent, including the Khyber Pass up on the border of Afghanistan" (Miles, *A Different Kind of War,* 268). Perhaps this is also what AZ was referring to when he commented to his wife, "The people needed to keep an eye on these supplies rotated out on leave through Karachi" (AZ letter to BSZ, 22 July 1944). Additional comments on the situation at that time in Afghanistan are from Buhite, *Hurley,* 133; G. Enders, "Report of Military Attaché, Kabul (5 pp.); and G. Enders, memorandum to Hurley, "Afghanistan in General" (5 pp.), both dated Kabul, 13 January 1944. The two five-page documents are both in OU Special Collections, Hurley Papers. The Report on Hurley's visit is in Box 83, Folder 7; and the memorandum to Hurley is in Box 493C, Folder 4.

15. Engert to Hunter, CVHE Papers, Box 8, Folder 21. Engert was being very circumspect, and he doesn't say what he was referring to in this message, or in others that were not preserved: However, he may have been referring to the recent trip of Enders in the NWFP: [Engert to Lt. Col. Edward O. Hunter, Rear Echelon Headquarters, U.S.A.F., A.P.O. 885, India] TLc (telegram) / Kabul, 15 January 1944. / "Secret. / Dear Colonel Hunter, / I have given your letter of December 30, 1943, a good deal of thought and have talked it over with Major Enders. / For obvious reasons I feel that your suggestion has to be handled with the utmost caution, and the Major agrees with me that the fewer people connected with the Legation are involved, the better."

16. Major General Sir Walter Joseph Cawthorn, CBE, CIE, CB (1896–1970) had been head of the Australian Secret Intelligence Service; he was director of military intelligence at general headquarters India; CVHE Papers, Box 8, Folder 21.

17. Miles, *A Different Kind of War,* 206–7. Miles was en route to Washington, DC, when he arrived at Karachi on 7 February. He was actually a captain

at that time, and was promoted to commodore in March 1944. On his return, he arrived in Bombay, and then went to Calcutta (where he learned that he had been promoted to commodore), and then to Chungking. Details are in Yu, *OSS in China*, 140. From 1943 to 1945 he served as second in command of a joint intelligence operation called the Sino-American Special Technical Cooperative Organization (SATO), also known as SACO. In 1944–45 he was also commander, U.S. Naval Group, China. He was promoted to the rank of vice admiral on his retirement in 1958.

18. Thayer, *Bears in the Caviar*, 299 ("heading an Anglo-American"); also see 296–7, 300–2. The formation of the European Advisory Commission (EAC) was agreed upon at the Moscow Conference in October 1943 between the foreign ministers of the United Kingdom, United States, and Union of Soviet Socialist Republics, and was confirmed at the Tehran Conference in November. Major General Sir Fitzroy Maclean, first baronet, KT, CBE (1911–1950) was in the Special Air Service (SAS) in North Africa, and in 1943, as a brigadier, he was personally selected by Winston Churchill to lead a mission to central Yugoslavia. He is said by some to be the model for Ian Fleming's James Bond.

19. Bromhead to AZ, 15 January 1944, from The Services Hotel, Peshawar.

20. Bromhead to AZ, 27 January 1944.

21. CVHE Papers, Box 8, Folder 21.

22. CVHE papers, Box 8, Folders 21–22. On 26 March 1944 Major Enders and Major Fox paid a courtesy call on the senior Afghan general in Kabul, Major General Daoud Shah. The general requested an exchange of American and Afghan officers for training, and this request was forwarded by Enders and Fox to the Department of State. It was rejected by Charles Bohlen on 22 August 1944. (See State Department Archives/ Microfilm Publication #1219, Afghanistan, Boxes 4–7, Afghanistan 1940–45, Box 4, Thayer file.

23. CVHE Papers, Box 8, Folder 22; Engert to Department of State, 14 February 1944.

24. Quotes are from Engert, *FRUS* 1944, vol. 5, 49 ("Middle Eastern country," "might rouse,"), 50 ("Moslem dissatisfaction") (25 August 1944), 54 ("Northwest Frontier"), 11 November 1944.

25. Saul Steinberg (1914–1999) was to become one of the most famous cartoonists for the *New Yorker*. A double-page of Steinberg's "India" cartoons from the *New Yorker* (24 February 1944, 6–7), are in AZ-WP, Scrapbook, page 18(V).

26. AZ to BSZ, "friends of Freeman" (mentioned in his letters of 7 September 1943 and 10 October 1943 prior to the NWFP trip, and after the trip on 4 March 1944, 9 March 1944, and thereafter); and 19 February 1944 ("I'm trying to write a story"). Few of the monthly reports were saved, but the reports in the summer of 1945 reference an instruction of February 1944, and it appears that a requirement for the reports was initiated at that time. The report for February 1944, which would have included a report in January on the trip to the NWFP, did not show this report as

being completed and submitted. We may conclude that either (1) the report was never prepared in an intelligence report format, or (2) it was completed in December, before the NLOs were informed that monthly reports were required. I believe it is more likely that it was never prepared as an intelligence report, but was circulated as an "eye's only" document.

27. Lieutenant Commander F. Howard Smith, USN, CO of NLO in Karachi, was relieved under a cloud, for reasons unknown, but probably related to the finances of the NLO. There were other improprieties alluded to, however. For example, Madame Dubash was Mrs. Nadia Dubash. She appeared at the NLO on the night that AZ arrived in Karachi and she is mentioned in many of his letters thereafter until 28 December 1943, but never again thereafter. AZ's "Superiors" at the ONI were "S & O" ("Sadler" and "Off," first names unknown, were mentioned in Winsor's letter to AZ of 21 February 1944. In this letter, Winsor told also AZ of a "bombshell" relating to an allegation of financial mismanagement at the NLO in Karachi, which eventually was resolved, after an inventory and audit, without docking of the junior officers' pay, but the CO, Lieutenant Commander Smith, was transferred out and received an unsatisfactory fitness report. Quote ("all of you junior officers") in Winsor to AZ, 21 February 1944, p. 1 of 2.

28. Charles B. B. Clee (also spelled Clie and Clees in AZ's letters), CIE, CSI, revenue commissioner of Sind, 1944, and wife Mary. The viceroy was the guest of honor at a party given by the governor of Sind Province. Invitation and instructions are in AZ-WP, Scrapbook. This was AZ's first meeting with Lord Wavell since he met the viceroy in Peshawar a little over three months before, in November 1943. John Harris was the chief of central intelligence in Karachi. He is in civilian clothes in other photos, and this is the first time AZ said that he is also a military person. The photo was published in an unknown newspaper, doubtless in Karachi. The Sardar was a member of the Sindh legislature in 1935, and leader of the opposition in the legislature in West Pakistan in 1956–58. His full name and title is in the caption of the photograph.

29. CVHE Papers, Box 8, Folder 22.

30. Richard (Dick) Carlyle Kelley Jr. (1919–2000), AZ's nephew, was a captain in the U.S. Army Ordnance Corps. Peachy Durand appears in AZ's photo album in Kandy, Ceylon. McIntosh, *Sisterhood of Spies*, 209, 226. Nine women were in the initial group that went to India including Durand and Julia McWilliams, who later married Paul Child. Durand was later one of ten women in the OSS who were flown "over the hump" to serve in China. Barbara S. Zimmermann, "This War—And Brave Little Women," *Vogue* (1 March 1944), 137, 140.

31. AZ to BSZ, 13 March 1944. John Harris is the chief of central intelligence in Karachi.

32. This brief statement is the only contemporaneous account of the departure of Lieutenant Commander Smith and the assumption by AZ of

responsibility as acting (or actual) CO at the NLO in Karachi. The expected "important visitors" that AZ mentioned in letter 55 are the "large group of officers" who were in Karachi when he wrote this letter. I suspect that the group was headed by Commodore Milton Miles. If so, they had come to evaluate the ruckus about Smith that had led to his being transferred by ONI and relieved with an unsatisfactory fitness report. Miles eventually sided with Smith.

33. Fox, *Travels in Afghanistan,* vii ("honor is their bond").

34. CVHE papers, Box 8, Folder 3.

35. Lieutenant Commander John D. Bulkeley took his PT boat across the Atlantic, but other PT boats may later have gone west from Australia, across the Indian Ocean, the Suez Canal, and the Mediterranean Sea. They would thus avoid the perilous crossing of the Atlantic Ocean, which was infested with German submarines. See Bachman, *An Honorable Profession,* 48–49.

36. Winsor to AZ, 6 April 1944.

37. Winsor to AZ, 21 April 1944. In 1964 Sidney S. Sweet was appointed to the Public Advisory Committee on Trade Negotiations. Captain Gene Markey, USNR, was the senior U.S. ALUSLO in I-B theater. AZ first encountered him in Cairo, and although he was the senior ALUSLO in the region and AZ must have had much correspondence with him, he only mentioned him in one other letter to his wife (7 June 1944). "The colonel" refers to Colonel W. L. Bales, USMC, Winsor's superior, whose initials appear in Winsor's letter of 9 March 1945. His name appeared to be "Bates" in many handwritten letters, but it is typed "Colonel W. L. Bales" in Winsor's letter to him of 9 March 1945.

38. Anne Carter Greene was regional director of the American Red Cross in the CBI theater during World War II, and a former president of the Junior League of Washington.

39. Elizabeth C. Enders (Mrs. Gordon B.) to BG [sic] Patrick J. Hurley, from 918 Highland Ave., Lafayette, IN, to War Department, Washington, DC, 22 April 1944, TLS. In Patrick J. Hurley Collection, University of Oklahoma Special Collections, Box 84, Folder 4.

40. Winsor to AZ, 23 May 1944. When the CO, Lieutenant Commander F. Howard Smith, was transferred out, he would ordinarily have written a fitness report on all of his subordinates before he left, and they were probably not rated highly because there was ill will between them and the CO. It would be a likely cause AZ's request for promotion to be set aside.

41. Winsor to AZ, 23 May 1944, p. 1 ("We would like you as a"). A major investigation and audit of the NLO in Karachi Navy mess took place in 1944, perhaps on the authority of the chief of naval operations himself, Admiral Ernest King. Commodore Milton Miles, the senior U.S. Navy officer in Southeast Asia, believed Smith was unfairly blamed for the problems in Karachi. Miles was a protégé of Admiral King, who is said to have detested reservists, on principle. Miles implies that Curt Winsor had a hand in Smith's downfall, and that perhaps AZ was not simply an innocent bystander.

42. In RG 165, Entry 77 India 4730–5900, Box 1629, Folder labeled #1, which is the third folder in the box, apparently misfiled, is a copy of the Port Summary of Karachi, India, 15 May 1944, from Op-16-FE, 40 pages, with map and photo, and no appendices. Mimeographed and stapled. A report on the NWFP trip is *not* here.

43. CVHE Papers, Box 7, Folder 65.

44. Five Ralli brothers started operations in India in 1851. The business closed under the Ralli name in 1931, passing to Argenti and Co. Vere Birdwood was Lady Elizabeth Vere Drummond Ogilvie Birdwood. AZ does not mention this, and he may not have known it: her mother-in-law was the aunt of his companion on the NWFP trip, Sir Benjamin Gonville Bromhead. Her husband, Christopher Birdwood, was in the Waziristan campaign with Bromhead in 1919–20. Vere Ogilvie Birdwood became Baroness Birdwood in 1951 upon the death of her father-in-law, when her husband acceded to the title. She was divorced two years later and Baron Birdwood remarried. She died 1 May 1997.

45. Leider, *Myrna Loy,* 272 ("nothing less"). See also 245–7, 256–8, 265, 271–6.

46. University of Virginia School of Medicine, History, www.medicine.virginia .edu/research/research-centers/cell-signaling/welcome-information /history-page

47. Brigadier General John A. Warden and Brigadier General Julian B. Haddon, USA; and "aur billi," presumably H. E., Governor Sir Hugh Dow. "Bahadur" is now a major training base for the Pakistan navy.

48. U.S. ALUSLO, Karachi, to JICA/CBI and DNI, 5 July 1944, Serial 18–44, "India—Political Parties and Groups," declassified under FOIA, nine pages. Quotations from p. 9.

49. Hampton (Hampy) Barnes was born in Philadelphia 1908 and died in Edgmont, Delaware, in 1993.

50. Captain Paul Glenwood Linaweaver Jr., USN, was the senior ALUSLO, Kandy, Ceylon, 1944–45, and thus the immediate senior to AZ. In turn, he would have been under the command of Captain Habecker in Ceylon.

51. The man to whom AZ reports is the senior U.S. ALUSLO, I-B Theater, who was also United States senior ALUSLO, New Delhi. The friend of AZ and BSZ, Peachy Durand, who appears in the photograph that AZ sent home after this trip, was stationed in Kandy as a civilian in the OSS. Her friend in the OSS, Julia McWilliams (later Julia Child), is reported to have said, "Kandy is dandy" (a paraphrase from Ogden Nash).

52. The letter is quoted exactly here. I cannot find this article in the files of the *Saturday Evening Post* at the New York Public Library. I suspect that it may have been submitted but never published.

53. The Naval attaché Chungking was Lieutenant Colonel James M. McHugh, USMC, a classmate of then Commodore Milton Miles. He was a brother-in-law of Brigadier General John Magruder, who had been in China with the U.S. Army, but was recalled by General Marshall. Colonel McHugh was the special representative of Navy Secretary Frank Knox. (Miles, *A Different Kind of War,* 335–6; and Yu, *OSS in China,* 27).

54. State Department archives Microfilm # 1219, Afghanistan / Boxes 4–7, Afghanistan 1940–45 / Box 4. Marshall Green had been secretary to the U.S. Ambassador to Japan, Joseph Grew. He returned to the United States shortly before Pearl Harbor was attacked, and entered the Navy, where he served in naval intelligence as a Japanese language translator. He became the U.S. ambassador to Indonesia, and was assistant secretary of State from 1969 to 1973. He was one of the few in the State Department who predicted correctly that China and the USSR did not have a common front—that China would go her own way—and he accompanied Nixon to China in 1972.

55. In the spring of 1944 the new military attaché, Ernest Fox, requested military training in the United States for Afghan Army officers, including medical officers. On 26 March 1944 Fox had been introduced by Gordon Enders to Major General Shah, commander of the central army forces in Kabul. On 22 August 1944, Bohlen, of the Division of Eastern European Affairs, recommended rejection of this request, and it was annotated "I agree," by his unnamed superior.

56. All quotations in this paragraph are from an unsigned handwritten letter, dated 22 August 1944, which was included with Winsor's letters to AZ. It appears to be in AZ's handwriting, and is difficult to read. The letter was probably written by Commodore Milton Miles, USN, and apparently refers to Winsor's letter to the DNI, RADM Roscoe E. Schuirmann, which Winsor enclosed to Col. Bales on 9 Mar 1945. The addressee is not named, and there is no signature on it, so I can only speculate that this letter was from Miles to Schuirmann, and that Winsor showed it to AZ when Winsor visited Karachi, and AZ then copied it. I believe the letter is not the original document but it is a fair copy, although some abbreviations may have been made in it by AZ. The letter begins with "If I am right, I think you may have to fire [?] somebody. If you will read the photoed [letter] a few times and take into account what has been going on, I think you will agree that there's skull-duggery about."

57. This is the only place where AZ describes what he believes was the purpose of the trip, to amplify what was in the message from IB Quetta in October 1943 and in his orders from the Navy Department in November 1943. The relationship of the trip to the independence movement in India is new here; it is not mentioned at all in any of his notes or in the trip narrative. He also states unequivocally that Enders "instigated" the trip.

58. Curt Winsor provided official permission from the ONI for AZ to submit his photos for publication, and BSZ then communicated with *Life* magazine, *Reader's Digest,* and *National Geographic* with regard to his photos and stories about his experiences in India. Bromhead also gave permission for AZ to use the photos he took on the NWFP trip. AZ then wrote to BSZ, "if what they have in hand, Life or Town & Country want to go ahead, I'm game" (5 September 1944, p. 4).

59. For descriptions of the photos and details of the trip, see AZ-WP file on the Baluchistan trip. One photo is shown here as an example: it is "the

thing" (a life raft from a Liberty ship) that washed ashore and was the object that AZ and his companions rode out on camels to examine. AZ's formal report on the trip to Baluchistan was filed on 13 October 1944, as "Serial 23–44, Monograph 602–300, From U.S.N.L.O. Karachi to ONI/ FE via JICA/CBI (2 pp.). Subj: LIFE RAFT—Washed ashore at 25°11'N— 66°45'E." The report includes a message from A. A. Lawson, RIN, saying that the S. S. William I. Kip was renamed S. S. Sampan. The inventory of the items found in the life raft includes "the cholocates and bisquites [sic] having disappeared in the interim." The document was found in NARA II, Record Group 38, Records of the Office of the Chief of Naval Operations, RG 38—ONI Monograph Files South Asia—ALUSLO 1-S-44. An unpublished typewritten MS by AZ, which he had hoped to submit to *Life* magazine, is filed in AZ-WP 1–9 Maps, Typed Letters, Notes— Baluchistan, entitled "Navy Men Go Funny Places on Funny Animals: A Trip into Baluchistan by Camel"(now in USNI Special Collections). AZ's captioned photos, taken on the trip, are also there.

60. Winsor to AZ, 15 September 1944. This is the last time that Markey was mentioned in any correspondence in the AZ-WP.

61. Bromhead to AZ, telegram 22 September 1944, original in AZ Wartime Scrapbook, p. 28.

62. Quotation from Lohbeck, *Hurley,* 280, citing letter from FDR to Chiang, 19 August 1944.

63. NARA II, Record Group 38- Records of the Office of the Chief of Naval Operations, RG 38—ONI Monograph Files South Asia—ALUSLO 1-S-44. In NARA II, RG38, AZ's message: "USNLO in Karachi to CNO (DNI) 1 Sep 1944 / Serial 960 / CONFIDENTIAL Subj.: Landing Beaches in the vicinity of Karachi, Study of. [s] Albert W. Zimmermann. Received in FE mail Room, 1042 AM, 11 Sep 44" The "admiral" was probably Rear Admiral C. Julian Wheeler, who was on his way to take a new job as U.S. ALUSLO at the British Eastern Fleet. Rear Admiral Wheeler, in a letter of 7 November 1944, thanked AZ for hosting him on his way to his new post, and he refers to a "big Navy Day cocktail party" that took place on the day he arrived at his new post, probably on 27 October. Another Navy Day party was hosted in Chungking on 27 October by the naval attaché, Captain H. T. Jarrell, who thanked AZ for help with the spirits. Jarrell was a Naval Academy classmate of Commodore Miles.

64. NARA II / State Department Archives / Microfilm Publication #1219, Afghanistan / Boxes 4–7, Afghanistan 1940–45 / Box 4: Engert letter to State Department, 15 July 1944, says that the rebel leader Abdurrahman, known as "Pak," was next in importance to the faqir of Ipi. Engert letter to State Department, 13 September 1944, says Mazrak Khan was a rebel in the South, in addition to "Pak" and the faqir of Ipi. He was known as "Mazrak."

65. Hauser, "A Reporter at Large." On 13 October AZ submitted his intelligence report on the life raft from the SS *Kip* (see above). Captain Harold G. Bowen Jr., USN, was deputy DNI, later vice admiral. His decorations included the Distinguished Service Medal with gold star, two Legion of

Merit medals with Combat V, three Bronze Star medals with gold star and Combat V, and three Navy Commendation medals.

66. Brigadier General John Warden was appointed commanding general, S.O.S., India, Burma Theater (SOS-IBT), 18 December 1944–10 February 1945.

67. Lieutenant General George Stratemeyer (1890–1969) went to the CBI theater in mid-1943. He was appointed commanding general of the Army Air Forces in the theater and air commander of the Allied Eastern Air Command. Part of Stratemeyer's command, the Tenth Air Force, had been integrated with the RAF Third Tactical Air Force in India in December 1943 and was operating under Mountbatten's command in SEAT. Lohbeck, *Hurley,* 205.

68. Smith, *OSS,* 248–9.

69. Harold G. Bowen Jr., to AZ, 20 November 1944, in Winsor folder. Captain Ransom Kirby Davis, business card in AZ-WP, Scrapbook, loose between sheets 17(L) and 18(R). Captain Davis became senior U.S. ALUSLO, I-B Theater. He had a career at sea, and then became a trainer and intelligence officer. As a lieutenant commander, Davis (1897–1995) was the sixth CO of USS *Worden* (DD-352), (June 1939–April 1941), which was awarded four battle stars in World War II. As a captain, Davis is mentioned in Fetridge, *Navy Reader,* 18: "To my most recent commanding officers, Captain Cary W. Magruder, USN, of the Naval Training Station, Newport, Rhode Island, and Captain Ransom K. Davis, USN, of the Naval Training School, Cedar Falls, Iowa, my sincere gratitude." Captain Ransom K. Davis appears in several citations within an on-line book: Hunt, *Secret Agenda.* "The decision to use Osenberg was made by" U.S. Navy Captain Ransom K. Davis, who was assigned to "Op-23 JIS, 5 March 1946."

70. From NLO Karachi to Chief of Naval Operations (Director of Naval Intelligence), 25 Nov 1944, Serial 1068 CONFIDENTIAL, Received A4b, 1028 AM, 6 December 44. "Subj: Records of Mess at the Office of U.S. Naval Liaison Officer, Karachi—Retention of. . . . The actions reflected therein did not have the approval of the full complement of officers." From NARA II, RG38, Records of the Office of the Chief of Naval Operations / Correspondence with Naval Attaches, Observers, and Liaison Officers, 1930–48, 370, 15/1/2, Box 8 (Hobart, Australia to Lima, Peru, includes Karachi, India), microfilm.

71. The three naval officers were Lieutenant (jg) C. Rollins Hanlon, MC, USNR (1915–2011); J. Murray Steele, M.D.; and a "Dr. Woods," who I have not been able to locate. Henry A. Schroeder, M.D., was at the University of Pennsylvania when the Zimmermanns knew him. By 1940 he had moved to the Rockefeller Institute in New York City, where he and Steele wrote several papers together. Hanlon's letter to AZ, written in Calcutta, 13 January 1945, is in AZ-WP, Scrapbook, p. 24(V). Dr. Hanlon was president of the American College of Surgeons in 1982, and I knew him when he was director of the College (1969–1986). On 4 March 2011

I spoke on the telephone with him. As with any intelligence officer, he was somewhat evasive, even long after the events. He said that they were not on a typhus mission; that was just a cover. He recommended Drea, *MacArthur's ULTRA,* to get some idea of what they were doing. He remembered staying at the NLO in Karachi in 1944 (especially the batman who helped him put on his trousers there), but he did not remember the Christmas party or his host, AZ. He died soon after I spoke with him.

72. Cyrus (Cy) H. Polley and AZ were members of the Merion Cricket Club. Polley was one of the best squash players in America; he would become the U.S. veterans champion in 1947. His obituary was in the *Buffalo News* (26 March 1997). It says that he joined the U.S. Army Air Forces and was made a lieutenant and later a major in General Claire Chennault's 14th Air Force, successor to the Flying Tigers. Polley was in charge of Special Forces in Kunming, China. John Browning Clement Jr. was a graduate of the University of Pennsylvania, AB 1908, LLB 1912, with a varsity letter in cricket. He was a member of the Colonial Society of Pennsylvania. He was a generation older than AZ, but was his friend in the Orpheus Club and the Merion Cricket Club. AZ knew Colonel Bryce Blynn as a member of the Merion Cricket Club. He was a member of Tau Chapter of the Psi Upsilon fraternity, Class of 1918.

73. Mitchell, *Cunningham,* 109 ("extreme friendliness").

74. Captain Frederick Shrom Habecker, USN (2 April 1905–12 May 1981), U.S. Naval Academy graduate, 1927. He received the Navy Cross for service as CO of DD-664, USS *Richard P. Leary,* on 24–25 October 1944, in the Battle of Leyte Gulf, and the Legion of Merit for service in the Cold War. He was transferred to ONI and was sent to India to be the senior U.S. naval officer at SACSEA [Supreme Allied Command, South East Asia] in January 1945. He retired as a rear admiral but is shown on one web page as "later VADM" so he apparently received a "tombstone" promotion, based on his receipt of the Navy Cross. Habecker wrote from Queen's Hotel, Kandy, where headquarters of SACSEA was located. The hotel was built in about 1850. Captain Paul Glenwood Linaweaver Jr., USN, was senior ALUSLO, Kandy, Ceylon, 1944–45.

75. Habecker to AZ and Voorhees, 23 January 1945, in Winsor file, AZ-WP, written: "Hdq. Sacsea, A.P.O. #432 / Jan 23rd [1945]."

76. The four articles eventually published in the *National Geographic* are Fisher, "India's Treasures Helped the Allies," Muir and Muir, "India Mosaic," Tolstoy, "Across Tibet from India to China," and Williams, "South of Khyber Pass."

77. With regard to Thornton, see AZ's letter to BSZ, 7 July 1943, in which he mentioned meeting Thornton in Cairo. The invitation for this event is in AZ-WP, Scrapbook, loose between pp. 25 and 26.

78. Winsor arrived "early in the morning" on 25 February and departed "after breakfast," presumably on the same day, because AZ says they spent only "a few minutes" together. However, Winsor's letter of 9 March to Colonel Bales at ONI, written while he was still in India (probably

in Delhi), shows that Winsor and AZ must have exchanged important information that AZ does not mention here. It is very likely that Winsor showed AZ photocopies that he brought with him of a two-page "personal" letter from Winsor to AZ (dated 21 February 1944), which had been intercepted by the then-CO at Karachi, Lieutenant Commander F. Howard Smith; and a one-page letter from Commodore Milton Miles to Rear Admiral Schuirmann, DNI (dated 22 August 1944), in which Miles suggested that Winsor ought to be fired. AZ to BSZ, 6 March 1945, 5 ("various people in to meet" and "hunch about this latest bomb shell").

79. Winsor to AZ, handwritten letter, 9 March 1945. The reference to the "CNO" (Fleet Admiral Ernest King) shows that King's attention must have been drawn to this matter by Commodore Miles, who was one of his protégés. Lieutenant Commander Henry Groman first appears in AZ's correspondence on 26 December 1944. On 19 February AZ wrote that Groman was still expected to leave for Karachi soon, and perhaps had even left already. On 6 March AZ wrote that he had just received a letter from Groman, saying that he would not be coming.

80. Lieutenant Commander Edward F. O'Connor, USNR, was appointed CO, NLO in Karachi. His arrival on 30 March 1945 is shown in AZ's last letter to BSZ from Karachi. After several days of familiarization, he relieved AZ, and as CO, he then signed orders detaching AZ to return to the United States on 9 April 1945.

81. Winsor refers to his letter of 21 February 1944 to AZ, which began, "Dear Al." Winsor and AZ had many more personal communications than Winsor acknowledged in his letter to Bales.

82. Winsor to Colonel W. L. Bales, Room 4625, Navy Department, Washington, DC, 9 March 1945, probably typed and sent from the NLO office in Delhi or New Delhi, copy in AZ-WP, Winsor File. The copy is unsigned, and was apparently provided to AZ as a blind copy. Winsor disappears at this point from the AZ-WP, and Curt Winsor was no longer AZ's desk officer after he left India. AZ and Curt Winsor were never friends after the war, although both moved in similar circles in Philadelphia; their relationship must have been poisoned by their work in the ONI. Curt Winsor was promoted to lieutenant commander, and then resigned his commission and returned to civilian life in Philadelphia. He was active in business and charitable and environmental organizations in Philadelphia until his death on 12 November 1998, at the age of ninety-two. The class of 1927 at Princeton, of which he was secretary, observed that in 1949 he founded American Competitive Enterprise System (ACES) in Pennsylvania, a nonprofit economic education organization. His stepson, William Donner Roosevelt (1932–2003), was the child of his first wife, Elizabeth Donner, and her first husband, Elliott Roosevelt, son of FDR. Curt and Elizabeth Donner had two children, born in Philadelphia: Curtin Winsor Jr. (b. 1939); and Joseph Donner Winsor (1941–1976). After she and Curt were divorced, Elizabeth raised all three children, and all three were involved with the Donner Foundation when they were adults. Curtin

Winsor III, son of Curtin Jr., was born in 1963, and is also involved with the Donner Foundation. Curt Sr. married (second), Margaretta Rowland, from whom he was divorced, (third) Catherine Horst, who died in 1971; and (fourth) in Bryn Mawr, Penn., Eleanor Webster, with whom he had a daughter. Curt Winsor's brother Jim and Jim's wife were good friends of the Zimmermanns and their children and the Zimmermann children were friends, too.

83. Roderick Engert in CVHE Papers, Box 7, Folder 57.
84. Thayer, *Hands across the Caviar,* 1–3, 17, 22–4, 50, 57, 119–20. In the 1980s I met McCrary on several occasions in connection with my Navy duties. I did not know of his interactions with Thayer until I began research for this book, so I never spoke with him about Thayer.
85. Smith, *OSS,* 145–6.
86. The military versus the civilians in the Indian government; aggressive action versus passive conciliation; Conservatives versus Liberals; the Forward Policy, or not. Wavell and Moon, *Wavell,* 179.
87. Mitchell, *Cunningham,* 177.
88. On 30 December 1945 he was addressed as lieutenant in a form letter from the secretary of the Navy, but on 16 February 1946 he was addressed as lieutenant commander by the Bureau of Personnel (BuPers).
89. Buhite, *Hurley,* 302 ("suspicion, insecurity" and "gadfly"), 315 ("superficially spectacular"), 322–3 ("cowboy").
90. This summary of Thayer is based on his biography on the dust jacket of *Diplomat* (Harper, 1959). He wrote many other books and articles, two of which were used as references in this work: The forced retirement of Thayer from the State Department is discussed in Hersh, *The Old Boys.*
91. Wavell and Moon, *Wavell,* 377 ("nice, friendly old man"), 378 ("pleasant to visit"); also see Fort, *Archibald Wavell,* 391.
92. Connell, *Wavell;* and Fort, *Archibald Wavell,* 362.
93. AZ to BSZ, 6 December 1943, handwritten letter from Wana, NWFP.
94. Roderick Engert, telephone conversation with the author, 13 August 2009: "Yes, I saw Enders several times, and he certainly was flamboyant, a blowhard in fact."
95. G. Enders, "The Nomad Woman." This was his only known postwar publication. The author is shown as Major Gordon B. Enders, so he apparently had not yet been promoted.

Chapter 5: Afterword and Closure, after September 11, 2001

1. AZ Trip Notes, 30 November 1943 (copy in AZ-WP, File 1–4, Chitral Trip): "most potentially powerfully position in world."
2. Somini Sengupta and Hari Kumar, "Sunk in Despair, Remote Villages Await Quake Aid. Long Treks to Seek Help. Pakistan Toll Put at 25,000—A Million Homeless, U.N. Estimates" *New York Times* (12 October 2005); "Racing against Winter to Reach Survivors" *[Newark, N.J.] Star-Ledger* (21 October 2005); and Somini Sengupta, "Quake Strains 58-Year-Old Fault Line. Disaster Highlights and Widens Split

Between India and Pakistan: Toll has risen to 78,000," *New York Times* (24 October 2005); Saeed Shah and Jonathan S. Landay, "Pakistan Flood Crisis Raises Concern about Government Destabilization" *[Newark, N.J.] Star-Ledger* (14 August 2010), 29; Eric Schmitt, "U.S. Extends a Hand to Rescue Pakistanis and Reclaim Its Image," *New York Times* (15 August 2010); Carlotta Gall, "With No Letup in Pakistan's Misery, U.S. Increases Aid" Map legend, Dir to Chitral, *New York Times* (20 August 2010); Carlotta Gall, "Pakistanis Tied to [14 May] 2007 Attack on Americans. New Details Emerge of Ambush at Border," *New York Times* (27 September 2011); Scott Wilson and Craig Whitlock, "'Justice Has Been Done': U.S. Raid Kills al Qaeda Chief in Pakistan after a 10-Year Hunt," *[Newark, N.J.] Star-Ledger* (2 May 2011), 1, 4; Eric Schmitt and Thom Shanker, "In Long Pursuit of Bin Laden, the '07 Raid, and Frustration," *New York Times* (6 May 2011).
3. Carlotta Gall, "Militant Commander in Pakistan is Reported Killed by U.S. Drone Strike," *New York Times* (5 June 2011).
4. Jack Healy and Alissa J. Rubin, "As Afghanistan's Ties to India Grow Stronger, Its Rift with Pakistan Widens," *New York Times* (5 October 2011); Jane Perlez, "Pakistan Pulls Closer to a Reluctant China," *New York Times* (7 October 2011); Scott Shane, "C.I.A. Is Disputed on Civilian Toll in Drone Strikes; U.S.: No Deaths in Year. Report Contests Count in Latest Anti-Qaeda Effort in Pakistan," *New York Times* (12 August 2011).

Selected Bibliography

The diaries, letters, and photos of Albert Zimmerman that formed the foundation for this work have been donated to the United States Naval Institute. The Albert Zimmerman Papers and Photos are now held in the U.S. Naval Institute Heritage Group Special Collections in Annapolis, Maryland.

Archival Sources

Franklin Delano Roosevelt Presidential Library, Hyde Park, New York (FDR Library)

Georgetown University, Washington, D.C., Special Collections, Cornelius Van Engert Papers (CVHE Papers)

University of Oklahoma Libraries, Western History Collections, Patrick J. Hurley Papers (Hurley Papers)

Foreign Relations of the United States (*FRUS*). Washington, D.C.: U.S. Government Printing Office, 1861 and annually thereafter.

National Archives and Records Administration II (NARA II), Archives at College Park, Md.:

    Office of the Chief of Naval Operations—Naval Archives Records (RG 38)

    War Department General and Special Staffs, U.S. Army Military Intelligence (MID Staff, G-2) (RG 165)

    Joint Chiefs of Staff records (RG 218)

    JICA Administrative and Serial Files, 1943–45 (JICA)

    Mediterranean Theater of Operations (RG 492)

    State Department Archives, State Department files, Microfilm (State Microfilm)

    M1332, Office of Naval Intelligence Reports, files (ONI Microfilm).

    FOIA: Freedom of Information Act. My request for "Intelligence Report, 5 July 1944, U.S. NLO Karachi, for JICA/CBI and DNI," was declassified on 8 December 2011 by DM at NARA, NW 36775.

Secondary Sources

Adams, Henry H. *Witness to Power: The Life of Fleet Admiral William D. Leahy.* Annapolis, Md.: Naval Institute Press, 1985.

Aldrich, Richard J. *American Intelligence and the British Raj: The OSS, the SSU and India, 1942–1947.* New York: Routledge, 1998.

Amis, Kingsley. *Rudyard Kipling and His World.* London: Thames and Hudson, 1975.

Andrew, Christopher. *Defend the Realm: The Authorized History of MI5.* New York: Vintage Books/Random House, 2009.

———. *For the President's Eyes Only: Secret Intelligence and the American Presidency from Washington to Bush.* New York: HarperPerennial, 1996.

Bachman, Bruce M. *An Honorable Profession: The Life and Times of One of America's Most Able Seamen: Rear Adm. John Duncan Bulkeley, USN.* New York: Vantage Press, 1989.

Baltzell, Edward Digby. *Philadelphia Gentlemen: The Making of a National Upper Class.* New Brunswick, N.J.: Transaction Publishers, 2009.

Beesley, Patrick. *Very Special Admiral: The Life of Admiral J. H. Godfrey, CB.* London: Hamish Hamilton, 1980.

Boulger, Demetrius Charles de Kavanagh. "Unity of Coinage for the Empire." *The Imperial and Asiatic Quarterly Review and Oriental and Colonial Period,* 3rd Series, 13 (nos. 25 & 26, Jan.–Apr. 1902).

Brobst, Peter John. *The Future of the Great Game: Sir Olaf Caroe, India's Independence, and the Defense of Asia.* Akron, Ohio: University of Akron Press, 2005.

Brown, Anthony Cave. *The Secret Servant: The Life of Sir Stewart Menzies. Churchill's Spymaster.* London: Michael Joseph, Published by the Penguin Group, 1988.

———. *The Last Hero: Wild Bill Donovan.* New York: Vintage Books/Random House, 1982.

Bryant, Arthur. *Triumph in the West: A History of the War Years Based on the Diaries of Field-Marshal Lord Alanbrooke, Chief of the Imperial General Staff.* Garden City, N.Y.: Doubleday, 1959.

———. *The Turn of the Tide: A History of the War Years Based on the Diaries of Field-Marshal Lord Alanbrooke, Chief of the Imperial General Staff, 1939–1943.* Garden City, N.Y.: Doubleday, 1957.

Buhite, Russell D. *Patrick J. Hurley and American Foreign Policy.* Ithaca, N.Y.: Cornell University Press, 1973.

Casey, William. *The Secret War against Hitler.* New York: Berkeley Books, 1989.

Chua, Amy. *Day of Empire: How Hyperpowers Rise to Global Dominance—And Why They Fall.* New York: Doubleday, 2007.

Churchill, Sir Winston. *A History of the English Speaking Peoples.* v.4. *The Great Democracies.* New York: Dodd, Mead, 1958.

———. *The Second World War.* 5 vols. Vol. 4: *The Hinge of Fate.* Vol. 5: *Closing the Ring.* Boston, Mass.: Houghton Mifflin, 1981.

———. *The Story of the Malakand Field Force: An Episode of Frontier War.* Lexington, Ky.: Seven Treasures, 2009. First published as *Malakand Field Force,* London: Longmans, Green and Co., 1898.

Coll, Steve. *Ghost Wars: The Secret History of the CIA, Afghanistan, and Bin Laden, from the Soviet Invasion to September 10, 2001.* New York: Penguin Group/Penguin Press, 2005.

Connell, John. *Wavell: Scholar and Soldier, to June 1941.* London: Collins, 1964.

Courcy, Anne de. *The Viceroy's Daughters: The Lives of the Curzon Sisters.* New York: HarperCollins/Perennial, 2002.

Crile, George. *Charlie Wilson's War: The Extraordinary Story of How the Wildest Man in Congress and a Rouge CIA Agent Changed the History of Our Times.* New York: Grove Press, 2003.

Curzon, George N. *The Pamirs and the Source of the Oxus.* London: The Royal Geographical Society, 1896.

———. *Persia and the Persian Question.* 2 vols. London: Frank Cass, 1966.

———. *Russia in Central Asia in 1889 and the Anglo-Russian Question.* London: Frank Cass, 1967.

Cutting, Col. C. Suydam. "Cheetah Hunting," in George Plimpton, editor and introduction to *As Told at the Explorers Club,* 167–72. Guilford, Conn.: Lyons Press, 2005.

Cutting, Suydam. *The Fire Ox and Other Years.* New York: Charles Scribner's Sons, 1940.

Denslow, William. *10,000 Famous Freemasons.* Phoenix Masonry, 2004. http://www.phoenixmasonry.org/10,000_famous_freemasons/Volume_3_K_to_P.htm

Dorril, Stephen. *MI6: Inside the Covert World of Her Majesty's Secret Intelligence Service.* New York: Simon & Schuster/A Touchstone Book, 2002.

Dorwart, Jeffery M. *Conflict of Duty: The U.S. Navy's Intelligence Dilemma, 1919–1945.* Annapolis, Md.: Naval Institute Press, 1983.

———. "The Roosevelt-Astor Espionage Ring." *Quarterly Journal of the New York State Historical Association* 62, no. 3 (July 1981): 307–22.

Drea, Edward J. *MacArthur's ULTRA: Codebreaking and the War against Japan, 1942–1945.* Lawrence: University Press of Kansas, 1992.

Dulles, Allen. *The Craft of Intelligence: America's Legendary Spy Master on the Fundamentals of Intelligence Gathering for a Free World.* Guilford, Conn.: Lyons Press, 2006.

———. *The Secret Surrender.* New York: Harper & Row, 1966.

Eisenhower, David. *Eisenhower at War, 1943–1945.* New York: Random House, 1986.

Enders, Elizabeth Crump. *Swinging Lanterns.* New York: D. Appleton, 1923.

———. *Temple Bells and Silver Sails.* New York: D. Appleton, 1925.

Enders, Gordon Bandy. "Afghanistan's Strategic Geography," Report 107-A, eight pages (four double-sided), 6 September 1943, in NARA II, RG 165, Entry 7 Afghanistan 5000–6400 Box 4 NND 745008. Geography (5900), 5930.

———. [published as Anon.] "Flying Gold Out of Tibet: Planes Invade Land of the Lamas." *Modern Mechanix Hobbies Inventions* (November 1936): 76–77, 120.

———. *Foreign Devil: An American Kim in Modern Asia.* New York: Simon and Schuster, 1942.

———. "The Nomad Woman." *Colliers* (7 October 1950), http://www.unz.org/Pub/Colliers-1950oct07–00016

———. "Prohibition in Old India." *Asia: The American Magazine on the Orient* 20, no. 10 (November 1920): 1003–4.

Enders, Gordon Bandy, and Edward Anthony. *Nowhere Else in the World.* New York: Farrar & Rinehart, 1935.

Engert, Cornelius. *A Report on Afghanistan*. Washington, D.C.: GPO, 1924.

Engert, Jane Morrison. *Tales from the Embassy: The Extraordinary World of C. Van H. Engert*. Westminster, Md.: Heritage Books/Eagle Editions, 2006.

Ewans, Sir Martin. *Afghanistan: A Short History of Its People and Politics*. New York: Perennial/HarperCollinsPublishers, 2002.

Fetridge, William Harrison. *The Navy Reader*. Indianapolis: Bobbs-Merrill, 1971.

Filkins, Dexter. *The Forever War*. New York: Alfred A. Knopf, Borzoi Book, 2008.

Fisher, John. "India's Treasures Helped the Allies." *National Geographic* 89 (April 1946): 501–22.

Fort, Adrian. *Archibald Wavell: The Life and Times of an Imperial Servant*. London: Jonathan Cape, 2009.

Fox, Ernest F. *By Compass Alone*. Philadelphia: Dorrance & Company, 1971.

———. *Travels in Afghanistan*. New York: The Macmillan Company, 1943.

Fraser, George MacDonald (Ed.). *Flashman in the Great Game: From the Flashman Papers 1856–1858*. New York: Penguin, 1989 [fiction].

Gilmour, David. *The Long Recessional: The Imperial Life of Rudyard Kipling*. New York: Farrar, Straus and Giroux, 2002.

Goodson, Larry P. *Afghanistan's Endless War: State Failure, Regional Politics, and the Rise of the Taliban*. Seattle: University of Washington Press, 2001.

Goradia, Nayana. *Lord Curzon: The Last of the British Moghuls*. Delhi: Oxford University Press, 1997.

Green, Peter. *Alexander of Macedon, 356–323 B.C.: A Historical Biography*. Berkeley: University of California Press, 1991.

Grose, Peter. *Gentleman Spy: The Life of Allen Dulles*. Amherst: University of Massachusetts Press, 1996.

Harlan, J[osiah]. *A Memoir of India and Avghanistaun with Observations on the Present Exciting and Critical State and Future Prospects of Those Countries. Comprising Remarks on the Massacre of the British Army in Cabul, British Policy in India, A Detailed Descriptive Character of Dost Mahomed and His Court, Etc.* Philadelphia: J. Dobson, 1842.

Harris, Charles H. III, and Louis R. Sadler. *The Archaeologist Was a Spy: Sylvanus G. Morley and the Office of Naval Intelligence*. Albuquerque: University of New Mexico Press, 2003.

Hauser, Ernest O. "A Reporter at Large: Pathans behind the Rocks." *New Yorker* 90 (30 September 1944): 169–222.

Hay, William Rupert. *Two Years in Kurdistan. Experiences of a Political Officer, 1918–1920*. London: Sidgwick and Jackson, 1921.

Hersh, Burton. *The Old Boys: The American Elite and the Origins of the CIA*. New York: Charles Scribner's Sons, 1992.

Hill, George J. *Intimate Relationships: Church and State in the U.S. and Liberia*. Saarbrucken: VDM Verlag Dr. Muller, 2008.

Holt, Thaddeus. *The Deceivers: Allied Military Deception in the Second World War*. New York: Skyhorse, 2007.

Hopkirk, Peter. *The Great Game: The Struggle for Empire in Central Asia*. New York: Kodansha Globe, 1992.

———. *Quest for Kim: In Search of Kipling's Great Game*. Ann Arbor: University of Michigan Press, 1999.

———. *Setting the East Ablaze: Lenin's Dream of an Empire in Asia*. New York: Kodansha International, 1995.

————. *Trespassers on the Roof of the World: The Secret Exploration of Tibet.* New York: Kodansha International, 1995.

Houston, Charles S., and Robert H. Bates. *K2: The Savage Mountain.* Seattle, WA: The Mountaineers, 1979.

Hunt, Linda. *Secret Agenda: The United States Government and Project Paperclip, 1945 to 1990.* New York: St. Martin's Press / Macmillan, 1991.

Hyde, H. Montgomery. *Room 3603: The Incredible True Story of Secret Intelligence Operations During World War II.* New York: Lyons Press, 2001.

Isaacson, Walter, and Evan Thomas. *The Wise Men: Six Friends and the World They Made. Acheson, Bohlen, Harriman, Kennan, Lovett, McCloy.* New York: Simon & Schuster / A Touchstone Book, 1988.

Jablonsky, David. *Churchill: The Great Game and Total War.* New York: Routledge, 1991.

Jeffers, H. Paul. *In the Rough Rider's Shadow: The Story of a War Hero— Theodore Roosevelt Jr.* New York: Presidio Press / Ballantine Publishing, Random House, 2003.

Jeffery, Keith. *The Secret History of MI6.* New York: Penguin, 2010.

Jeffreys, Alan, and Duncan Anderson. *British Army in the Far East 1941– 1945.* Oxford: Osprey, 2005.

Jones, Seth G. *In the Graveyard of Empires: America's War in Afghanistan.* New York: W. W. Norton, 2010.

Kaplan, Robert D. *Monsoon: The Indian Ocean and the Future of American Power.* New York: Random House, 2010.

Khan, Mohammad. "A Short History of Chitral and Kafirstan." www.anusha .com/chitralh.htm

Kiernan, Frances. *The Last Mrs. Astor: A New York Story.* New York: W. W. Norton & Company / Norton paperback, 2008.

Kipling, Rudyard. *Kim.* Mineola, N.Y.: Dover, 2005.

————. *Kipling Stories: Twenty-eight Exciting Tales by the Master Storyteller.* New York: Platt & Munk, 1960.

————. *The Writings in Prose and Verse of Rudyard Kipling.* New York: Charles Scribner's Sons, 1897–98. 12 vols. *Under the Deodar, The Story of the Gadsbys, Wee Willie Winkie* (vol. 6). *Verses, 1889–1896* (vol. 11).

Kleveman, Lutz. *The New Great Game: Blood and Oil in Central Asia.* New York: Grove Press, 2003.

Leider, Emily W. *Myrna Loy: The Only Good Girl in Hollywood.* Berkeley: University of California Press, 2011.

Lewin, Ronald. *The Chief: Field Marshal Lord Wavell, Commander-in-Chief and Viceroy, 1939–1947.* New York: Farrar, Straus and Giroux, 1980.

Liddell, Guy Maynard, and Nigel West. *The Guy Liddell Diaries: MI5's Director of Counter-Espionage in World War II.* Florence, Ky.: Taylor & Francis, 2005.

Lieven, Anatol. *Pakistan: A Hard Country.* New York: Public Affairs, 2011.

Lohbeck, Don. *Patrick J. Hurley.* Chicago: Henry Regnery, 1956.

Lukacs, John (ed.) *Through the History of the Cold War: The Correspondence of George F. Kennan and John Lukacs.* Philadelphia: University of Pennsylvania Press, 2010.

Manchester, William. *The Last Lion: Winston Spencer Churchill. Visions of Glory, 1874–1932.* Boston: Little, Brown, 1983.

Markey, Gene. *His Majesty's Pyjamas.* New York: Covici-Friede, 1934.

———. *Women, Women, Everywhere.* New York: Bobbs-Merrill, 1964.

Marston, Daniel. *Phoenix from the Ashes: The Indian Army in the Burma Campaign.* Westport, Conn.: Praeger, 2003.

McIntosh, Elizabeth P. *Sisterhood of Spies: The Women of the OSS.* Annapolis, Md.: Naval Institute Press, 1998.

Meyer, Karl Ernest, and Shareen Blair Brysac. *Tournament of Shadows: The Great Game and the Race for Empire in Central Asia.* New York: Basic Books, 1999.

Miles, Milton E. *A Different Kind of War: The Unknown Story of the U.S. Navy's Guerilla Forces in World War II China.* Garden City, N.Y.: Doubleday, 1967.

Mills, Eric. "John Ford, USN." *Naval History* 27, no. 2 (April 2013): 48–55.

Mitchell, Norval. *Sir George Cunningham: A Memoir.* Edinburgh: William Blackwood, 1968.

Moran, Lord (Charles Wilson). *Churchill: Taken From the Diaries of Lord Moran. The Struggle for Survival, 1940–1965.* Boston: Houghton Mifflin, 1966.

Morison, Samuel Eliot. *The Two Ocean War: A Short History of the United States Navy in the Second World War.* Boston: Little, Brown, 1963.

Muir, Peter, and Frances Muir. "India Mosaic." *National Geographic* 89 (April 1946): 442–70.

New Encyclopaedia Britannica. Chicago: University of Chicago, 1989.

Osborne, Frances. *The Bolter.* New York: Vintage Books, 2010.

Page, Bruce, David Leitch, and Phillip Knightley. *Philby: The Spy Who Betrayed a Generation.* London: Andre Deutsch, 1968.

Persico, Joseph. *Roosevelt's Secret War: FDR and World War II Espionage.* New York: Random House, 2002.

Pfeiffer, David A. "Sage Prophet or Loose Cannon? Skilled Intelligence Officer in World War II Foresaw Japan's Plans, but Annoyed Navy Brass." *Prologue Magazine* [National Archives] 40, no. 2 (Summer 2008).

Philby, Kim. *My Silent War: The Autobiography of a Spy.* New York: Modern Library, 2002.

Powers, Thomas. *Intelligence Wars: American Secret History from Hitler to Al-Qaeda.* New York: New York Review of Books, 2004.

Prescott, Kenneth W. (Captain, USNR, ret.). *A PT Skipper in the South Pacific: A Naval Officer's Memoir of Service on PTs and a PT Boat Tender.* Bennington, Vt.: Miriam Press, 2009.

Rasanayagam, Angelo. *Afghanistan: A Modern History.* London: I. B. Tauris, 2005.

Rashid, Ahmed. *Taliban: Militant Islam, Oil and Fundamentalism in Central Asia.* New Haven, Conn.: Yale University Press, 2001.

Reeve, Walter. "Peshawar Remembered." www.khyberlodge.co.uk/about-khyber-mainmenu-26/peshawar-remembered-mainmenu-43.html

Renault, Mary. *The Persian Boy.* New York: Bantam Books, 1974.

Rhodes, Richard. *Hedy's Folly: The Life and Breakthrough Inventions of Hedy*

Lamarr, the Most Beautiful Woman in the World. New York: Doubleday, 2011.

Ricketts, Harry. *Rudyard Kipling: A Life.* New York: Carroll & Graf, 2001.

Rolandshay, The Rt. Hon., the Earl of. *The Life of Lord Curzon: Being the Authorized Biography of George Nathaniel, Marquess Curzon of Kedleston, K.G.* London: Ernest Benn, 1927.

Ross, Nancy Wilson. *Buddhism: A Way of Life and Thought.* New York: Vintage Books / Random House, 1981.

Shirazi, S. A. "Chitral: A Bloody History and a Glorious Geography." www.chitral.weebly.com/history-of-chitral.html.

Smith, Richard Harris. *OSS: The Secret History of America's First Central Intelligence Agency.* Guilford, Conn.: Lyons Press, an imprint of The Globe Pequot Press, 2005.

Stevenson, William. *Intrepid's Last Case.* New York: Ballantine Books / Random House, 1984.

———. *A Man Called Intrepid: The Secret War.* Guilford, Conn.: Lyons Press / Globe Pequot Press, 2000.

Sutton, Antony G. *America's Secret Establishment: An Introduction to the Order of Skull & Bones.* Walterville, Ore.: Trine Day, 2002.

Swayne-Thomas, April. *Indian Summer: A Mem-sahib in India and Sind.* London: New English Library, Barnard's Inn, Holborn, 1981.

Taylor, Edmond. *Richer by Asia.* New York: Time Life Books, 1964.

Taylor, Mark. "What Happened to the Sandia Bighorn Herd? Gordon Enders Focused on Sheep" probably *Albuquerque Journal* (22 December 1986): A1, A6.

Thayer, Charles W. *Bears in the Caviar.* Philadelphia: J. B. Lippincott, 1951.

———. *Diplomat.* New York: Harper & Brothers, 1959.

———. *Guerrilla.* New York: Harper & Row, 1963.

———. *Hands across the Caviar.* Philadelphia: J. B. Lippincott, 1952.

Thomas, Evan. *The Very Best Men: The Daring Early Years of the CIA.* New York: Simon & Schuster, 2006.

Thomas, Lowell. *Beyond Khyber Pass into Forbidden Afghanistan.* New York: Grosset & Dunlap, by arrangement with The Century Company, rev. ed., 1925.

Thompson, Nicholas. *The Hawk and the Dove: Paul Nitze, George Kennan and the History of the Cold War.* New York: Henry Holt / Picador, 2009.

Tolstoy, Ilia. "Across Tibet from India to China." *National Geographic* 89 (August 1946): 169–222.

Treanor, Tom. *One Damn Thing after Another.* Garden City, N.Y.: Doubleday, Doran & Co., 1944.

Tung, Rosemary Jones. *A Portrait of Lost Tibet.* New York: Holt, Rinehart and Winston, 1980.

Viesturs, Ed, and David Roberts. *K2: Life and Death on the World's Most Dangerous Mountain.* New York: Broadway Books, 2009.

Wake, Jehanne. "Benson, Sir Reginald Lindsay (1889–1968)." *Oxford Dictionary of National Biography,* vol. 5. Oxford: Oxford University Press, 2004.

———. *Kleinwort Benson: The History of Two Families in Banking.* Oxford: Oxford University Press, 1997.

Warner, Philip. *Auchinleck: The Lonely Soldier.* Barnsley, South Yorkshire, UK: Pen & Sword Books, 2006.

Wavell, A. P. [Archibald Percivall] (Field Marshall Viscount Wavell). *Other Men's Flowers: An Anthology of Verse.* New York: G. P. Putnam's Sons, 1945.

Wavell, A. P. [Archibald Percivall] (Field Marshall Viscount Wavell), and Penderel Moon. *Wavell: The Viceroy's Journal.* London: Oxford, 1973.

Wedemeyer, Albert C. *Wedemeyer Reports!* New York: Henry Holt, 1958.

Weiner, Tim. *Legacy of Ashes: The History of the CIA.* New York: Random House / Anchor Books, 2008.

Wilhelm, Maria. *The Man Who Watched the Rising Sun: The Story of Admiral Ellis M. Zacharias.* New York: Franklin Watts, 1967.

Williams, Maynard Owen. "South of Khyber Pass." *National Geographic* 89 (April 1946): 471–500.

Wolpert, Stanley. *Shameful Flight: The Last Years of the British Empire in India.* New York: Oxford, 2009.

Young, Desmond. *Rommel.* London: Collins, 1954.

Yu, Maochun. *The Dragon's War: Allied Operations and the Fate of China, 1937–1947.* Annapolis, Md.: Naval Institute Press, 2006.

———. *OSS in China: Prelude to Cold War.* New Haven, Conn.: Yale University Press, 1997.

Zacharias, Ellis M. *Behind Closed Doors: The Secret History of the Cold War.* New York: G. P. Putnam's Sons, 1950.

———. *Secret Missions: The Story of an Intelligence Officer.* Annapolis, Md.: Naval Institute Press, 2003.

Zareef, Adil. "Dean's Hotel: Every Stone Has a History," *The Most Famous Hotels in the World.* http://www.khyber.org/places/2005/Deans_Hotel_-_Every_Stone_has_.shtml

Ziegler, Philip. *Mountbatten.* New York: Alfred A. Knopf, 1985.

Zimmermann, Barbara S. *Mutterings.* Wynnewood, Penn.: Livingston, 1969.

Zimmermann, Warren. *First Great Triumph: How Five Americans Made Their Country a World Power.* New York: Farrar, Straus and Giroux, 2002.

Interviews and Correspondence

Brady, The Honorable Nicholas F. Letter, 14 October 2009.

Creel, Maynard. Correspondence, 29–30 August 2010.

Dahl, Sheila (Kane). Phone conversation, 2008.

Enders, Dr. Allen Coffin. Correspondence and phone conversation, 16–20 August 2009.

Engert, Roderick. Phone conversation, 13 August 2009.

Frazier, Mrs. Lois (Thayer) Wesley. Phone conversation, 2008.

Hanlon, C. Rollins, M.D., F.A.C.S. Phone conversation, 4 March 2011.

Hegge, Amanda. Correspondence, 27 September–4 October 2011.

Hovde, David M. Letter, 19 May 2009.

Huntington, Dr. Gertrude Enders. Correspondence and phone conversations, 24 August 2009–10 January 2010.

Lillien, Susan. Conversation, 10 December 2011.

Streather, Colonel Tony. Phone conversation, 20 January 2010.

Thayer, Dodie. Conversation, 29 April 2011.

Ushack, Sarah. Letters, 20 May–8 June 2009.

Index

Abbotabad, 5, 178

Afghanistan: Allies policy in, 20, 62–63; attacks on and ambush of US military personnel, 178, 179; Axis policy and sympathizers, 45, 62, 172; bleakness of life in, xi, 125; border areas, 2, 3, 4, 5, 7, 175; border unrest, 45, 47, 147, 151, 204n64; British interests in, 6–10, 60–61, 172; changeless nature of area, 178–79; conditions and cultural traditions in, xii–xiii, 63, 76, 125, 177; demographics and geography of, 3–5; economic opportunities in, xi, 173; Enders travel through, 20; exchange of American and Afghan officers, 148, 199n22, 203n55; Great Game from viewpoint of, 60–61; Great Game role of, 1–2, 169–70; history of, 5–10; imports, exports, and trade, 28, 136–37, 142, 173; neutrality policy, xii, 9–10, 19–20, 172; Pakistan creation and effects on, 41–42; Russian interests in, 6–10, 41, 60–61, 62–63, 136, 172; Soviet invasion of, 177; supply route and supply stashes in, 134–35, 173–74, 187n48, 198n14; US drone use in, 177, 179; US role in, 9–10, 19, 37, 38–39, 40–41, 61, 169–70, 179; US support for, 177; wars between Britain and, 2

Afridi tribe, 33, 96, 111–12, 113, 117, 120, 156, 164, 186n42

Astor, Vincent, 24–25, 80, 84–85, 184–85n25

Auchinleck, Claude J. E. "the Auk," xxiv, 33, 57, 58, 79–80, 86, 94, 99

Baluchistan province, 3, 4, 5, 124–27, 148, 177, 196–97n62, 203–4n59

Benson, Reginald Lindsay "Rex": banking career, 131, 197n2; birth and early life of, 50; discharge of, 131; Donovan relationship with, 54; Enders letter of introduction from, 17, 49, 53; Enders meeting with, 14; intelligence career of, 49–50, 51–54, 85, 188n84, 188n88; Japanese attack plans, 53–54; Khyber Pass travel by, 114; leaking information by, 54; marriage and family of, 52, 197n2; Menzies relationship with, 50, 81; military service of, 50–51; popularity of, 53; recall to Britain, 54, 131; role in trip, xxiv; Washington position of, 52–54, 183n12

bin Laden, Osama, 117, 177, 178

Bolan Pass, 115, 127, 176

Bromhead, Benjamin: appearance of, xv, 93; AZ meeting in Peshawar, 92–93; birth and early life of, 22; communications to AZ, 136, 141,

About the Author

George Hill graduated from Yale University and the Harvard Medical School. He served in the U.S. Marine Corps and the Public Health Service, and he retired as a captain in the USNR in 1992. He has received the Navy and Marine Corps Parachute Badge, the Vietnam Service Medal, and the Meritorious Service Medal.